MORAL DUTY AND
RESPONSIBILITY

THE CENTURY PHILOSOPHY SERIES

Justus Buchler and Sterling P. Lamprecht, EDITORS

MORAL DUTY AND LEGAL RESPONSIBILITY

A PHILOSOPHICAL-LEGAL CASEBOOK

EDITED BY

PHILIP E. DAVIS
SAN JOSE STATE COLLEGE

NEW YORK

APPLETON-CENTURY-CROFTS
DIVISION OF MEREDITH PUBLISHING COMPANY

PRINTED IN THE UNITED STATES OF AMERICA

E 25535

PREFACE

The questions which philosophers ask about duty and responsibility tend to be very general and abstract. Practical persons ask relatively specific and concrete questions such as the following: "Should I break a promise I have made? "Is it right, under these circumstances, to lie?" "Should a child be held responsible for the injuries he causes?" "What are my duties as a parent, a citizen, or a neighbor?" The philosopher prefers to abstract the problems from their practical settings and generalize them. He asks such questions as the following: "What does it mean to be a morally dutiful person?" "What does it mean to say that an action is right or ought to be done?" "What are the conditions which must exist before anyone can be held responsible for his acts?"

The abstract and generalizing character of philosophy is one of its chief merits. The philosophical generalization of the problem of responsibility, for instance, provides a kind of map, a framework of concepts within which the more specific and practical questions about responsibility, blame, and punishment can more intelligently be asked.

Nevertheless, as Francis Bacon once said, there comes a time when the philosopher needs to imitate the bee rather than the spider. He needs sustenance other than that which he is capable of producing from his own mind and experience. Generalization is possible only if there is something to generalize about; abstraction is possible only if there is something to abstract from.

This collection of legal cases is an attempt to provide some specific content to ethical theory, not only by way of concrete ex-

v

amples of different human relationships and situations in which specific questions of moral, as well as legal, responsibility arise, but also by demonstrating the manner in which the concept of moral duty often enters into the assignment of legal responsibility. Furthermore, it calls attention to certain legal distinctions and procedures which the philosopher, or student of philosophy, may well find suggestive and useful for his own purposes, and in his own way.

The volume is divided into two parts. The first concerns problems of assigning responsibility. It is not concerned, as an ordinary legal treatise or casebook might be, with all the special requirements or "elements" which must be proved in order to establish legal liability for specific kinds of acts. It is concerned, however, with one relatively specific and concrete problem, or predicament, which fairly often confronts the judge in assigning legal responsibility, namely, "What recognition should moral duties be given in deciding legal issues?" Sometimes the question is explicitly so stated, e.g., "Is a promise which is supported only by a moral obligation legally enforceable?" At other times, the role of a moral duty in the general problem of assigning legal responsibility is only implicitly recognized, but rejected as having no direct bearing. This is especially apparent in decisions assigning "liability without fault."

The cases that have been selected raise these kinds of problems in a variety of different ways. It seemed appropriate to begin by considering many types of moral duties. Although by no means exhaustive, the classification given in Chapter 1 follows, more or less, the list of *prima facie* moral duties which Sir David Ross offers in his book, *The Right and the Good*.[1]

Ross lists some six or eight kinds of duties, depending upon how one takes his classification. Only one of the kinds he mentions is stated negatively, namely, the "duty not to harm others." He defends this as a distinctive kind to be contrasted specifically with our duty to benefit others in need (the "duty of beneficence," which in this book is treated more narrowly in terms of the legal "duty to rescue"). Since the violation of any of the other kinds of duty usually involves harm to someone, it could be debated that this last type overlaps with, or is implied by, the

1 The Clarendon Press, 1930, Chapter II.

other types. But whether Ross is correct or not, his last classification does suggest a second major problem about the assigning of responsibility. Besides the problem of determining whether a moral obligation will support a claim of legal responsibility, there is also the problem of assigning responsibility where a duty not to harm is apparent, a harm has occurred, but where an excuse or justification for it is offered. This gives us the rationale of Chapters 2 and 3.

Part II is concerned with problems of making and justifying a judgment of legal responsibility. It is one thing to judge a person responsible, and another to justify such a judgment. What I have in mind here are certain methodological problems as compared with the relatively more substantive questions of Part I. The cases have been selected primarily from this standpoint, although they have been selected for their moral content as well. Thus, the issues of the first part continue to appear throughout the book.

If a person is responsible, he must be responsible for something, and so the first requisite in justifying as well as in making a judgment is the clarification of the notion of an "act." It may well be that men are sometimes held morally responsible for their thoughts as well as their acts, but they are never held legally responsible for them. The law requires an act in all cases. Our coverage of this topic, therefore, is limited to what can be learned from the legal analysis of acts. Yet, since not all acts are those for which the law holds men responsible, it must also be made clear which kinds of acts will give rise to "causes of action," i.e., grounds for holding a person legally responsible. These matters are discussed in Chapter 4.

The grounds of responsible judgment inevitably include reference to, and the application of, some kind of legal norm. These include legal concepts, statutory and common-law rules, standards, legal maxims, and legal canons. Consideration is given to their logical and practical differences, and to their roles in legal reasoning, in Chapter 5.

The final chapter raises questions about the kinds of evidence or proof which are relevant and appropriate to the justification of judgments of responsibility. At the beginning of this chapter, as well as at the beginning of each of the others, I have taken the liberty of suggesting the possible significance of legal methods, distinctions, and procedures in the analysis of analogous problems in ethics and morals. At the end of each chapter, I have included some critical comments and questions under the heading, Notes, which presuppose a reading of the preceding cases.

So much for the format of the book. A few words perhaps need to be said regarding the cases themselves. They have been drawn from various branches of the law. Some are landmark cases establishing precedent which is still binding on the courts. Others have been more or less superseded by contrary decisions, and so perhaps are not "good law" today, as the lawyers say. Some deal with important issues; others with what may seem trivial matters. Most of the cases are illustrative of commonly recognized moral issues, although a few are restricted to purely technical or methodological considerations. The aim throughout has not been to present up-to-date law, or even examples of legal reasoning at its best. The aim has rather been to select those cases which suggest whole ranges of problems upon which to work the philosophical imagination. Perhaps a solution to a puzzlement, or a hint of an overlooked distinction, may thus be engendered.

The philosopher, or the student of philosophy, as the case may be, is asked in one other respect to become a student of law. Instead of giving distilled summaries of the cases, and putting them into layman's English, I have thought it of some value for the reader to struggle with the legal terminology of the actual law reports themselves. The language of the law is not as difficult to comprehend as it may at first appear, and, in any case, an introduction to the way lawyers use language may, for some, be highly instructive. However, some of the purely procedural aspects of the cases, though not all, have been deleted, along with some of the supporting case citations, since these are of use only to those having a professional interest in the law. A glossary of some of the more technical legal terms appearing in this book has been supplied at the end. An appendix of legal abbreviations has also been added.

I am greatly indebted to my colleagues in philosophy at San Jose State College for their critical advice, literary suggestions, and general encouragement—most notably to Professors Ved

Sharma, Arthur Cody, John Dutton, Whitaker Deininger, and Frederick Scott. I also wish to thank Professor Edward Madden of the University of Buffalo for encouraging me to undertake a study of the works of a great American legal scholar, James Bradley Thayer, which helped immensely in the preparation of Chapter 6. I am grateful to Mr. Kenneth J. Enkel, friend, former colleague, and Minneapolis attorney, for his generous gift of time and expert legal knowledge, which was so useful in the writing of the glossary. To Professor Harry Kalven, Jr. of the University of Chicago Law School, and to Dean John W. Wade of the Vanderbilt University Law School, I am indebted for their many instructive insights into the law of torts. Acknowledgements are also due to the Social Science Research Council and to the American Philosophical Society (Penrose Fund) for two grants which provided valuable research opportunities, and which contributed both directly and indirectly to the writing of this volume. Finally, I am indebted to my wife, Laura, for her loyal support and assistance with the manuscript. Needless to say, no one except myself is to be held in any way responsible for the errors or inadequacies of this book.

P.E.D.

CONTENTS

Preface   v

I. PROBLEMS OF ASSIGNING RESPONSIBILITY

1. DUTIES   3

Duty to Keep Promises   BRITTON V. TURNER   8
Duty to Tell the Truth   SWINTON V. WHITINSVILLE
   SAVINGS BANK   13
Duty to Make Reparations   MITCHELL V. ROCHESTER
   RY. Co.   15
Duty to Be Grateful   WEBB V. McGOWIN   18
Duty to Prevent Injustice   RIGGS V. PALMER   23
Duty to Rescue   WAGNER V. INTERNATIONAL RY. Co.   34
Duty to Be Intelligent   MARENGO V. ROY   38

2. WRONGS: EXCUSES   43

Intervening Cause   WATSON V. KENTUCKY & INDIANA
   BRIDGE & R.R. Co.   47
Insanity (Crime)   PEOPLE V. SCHMIDT   58
Insanity (Tort)   McGUIRE V. ALMY   69
Drunkenness   PEOPLE V. KOERBER   73
Ignorance of Fact   PEOPLE V. WERNER   81
Faultlessness   LUTHRINGER V. MOORE   83

3. WRONGS: JUSTIFICATIONS   93

Reasonableness   TEDLA V. ELLMAN   96
Physical Necessity   UNITED STATES V. HOLMES   102
Self-Defense   BROWN V. UNITED STATES   119
Defense of Property   STATE V. CHILDERS   122
Privilege   WATT V. LONGSDON   126

II. Problems of Justifying a Judgment

4. ACTS AND CAUSES OF ACTION   143

An Act of God   KIMBLE V. MACKINTOSH
                                HEMPHILL CO.   147
An Overt Act   STATE V. RIDER   153
An Intentional Act   VOSBURG V. PUTNEY   156
An Intervening Act   PEOPLE V. LEWIS   159
A Negligent Act   PALSGRAF V. LONG ISLAND R. R. CO.   164
A First Case   HINISH V. MEIER & FRANK CO.   178

5. LEGAL NORMS   187

Legal Concepts   DURFEE V. JONES   191
Competitive Rules   HYNES V. NEW YORK CENTRAL
                                R. CO.   194
Rules Versus Standards   BALTIMORE & OHIO R.R.
                                v. GOODMAN   199
Standards Versus Rules   POKORA V. WABASH RY. CO.   201
General Law   ERIE RAILROAD CO. V. TOMPKINS   205
The Due Process Clause   ROCHIN V. CALIFORNIA   211

6. THE MEANS AND LIMITS OF PERSUASION   223

Incompetent Evidence   PEOPLE V. ZACKOWITZ   227
Presumptions and Burden of Proof   WORTH V.
                                WORTH   234
Finding of Fact   BAUMGARTNER V. UNITED STATES   242
Circumstantial Evidence   WARMKE V.
                                COMMONWEALTH   250
Judicial Notice and General Knowledge   MULLER
                                v. OREGON   254
Difficulty of Proof   WOODS V. LANCET   261

Glossary of Legal Terms   269

Appendix: Legal Abbreviations   277

Index   283

I

PROBLEMS OF
ASSIGNING RESPONSIBILITY

1

DUTIES

The legal cases in this chapter are all decided against the background and in terms of some recognized moral duty. This is not to say that in every case the judge finds a moral duty related to the facts of the case, takes it into consideration, and allows it to decide the issue. In some of the cases the judge refuses, or simply fails, to recognize the presence of a moral obligation. In others, he recognizes it, perhaps even takes it into consideration, but does not allow it a decisive influence. All that is claimed for the following cases is that each of them presents a moral duty which is relevant to the settlement of the issue, whether it is taken into consideration by the judge or not.

The case of *Riggs v. Palmer,* for example, is a classic illustration of the fact that moral obligations are not unrelated to legal decision making. In this case, a convicted murderer attempts to claim his share of his victim's will. Against the view that a will is entitled to strict legal enforcement, the view that no man ought to profit from his own iniquity wins out. Against the view that the civil courts may not add to the penalties for crimes, the same moral sentiment wins out, but not without a struggle. Of especial note in this case is the fact that the legal judgment is not directly concerned with assigning responsibility for the murderer's previous act of murder, but only with the consequences of such an assignment, namely, the prevention of further injustice.

In another case, a specific moral duty is recognized but is not allowed a decisive influence. The defendant in *Swinton v. Whitinsville Savings Bank* sold a house to the plaintiff without telling him that the house was infested with termites. The judge explicitly recognizes the moral obligation to tell the truth, but finds that although the defendant didn't tell the truth, he didn't lie either. He merely failed "to disclose the truth," and it is decided that he was under no special obligation to act otherwise. Although the judge refuses to apply the highest standard

3

of truth-telling to such a transaction (requiring the seller to disclose to the buyer all nonapparent defects known to him), he does recognize the relevance of the moral obligation, and gives it an appropriate, even if not a decisive, weight in his deliberations.

Sometimes a judge fails to take account of, or even to recognize, the presence of a moral duty in certain types of cases. For example, *Mitchell v. Rochester Ry. Co.* is a case dealing with the infliction of mental shock to a pregnant woman who thereafter suffers a miscarriage. Some may think the court's decision a miscarriage of justice. It is decided that she may not receive compensation for her loss even though negligently caused by another. In fact, it is only very recently that the courts have even begun to allow recovery for mental shock unaccompanied by immediate bodily injury to the complaining party. What is particularly puzzling about the Mitchell case is how the judge could fail to see, not only that mental injury is as much a harm as other harms which the law does recognize, but also that the one who wrongfully causes it is morally obligated to make reparations for it. This particular moral obligation is not expressly taken into account. Yet the failure of the judge, along with almost the entire legal tradition, to recognize it in cases of this kind only underlines its relevance.

There are some persons, of course, who hold the view that neither legal issues nor legal decisions are ever specifically moral in character. Legality is one thing, they say, and morality is another. Undoubtedly there are many legal cases in which the moral content is minimal, consisting perhaps only in the observance of the principle of impartiality, or the principle of equal treatment before the law. One can even find cases in which these simple canons of justice go unobserved. And certainly there are many cases in which a well-recognized moral obligation is not even suggested as a factor for consideration. The following cases, however, are not of those types. They have been selected precisely because certain commonly acknowledged moral obligations are involved in them in one way or another, and, in most of the cases, are explicitly avowed as such by the judge himself.

In one obvious sense of the term "moral decision," then, some legal decisions are moral decisions. All this means, of course, is that certain legal controversies involve moral factors which influence the final decision. The following cases themselves will repeatedly illustrate and verify this point. However, there are many who, while admitting the influence of moral considerations upon legal decisions, would still say that moral factors are allowed to enter into the judicial process only because of some constitutional, statutory, or other specifically legal enactment, definition, or rule. In short, that the influence of moral considerations is ultimately controlled by principles of pure legality. The resulting decisions are therefore strictly legal, but non-moral, in character, even though the subject of dispute may involve moral considerations.

Some of the following cases tend to support this view. For example, in *Webb v. McGowin* the question is raised whether a moral obligation is a sufficient consideration for a contract. The moral obligation involved is the duty of a person to be grateful to another who has saved his life. It is adjudged a sufficient consideration on the basis of a distinction between a "mere moral obligation" or conscientious duty unconnected with a receipt of a material or pecuniary benefit, and a moral obligation having such a connection. Since the obligation in question is found to be of the latter type (a life saved is worth something), and the *law* recognizes material benefits to the promisor as a valid legal consideration for a promise, the moral obligation is allowed to control the legal decision in the plaintiff's favor.

On the other hand, there are cases in this chapter, as well as throughout the book, which throw suspicion on this interpretation of the role of moral factors, especially moral obligations, in determining the legal judgment. For example, when we find a judge like Judge Parker in *Britton v. Turner* saying, "That such a rule in its operation may be very unequal, not to say unjust, is apparent," or Justice Qua in *Swinton v. Whitinsville Savings Bank* saying, "That the particular case here stated by the plaintiff possesses a certain appeal to the moral sense is scarcely to be denied," we are initially aware only that they are sensitive to the minimal requirements of justice—equality, impartiality, and the like—all of which they are *constitutionally* bound to uphold. But when Judge Parker goes on to appeal, not to precedent, or to statute, or to a constitutional provision, but rather to the "general understanding of the community" in order to decide the case in opposition to what was considered "the settled rule of law upon this subject," one may well inquire what principles of pure legality are controlling his decision in the case, and whether it isn't as much a moral decision as a legal one.

Perhaps it is *more* of a moral decision than a legal one, and there are those who would regard this as a criticism. They would regard it as an extra-judicial act, one in which the judge acts in his capacity as a moral man and not as a duly appointed judge. It is difficult, however, to square this view with the fact that such decisions are often regarded as "landmark" decisions in the law, and with the fact that they have been cited as authoritatively as any of the more "legal" decisions.

Another point worth mentioning, although it will be dealt with more particularly in Chapter 5, is concerned with the moral status of the laws or "principles of pure legality" which are said to control the employment of moral considerations in determining legal responsibility. If it is true that moral factors operate in the law only because of "legal" permission, and these purely legal principles are in fact morally neutral, then the claim that legality is one thing and morality another makes sense. If, on the contrary, the principles of legality are themselves dictates of morality, what then becomes of the contention that law and morality are distinct and separate realms?

This last issue, however, is not one with which we are immediately concerned. No position is taken in this book with regard to it, although the materials are calculated to throw some light upon it. Our immediate purposes are more restricted. They are, first, to call attention to the manner in which moral duties are taken into account in the settlement of legal controversies, and second, to point out how the judicial treatment of problems of legal responsibility provides a new perspective on the problems of moral responsibility.

Of course, the precise manner in which questions of morality are taken into account in deciding certain legal controversies is by no means evident. Although promise keeping is generally regarded as a moral duty, that fact does not imply that every breach of contract suit involves the settlement of a moral issue. Nor does it follow that because one is morally obligated to act reasonably, intelligently, or in anticipation of the conduct of others, a failure to do so will automatically mean the ascription of legal responsibility. As the cases will show, sometimes moral obligations do support judgments of legal responsibility. Occasionally, they do not. That is to say, one can be morally obligated and yet not be held legally responsible. As we shall see in a subsequent chapter, the converse—one can be held legally responsible even though he is morally blameless—also occurs. The reader should be careful to distinguish the way in which each moral issue arises, how it is taken into account or disposed of.

One of the most instructive aspects of the following cases, from a philosophical point of view, is that they raise old philosophical issues in a different way. For example, according to Hobbes' fourth "Law of Nature," one should be grateful for benefits received. This so-called natural law presumably imposes a moral duty under the appropriate circumstances. Does it also convey a moral right to someone else? Whether to every duty there is a corresponding right is a question that has long been debated. The case of *Webb v. McGowin* raises it anew by inquiring whether a person who has performed a service to another, by saving his life, and is gratefully promised a life-time pension, has a right to demand its payment.

In a somewhat similar fashion, the case of *Wagner v. International*

Ry. Co. raises questions as old as Aristotle about the "reasonable man," and more specifically about the role of reason, as contrasted with instinct or passion, in determining what are our duties to a fellow human being in distress.

Marengo v. Roy raises, among others, questions about the relationship between our duty to anticipate the conduct of others (particularly that of children) and the practical limits of human foresight. Or to put it in traditional ethical language reminiscent of Kant, whether what one "ought" to do is circumscribed by what one, practically speaking, "can" do.

DUTY TO KEEP PROMISES

Britton v. Turner*

SUPERIOR COURT OF JUDICATURE OF NEW HAMPSHIRE,
1834
6 N.H. 481, 26 AM. DEC. 713

PARKER, J.† It may be assumed that the labor performed by the plaintiff, and for which he seeks to recover a compensation in this action, was commenced under a special contract to labor for the defendant the term of one year, for the sum of one hundred and twenty dollars, and that the plaintiff has labored but a portion of that time, and has voluntarily failed to complete the entire contract. It is clear, then, that he is not entitled to recover upon the contract itself, because the service, which was to entitle him to the sum agreed upon, has never been performed.

But the question arises, can the plaintiff, under these circumstances, recover a reasonable sum for the service he has actually performed, under the count in quantum meruit?‡ Upon this, and questions of a similar nature, the decisions to be found in the books are not easily reconciled. It has been held, upon contracts of this kind for labor to be performed at a specified price, that the party who voluntarily fails to fulfil the contract by performing the whole labor contracted for, is not entitled to recover anything for the labor actually performed, however much he may have done toward the performance; and this has been considered the settled rule of law upon this subject. . . .

---

* See Appendix for an explanation of the law reporting system and the method of case citation.
† Judge. See Appendix for other abbreviations.
‡ See Glossary.

8

That such a rule in its operation may be very unequal, not to say unjust, is apparent. A party who contracts to perform certain specified labor, and who breaks his contract in the first instance, without any attempt to perform it, can only be made liable to pay the damages which the other party has sustained by reason of such non-performance, which in many instances may be trifling; whereas a party who in good faith has entered upon the performance of his contract, and nearly completed it, and then abandoned the further performance,—although the other party has had the full benefit of all that has been done, and has perhaps sustained no actual damages,—is in fact subjected to a loss of all which has been performed, in the nature of damages for the non-fulfilment of the remainder, upon the technical rule, that the contract must be fully performed in order to [permit] a recovery of any part of the compensation.

By the operation of this rule, then, the party who attempts performance may be placed in a much worse situation than he who wholly disregards his contract, and the other party may receive much more, by the breach of the contract, than the injury which he has sustained by such breach, and more than he could be entitled to were he seeking to recover damages by an action.

The case before us presents an illustration. Had the plaintiff in this case never entered upon the performance of his contract, the damage could not probably have been greater than some small expense and trouble incurred in procuring another to do the labor which he had contracted to perform. But having entered upon the performance, and labored nine and a half months, the value of which labor to the defendant as found by the jury is $95, if the defendant can succeed in this defense, he in fact receives nearly five sixths of the value of a whole year's labor, by reason of the breach of contract by the plaintiff, a sum not only utterly disproportionate to any probable, not to say possible damage which could have resulted from the neglect of the plaintiff to continue the remaining two and a half months, but altogether beyond any damage which could have been recovered by the defendant, had the plaintiff done nothing towards the fulfilment of his contract. . . .

It is said that where a party contracts to perform certain work, and to furnish materials, as, for instance, to build a house, and the work is done, but with some variations from the mode prescribed by the contract, yet if the other party has the benefit of the labor and materials he should be bound to pay so much as they are reasonably worth. . . .

Those cases are not to be distinguished, in principle, from the present, unless it be in the circumstance that where the party has contracted to furnish materials, and do certain labor, as to build a house in a specified manner, if it is not done according to the contract, the party for whom it is built may refuse to receive it,—elect to take no benefit from what has been performed and therefore if he does receive, he shall be bound to pay the value—whereas in a contract for labor, merely, from day to day, the party is continually receiving the benefit of the contract under an expectation that it will be fulfilled, and cannot, upon the breach of it, have an election to refuse to receive what has been done, and thus discharge himself from payment. But we think this difference in the nature of the contracts does not justify the application of a different rule in relation to them.

The party who contracts for labor merely, for a certain period, does so with full knowledge that he must, from the nature of the case, be accepting part performance from day to day, if the other party commences the performance, and with knowledge also that the other may eventually fail of completing the entire term.

If under the circumstances he actually receives a benefit from the labor performed, over and above the damage occasioned by the failure to complete, there is as much reason why he should pay the reasonable worth of what has thus been done for his benefit, as there is when he enters and occupies the house which has been built for him, but not according to the stipulations of the contract, and which he perhaps enters, not because he is satisfied with what has been done, but because circumstances compel him to accept it such as it is, that he should pay for the value of the house. . . .

In neither case has the contract been performed. In neither can an action be sustained on the original contract. In both the party has assented to receive what is done. The only difference is, that in the one case the assent is prior, with a knowledge that all may not be performed, in the other it is subsequent, with a knowledge that the whole has not been accomplished. . . .

We hold then, that where a party undertakes to pay upon a

special contract for the performance of labor, or the furnishing of materials, he is not to be charged upon such special agreement until the money is earned according to the terms of it; and where the parties have made an express contract the law will not imply and raise a contract different from that which the parties have entered into, except upon some farther transaction between the parties.

In case of a failure to perform such special contract, by the default of the party contracting to do the service, if the money is not due by the terms of the special agreement he is not entitled to recover for his labor, or for the materials furnished, unless the other party receives what has been done, or furnished, and upon the whole case derives a benefit from it. Taft v. Inhabitants of Montague, 14 Mass. 282, 7 Am. Dec. 215; 2 Starkie, Ev. 644.

But if, where a contract is made of such a character, a party actually receives labor or materials, and thereby derives a benefit and advantage, over and above the damage which has resulted from the breach of the contract by the other party, the labor actually done, and the value received, furnish a new consideration, and the law thereupon raises a promise to pay to the extent of the reasonable worth of such excess. This may be considered as making a new case, one not within the original agreement, and the party is entitled to "recover on his new case, for the work done, not as agreed, but yet accepted by the defendant." 1 Dane's Abr. 224. . . .

In fact we think the technical reasoning, that the performance of the whole labor is a condition precedent, and the right to recover anything dependent upon it; that the contract being entire there can be no apportionment; and that there being an express contract no other can be implied, even upon the subsequent performance of service,—is not properly applicable to this species of contract, where a beneficial service has been actually performed; for we have abundant reason to believe, that the general understanding of the community is that the hired laborer shall be entitled to compensation for the service actually performed, though he do not continue the entire term contracted for, and such contracts must be presumed to be made with reference to that understanding, unless an express stipulation shows the contrary. . . .

It is easy, if parties so choose, to provide by an express agreement that nothing shall be earned, if the laborer leaves his employer without having performed the whole service contemplated, and then there can be no pretence for a recovery if he voluntarily deserts the service before the expiration of the time. . . .

This rule, by binding the employer to pay the value of the service he actually receives, and the laborer to answer in damages where he does not complete the entire contract, will leave no temptation to the former to drive the laborer from his service, near the close of his term, by ill treatment, in order to escape from payment; nor to the latter to desert his service before the stipulated time, without a sufficient reason; and it will in most instances settle the whole controversy in one action, and prevent a multiplicity of suits and cross actions. . . .

Judgment on the verdict.

DUTY TO TELL THE TRUTH

SWINTON v. WHITINSVILLE SAVINGS BANK

SUPREME JUDICIAL COURT OF MASSACHUSETTS, 1942
311 MASS. 677, 42 N.E.2D 808

Action by Neil W. Swinton against Whitinsville Savings
Bank to recover damages for alleged fraudulent concealment by
defendant in sale of a house to plaintiff. From an order sustaining a demurrer to plaintiff's declaration, the plaintiff appeals.

QUA, JUSTICE. The declaration alleges that on or about September 12, 1938, the defendant sold the plaintiff a house in New-
ton to be occupied by the plaintiff and his family as a dwelling;
that at the time of the sale the house "was infested with termites,
an insect that is most dangerous and destructive to buildings";
that the defendant knew the house was so infested; that the plaintiff could not readily observe this condition upon inspection; that
"knowing the internal destruction that these insects were creating
in said house," the defendant falsely and fraudulently concealed
from the plaintiff its true condition; that the plaintiff at the time
of his purchase had no knowledge of the termites, exercised due
care thereafter, and learned of them about August 30, 1940; and
that, because of the destruction that was being done and the dangerous condition that was being created by the termites, the plaintiff was put to great expense for repairs and for the installation
of termite control in order to prevent the loss and destruction of
said house.

There is no allegation of any false statement or representa-
tion, or of the uttering of a half truth which may be tantamount
to a falsehood. There is no intimation that the defendant by any

means prevented the plaintiff from acquiring information as to the condition of the house. There is nothing to show any fiduciary relation between the parties, or that the plaintiff stood in a position of confidence toward or dependence upon the defendant. So far as appears the parties made a business deal at arm's length. The charge is concealment and nothing more; and it is concealment in the simple sense of mere failure to reveal, with nothing to show any peculiar duty to speak. The characterization of the concealment as false and fraudulent of course adds nothing in the absence of further allegations of fact. . . .

If this defendant is liable on this declaration every seller is liable who fails to disclose any nonapparent defect known to him in the subject of the sale which materially reduces its value and which the buyer fails to discover. Similarly it would seem that every buyer would be liable who fails to disclose any nonapparent virtue known to him in the subject of the purchase which materially enhances its value and of which the seller is ignorant. . . . The law has not yet, we believe, reached the point of imposing upon the frailties of human nature a standard so idealistic as this. That the particular case here stated by the plaintiff possesses a certain appeal to the moral sense is scarcely to be denied. Probably the reason is to be found in the facts that the infestation of buildings by termites has not been common in Massachusetts and constitutes a concealed risk against which buyers are off their guard. But the law cannot provide special rules for termites and can hardly attempt to determine liability according to the varying probabilities of the existence and discovery of different possible defects in the subjects of trade. The rule of nonliability for bare nondisclosure has been stated and followed by this court. . . . It is adopted in the American Law Institute's Restatement of Torts §551. See Williston on Contracts, Rev. Ed., §§1497, 1498, 1499.

The order sustaining the demurrer is affirmed, and judgment is to be entered for the defendant. . . .

So ordered.

DUTY TO MAKE REPARATIONS

MITCHELL V. ROCHESTER RY. CO.

COURT OF APPEALS OF NEW YORK, 1896
151 N.Y. 107, 45 N.E. 354

Action by Annie Mitchell against the Rochester Railway
Company. From an order (28 N.Y. Supp. 1136) affirming an order
(25 N.Y. Supp. 744) setting aside a nonsuit, defendant appeals.
Reversed.

MARTIN, J. The facts in this case are few, and may be briefly
stated. On the 1st day of April, 1891, the plaintiff was standing
upon a crosswalk on Main Street, in the city of Rochester, await-
ing an opportunity to board one of the defendant's cars which
had stopped upon the street at that place. While standing there,
and just as she was about to step upon the car, a horse car of the
defendant came down the street. As the team attached to the car
drew near, it turned to the right, and came close to the plaintiff, so that she stood between the horses' heads when they were
stopped. She testified that from fright and excitement caused by
the approach and proximity of the team she became unconscious,
and also that the result was a miscarriage, and consequent illness.
Medical testimony was given to the effect that the mental shock
which she then received was sufficient to produce that result. Assuming that the evidence tended to show that the defendant's
servant was negligent in the management of the car and horses,
and that the plaintiff was free from contributory negligence, the
single question presented is whether the plaintiff is entitled to recover for the defendant's negligence which occasioned her fright

and alarm, and resulted in the injuries already mentioned. While the authorities are not harmonious upon this question, we think the most reliable and better-considered cases, as well as public policy, fully justify us in holding that the plaintiff cannot recover for injuries occasioned by fright, as there was no immediate personal injury. Lehman v. Railroad Co., 47 Hun, 335; Commissioners v. Coultas, 13 App. Cas. 222; Ewing v. Railway Co., 147 Pa. St. 40, 23 Atl. 340. The learned counsel for the respondent in his brief very properly stated that "the consensus of opinion would seem to be that no recovery can be had for mere fright," as will be readily seen by an examination of the following additional authorities. [Citations omitted.] If it be admitted that no recovery can be had for fright occasioned by the negligence of another, it is somewhat difficult to understand how a defendant would be liable for its consequences. Assuming that fright cannot form the basis of an action, it is obvious that no recovery can be had for injuries resulting therefrom. That the result may be nervous disease, blindness, insanity, or even a miscarriage, in no way changes the principle. These results merely show the degree of fright, or the extent of the damages. The right of action must still depend upon the question whether a recovery may be had for fright. If it can, then an action may be maintained, however slight the injury. If not, then there can be no recovery, no matter how grave or serious the consequences. Therefore the logical result of the respondent's concession would seem to be, not only that no recovery can be had for mere fright, but also that none can be had for injuries which are the direct consequences of it. If the right of recovery in this class of cases should be once established, it would naturally result in a flood of litigation in cases where the injury complained of may be easily feigned without detection, and where the damages must rest upon mere conjecture or speculation. The difficulty which often exists in cases of alleged physical injury, in determining whether they exist, and, if so, whether they were caused by the negligent act of the defendant, would not only be greatly increased, but a wide field would be opened for fictitious or speculative claims. To establish such a doctrine would be contrary to principles of public policy. Moreover, it cannot be properly said that the plaintiff's miscarriage was the proximate result of the defendant's negligence. Proximate damages are such as are the ordinary and natural results of the negligence charged, and those that are usual, and may, therefore, be expected. It is quite obvious that the plaintiff's injuries do not fall within the rule as to proximate damages. The injuries to the plaintiff were plainly the result of an accidental or unusual combination of circumstances, which could not have been reasonably anticipated, and over which the defendant had no control, and hence her damages were too remote to justify a recovery in this action. These considerations lead to the conclusion that no recovery can be had for injuries sustained by fright occasioned by the negligence of another, where there is no immediate personal injury. The orders of the general and special terms should be reversed, and the order of the trial term granting a nonsuit affirmed, with costs. . . . Ordered accordingly.

DUTY TO BE GRATEFUL

WEBB v. McGowin

COURT OF APPEALS OF ALABAMA, 1935
27 ALA. APP. 82, 168 SO. 196

Action by Joe Webb against N. Floyd McGowin and Joseph F. McGowin, as executors of the estate of J. Greeley McGowin, deceased. From a judgment of nonsuit, plaintiff appeals.
Reversed and remanded.
Certiorari denied by Supreme Court in Webb v. McGowin (3 Div. 170) 232 Ala. 374, 168 So. 199.

BRICKEN, PRESIDING JUDGE. This action is in assumpsit. The complaint as originally filed was amended. The demurrers to the complaint as amended were sustained, and because of this adverse ruling by the court the plaintiff took a nonsuit, and the assignment of errors on this appeal are predicated upon said action or ruling of the court.

A fair statement of the case presenting the questions for decision is set out in appellant's brief, which we adopt.

"On the 3d day of August, 1925, appellant while in the employ of the W. T. Smith Lumber Company, a corporation, and acting within the scope of his employment, was engaged in clearing the upper floor of mill No. 2 of the company. While so engaged he was in the act of dropping a pine block from the upper floor of the mill to the ground below; this being the usual and ordinary way of clearing the floor, and it being the duty of the plaintiff in the course of his employment to so drop it. The block weighed about 75 pounds.

"As appellant was in the act of dropping the block to the ground below, he was on the edge of the upper floor of the mill. As he started to turn the block loose so that it would drop to the ground, he saw J. Greeley McGowin, testator of the defendants, on the ground below and directly under where the block would have fallen had appellant turned it loose. Had he turned it loose it would have struck McGowin with such force as to have caused him serious bodily harm or death. Appellant could have remained safely on the upper floor of the mill by turning the block loose and allowing it to drop, but had he done this the block would have fallen on McGowin and caused him serious injuries or death. The only safe and reasonable way to prevent this was for appellant to hold to the block and divert its direction in falling from the place where McGowin was standing and the only safe way to divert it so as to prevent its coming into contact with Mc-Gowin was for appellant to fall with it to the ground below. Appellant did this, and by holding to the block and falling with it to the ground below, he diverted the course of its fall in such way that McGowin was not injured. In thus preventing the injuries to McGowin appellant himself received serious bodily injuries, resulting in his right leg being broken, the heel of his right foot torn off and his right arm broken. He was badly crippled for life and rendered unable to do physical or mental labor.

"On September 1, 1925, in consideration of appellant having prevented him from sustaining death or serious bodily harm and in consideration of the injuries appellant had received, McGowin agreed with him to care for and maintain him for the remainder of appellant's life at the rate of $15 every two weeks from the time he sustained his injuries to and during the remainder of appellant's life; it being agreed that McGowin would pay this sum to appellant for his maintenance. Under the agreement McGowin paid or caused to be paid to appellant the sum so agreed on up until McGowin's death on January 1, 1934. After his death the payments were continued to and including January 27, 1934, at which time they were discontinued. Thereupon plaintiff brought suit to recover the unpaid installments accruing up to the time of the bringing of the suit. . . ."

The action was for the unpaid installments accruing after January 27, 1934, to the time of the suit.

The principal grounds of demurrer to the original and amended complaint are: (1) It states no cause of action; (2) its averments show the contract was without consideration; (3) it fails to allege that McGowin had, at or before the services were rendered, agreed to pay appellant for them; (4) the contract declared on is void under the statute of frauds.

The averments of the complaint show that appellant saved McGowin from death or grievous bodily harm. This was a material benefit to him of infinitely more value than any financial aid he could have received. Receiving this benefit, McGowin became morally bound to compensate appellant for the services rendered. Recognizing his moral obligation, he expressly agreed to pay appellant as alleged in the complaint and complied with this agreement up to the time of his death; a period of more than 8 years.

Had McGowin been accidentally poisoned and a physician, without his knowledge or request, had administered an antidote, thus saving his life, a subsequent promise by McGowin to pay the physician would have been valid. Likewise, McGowin's agreement as disclosed by the complaint to compensate appellant for saving him from death or grievous bodily injury is valid and enforceable.

Where the promisee cares for, improves, and preserves the property of the promisor, though done without his request, it is sufficient consideration for the promisor's subsequent agreement to pay for the service, because of the material benefit received. . . . Edison v. Poppe, 24 S.D. 466, 124 N.W. 441, 26 L.R.A., N.S., 534.

In Boothe v. Fitzpatrick, 36 Vt. 681, the court held that a promise by defendant to pay for the past keeping of a bull which had escaped from defendant's premises and been cared for by plaintiff was valid, although there was no previous request, because the subsequent promise obviated that objection; it being equivalent to a previous request. On the same principle, had the promisee saved the promisor's life or his body from grievous harm, his subsequent promise to pay for the services rendered would have been valid. Such service would have been far more material than caring for his bull. Any holding that saving a man from death or grievous bodily harm is not a material benefit sufficient to uphold a subsequent promise to pay for the service, necessarily rests on the assumption that saving life and preservation of the body from harm have only a sentimental value. The converse of this is true. Life and preservation of the body have material, pecuniary values, measurable in dollars and cents. Because of this, physicians practice their profession charging for services rendered in saving life and curing the body of its ills, and surgeons perform operations. The same is true as to the law of negligence, authorizing the assessment of damages in personal injury cases based upon the extent of the injuries, earnings, and life expectancies of those injured.

In the business of life insurance, the value of a man's life is measured in dollars and cents according to his expectancy, the soundness of his body, and his ability to pay premiums. The same is true as to health and accident insurance.

It follows that if, as alleged in the complaint, appellant saved J. Greeley McGowin from death or grievous bodily harm, and McGowin subsequently agreed to pay him for the service rendered, it became a valid and enforceable contract.

It is well settled that a moral obligation is a sufficient consideration to support a subsequent promise to pay where the promisor has received a material benefit, although there was no original duty or liability resting on the promisor. . . .

The case at bar is clearly distinguishable from that class of cases where the consideration is a mere moral obligation or conscientious duty unconnected with receipt by promisor of benefits of a material or pecuniary nature. . . . Here the promisor received a material benefit constituting a valid consideration for his promise.

Some authorities hold that, for a moral obligation to support a subsequent promise to pay, there must have existed a prior legal or equitable obligation, which for some reason had become unenforceable, but for which the promisor was still morally bound. This rule, however, is subject to qualification in those cases where the promisor, having received a material benefit from the promisee, is morally bound to compensate him for the services rendered and in consideration of this obligation promises to pay. In such cases the subsequent promise to pay is an affirmance or ratification of the services rendered carrying with it the presumption that a previous request for the service was made. . . .

Under the decisions above cited, McGowin's express promise to pay appellant for the services rendered was an affirmance or ratification of what appellant had done raising the presumption that the services had been rendered at McGowin's request.

The averments of the complaint show that in saving McGowin from death or grievous bodily harm, appellant was crippled for life. This was part of the consideration of the contract declared on. McGowin was benefited. Appellant was injured. Benefit to the promisor or injury to the promisee is a sufficient legal consideration for the promisor's agreement to pay. . . .

Under the averments of the complaint the services rendered were not gratuitous. The agreement of McGowin to pay and the acceptance of payment by appellant conclusively shows the contrary.

The contract declared on was not void under the statute of frauds (Code 1923, § 8034). . . .

From what has been said, we are of the opinion that the court below erred in the ruling complained of; that is to say, in sustaining the demurrer, and for this error the case is reversed and remanded.

Reversed and remanded.

SAMFORD, JUDGE (concurring). The questions involved in this case are not free from doubt, and perhaps the strict letter of the rule, as stated by judges, though not always in accord, would bar a recovery by plaintiff, but following the principle announced by Chief Justice Marshall in Hoffman v. Porter, Fed. Cas. No. 6,577, 2 Brock. 156, 159, where he says, "I do not think that law ought to be separated from justice, where it is at most doubtful," I concur in the conclusions reached by the court.

DUTY TO PREVENT INJUSTICE

RIGGS V. PALMER

COURT OF APPEALS OF NEW YORK, 1889
115 N.Y. 506, 22 N.E. 188

EARL, J. On the 13th day of August, 1880, Francis B. Palmer made his last will and testament, in which he gave small legacies to his two daughters, Mrs. Riggs and Mrs. Preston, the plaintiffs in this action, and the remainder of his estate to his grandson, the defendant Elmer E. Palmer, subject to the support of Susan Palmer, his mother, with a gift over to the two daughters, subject to the support of Mrs. Palmer in case Elmer should survive him and die under age, unmarried, and without any issue. The testator, at the date of his will, owned a farm, and considerable personal property. He was a widower, and thereafter, in March, 1882, he was married to Mrs. Bresee, with whom, before his marriage, he entered into an antenuptial contract, in which it was agreed that in lieu of dower and all other claims upon his estate in case she survived him she should have her support upon his farm during her life, and such support was expressly charged upon the farm. At the date of the will, and subsequently to the death of the testator, Elmer lived with him as a member of his family, and at his death was 16 years old. He knew of the provisions made in his favor in the will, and, that he might prevent his grandfather from revoking such provisions, which he had manifested some intention to do, and to obtain the speedy enjoyment and immediate possession of his property, he willfully murdered him by poisoning him. He now claims the property, and the sole question for our determination is, can he have it?

The defendants say that the testator is dead; that his will was made in due form, and has been admitted to probate; and that therefore it must have effect according to the letter of the law. It is quite true that statutes regulating the making, proof, and effect of wills and the devolution of property, if literally construed, and if their force and effect can in no way and under no circumstances be controlled or modified, give this property to the murderer. The purpose of those statutes was to enable testators to dispose of their estates to the objects of their bounty at death, and to carry into effect their final wishes legally expressed; and in considering and giving effect to them this purpose must be kept in view. It was the intention of the law-makers that the donees in a will should have the property given to them. But it never could have been their intention that a donee who murdered the testator to make the will operative should have any benefit under it. If such a case had been present to their minds, and it had been supposed necessary to make some provision of law to meet it, it cannot be doubted that they would have provided for it. It is a familiar canon of construction that a thing which is within the intention of the makers of a statute is as much within the statutes as if it were within the letter; and a thing which is within the letter of the statute is not within the statute unless it be within the intention of the makers. The writers of laws do not always express their intention perfectly, but either exceed it or fall short of it, so that judges are to collect it from probable or rational conjectures only, and this is called "rational interpretation;" and Rutherford, in his Institutes, (page 420) says: "Where we make use of rational interpretation, sometimes we restrain the meaning of the writer so as to take in less, and sometimes we extend or enlarge his meaning so as to take in more, than his words express." Such a construction ought to be put upon a statute as will best answer the intention which the makers had in view, for *qui haeret in litera, haeret in cortice* ["He who clings to the letter has nothing but the outer shell"]. . . . Many cases are mentioned where it was held that matters embraced in the general words of statutes nevertheless were not within the statutes, because it could not have been the intention of the law-makers that they should be included. They were taken out of the statutes by an equitable construction; and it is said in Bacon: "By an equitable construc-

tion a case not within the letter of a statute is sometimes holden
to be within the meaning, because it is within the mischief for
which a remedy is provided. The reason for such construction is
that the law-makers could not set down every case in express
terms. In order to form a right judgment whether a case be within
the equity of a statute, it is a good way to suppose the law-maker
present, and that you have asked him this question: Did you intend to comprehend this case? Then you must give yourself such
answer as you imagine he, being an upright and reasonable man,
would have given. If this be that he did mean to comprehend it,
you may safely hold the case to be within the equity of the statute; for while you do no more than he would have done, you do
not act contrary to the statute, but in conformity thereto." 9 Bac.
Abr. 248. In some cases the letter of a legislative act is restrained
by an equitable construction; in others, it is enlarged; in others,
the construction is contrary to the letter. The equitable construction which restrains the letter of a statute is defined by Aristotle
as frequently quoted in this manner: *Aequitas est correctio legis
generaliter latae qua parte deficit* ["Equity is the correction of the
law wherein it is deficient by reason of its generality"]. If the law-
makers could, as to this case, be consulted, would they say that
they intended by their general language that the property of a
testator or of an ancestor should pass to one who had taken his
life for the express purpose of getting his property? . . .

What could be more unreasonable than to suppose that it
was the legislative intention in the general laws passed for the
orderly, peaceable, and just devolution of property that they
should have operation in favor of one who murdered his ancestor
that he might speedily come into the possession of his estate? Such
an intention is inconceivable. We need not, therefore, be much
troubled by the general language contained in the laws. Besides,
all laws, as well as all contracts, may be controlled in their operation and effect by general, fundamental maxims of the common
law. No one shall be permitted to profit by his own fraud, or to
take advantage of his own wrong, or to found any claim upon
his own iniquity, or to acquire property by his own crime. These
maxims are dictated by public policy, have their foundation in
universal law administered in all civilized countries, and have no-
where been superseded by statutes. They were applied in the de-

cision of the case of Insurance Co. v. Armstrong, 117 U.S. 599, 6 Sup. Ct. Rep. 877. There it was held that the person who procured a policy upon the life of another, payable at his death, and then murdered the assured to make the policy payable, could not recover thereon. Mr. Justice Field, writing the opinion, said: "Independently of any proof of the motives of Hunter in obtaining the policy, and even assuming that they were just and proper, he forfeited all rights under it when, to secure its immediate payment, he murdered the assured. It would be a reproach to the jurisprudence of the country if one could recover insurance money payable on the death of a party whose life he had feloniously taken. As well might he recover insurance money upon a building that he had willfully fired." These maxims, without any statute giving them force or operation, frequently control the effect and nullify the language of wills. A will procured by fraud and deception, like any other instrument, may be decreed void, and set aside; and so a particular portion of a will may be excluded from probate, or held inoperative, if induced by the fraud or undue influence of the person in whose favor it is. Allen v. McPherson, 1 H.L. Cas. 191; Harrison's Appeal, 48 Conn. 202. So a will may contain provisions which are immoral, irreligious, or against public policy, and they will be held void.

Here there was no certainty that this murderer would survive the testator, or that the testator would not change his will, and there was no certainty that he would get this property if nature was allowed to take its course. He therefore murdered the testator expressly to vest himself with an estate. Under such circumstances, what law, human or divine, will allow him to take the estate and enjoy the fruits of his crime? The will spoke and became operative at the death of the testator. He caused that death, and thus by his crime made it speak and have operation. Shall it speak and operate in his favor? If he had met the testator, and taken his property by force, he would have had no title to it. Shall he acquire title by murdering him? If he had gone to the testator's house, and by force compelled him, or by fraud and undue influence had induced him, to will him his property, the law would not allow him to hold it. But can he give effect and operation to a will by murder, and yet take the property? To answer these questions in the affirmative it seems to me would be a reproach to the jurisprudence of our state, and an offense against public policy. Under the civil law, evolved from the general principles of natural law and justice by many generations of jurisconsults, philosophers, and statesmen, one cannot take property by inheritance or will from an ancestor or benefactor whom he has murdered. Dom. Civil Law, pt. 2, bk. 1, tit. 1, § 3; Code Nap. § 727; Mack. Rom. Law, 530, 550. In the Civil Code of Lower Canada the provisions on the subject in the Code Napoleon have been substantially copied. But, so far as I can find, in no country where the common law prevails has it been deemed important to enact a law to provide for such a case. Our revisers and law-makers were familiar with the civil law, and they did not deem it important to incorporate into our statutes its provisions upon this subject. This is not a *casus omissus* [i.e., a case or contingency for which no legal provision has been made]. It was evidently supposed that the maxims of the common law were sufficient to regulate such a case, and that a specific enactment for that purpose was not needed. For the same reasons the defendant Palmer cannot take any of this property as heir. Just before the murder he was not an heir, and it was not certain that he ever would be. He might have died before his grandfather, or might have been disinherited by him. He made himself an heir by the murder, and he seeks to take property as the fruit of his crime. What has before been said as to him as legatee applies to him with equal force as an heir. He cannot vest himself with title by crime. My view of this case does not inflict upon Elmer any greater or other punishment for his crime than the law specifies. It takes from him no property, but simply holds that he shall not acquire property by his crime, and thus be rewarded for its commission.

Our attention is called to Owens v. Owens, 100 N.C. 240, 6 S.E. Rep. 794, as a case quite like this. There a wife had been convicted of being an accessory before the fact to the murder of her husband, and it was held that she was nevertheless entitled to dower. I am unwilling to assent to the doctrine of that case. The statutes provide dower for a wife who has the misfortune to survive her husband, and thus lose his support and protection. It is clear beyond their purpose to make provision for a wife who by her own crime makes herself a widow, and willfully and intentionally deprives herself of the support and protection of her husband. As she might have died before him, and thus never have been his widow, she cannot by her crime vest herself with an estate. The principle which lies at the bottom of the maxim *volenti non fit injuria* ["No injury is done to one who consents"] should be applied to such a case, and a widow should not, for the purpose of acquiring, as such, property rights, be permitted to allege a widowhood which she has wickedly and intentionally created.

The facts found entitled the plaintiffs to the relief they seek. The error of the referee was in his conclusion of law. Instead of granting a new trial, therefore, I think the proper judgment upon the facts found should be ordered here. The facts have been passed upon twice with the same result,—first upon the trial of Palmer for murder, and then by the referee in this action. We are therefore of opinion that the ends of justice do not require that they should again come in question. The judgment of the general term and that entered upon the report of the referee should therefore be reversed, and judgment should be entered as follows: That Elmer E. Palmer and the administrator be enjoined from using any of the personalty or real estate left by the testator for Elmer's benefit; that the devise and bequest in the will to Elmer be declared ineffective to pass the title to him; that by reason of the crime of murder committed upon the grandfather he is deprived of any interest in the estate left by him; that the plaintiffs are the true owners of the real and personal estate left by the testator, subject to the charge in favor of Elmer's mother and the widow of the testator, under the antenuptial agreement, and that the plaintiffs have costs in all the courts against Elmer. All concur, except GRAY, J., who reads dissenting opinion, and DANFORTH, J., concurs.

GRAY, J. (dissenting). This appeal presents an extraordinary state of facts, and the case, in respect of them, I believe, is without precedent in this state. The respondent, a lad of 16 years of age, being aware of the provisions in his grandfather's will, which constituted him the residuary legatee of the testator's estate, caused his death by poison, in 1882. For this crime he was tried, and was convicted of murder in the second degree, and at the time of the commencement of this action he was serving out his sentence in the state reformatory. This action was brought by two of the children of the testator for the purpose of having those provisions of the will in the respondent's favor canceled and annulled. The appellants' argument for a reversal of the judgment, which dismissed their complaint, is that the respondent unlawfully prevented a revocation of the existing will, or a new will from being made, by his crime; and that he terminated the enjoyment by the testator of his property, and effected his own succession to it, by the same crime. They say that to permit the respondent to take the property willed to him would be to permit him to take advantage of his own wrong. To sustain their position the appellants' counsel has submitted an able and elaborate brief, and, if I believed that the decision of the question could be effected by considerations of an equitable nature, I should not hesitate to assent to views which commend themselves to the conscience. But the matter does not lie within the domain of conscience. We are bound by the rigid rules of law, which have been established by the legislature, and within the limits of which the determination of this question is confined. The question we are dealing with is whether a testamentary disposition can be altered, or a will revoked, after the testator's death, through an appeal to the courts, when the legislature has by its enactments prescribed exactly when and how wills may be made, altered, and revoked, and apparently, as it seems to me, when they have been fully complied with, has left no room for the exercise of an equitable jurisdiction by courts over such matters. Modern jurisprudence, in recognizing the right of the individual, under more or less restrictions, to dispose of his property after his death, subjects it to legislative control, both as to extent and as to mode of exercise. Complete freedom of testamentary disposition of one's property has not been and is not the universal rule, as we see from the provisions of the Napoleonic Code, from the systems of jurisprudence in countries which are modeled upon the Roman law, and from the statutes of many of our states. To the statutory restraints which are imposed upon the disposition of one's property by will are added strict and systematic statutory rules for the execution, alteration, and revocation of the will, which must be, at least substantially, if not exactly, followed to insure validity and performance. The reason for the establishment of such rules, we may naturally assume, consists in the purpose to create those safeguards about these grave and important acts which experience has demonstrated to be the wisest and surest. That freedom which is permitted to be exercised in the testamentary disposition of one's estate by the laws of the state is subject to its being exercised in conformity with the regulations of the statutes. The capacity and the power of the individual to dispose of his property after death, and the mode by which that power can be exercised, are matters of which the legislature has assumed the entire control, and has undertaken to regulate with comprehensive particularity.

The appellants' argument is not helped by reference to those rules of the civil law, or to those laws of other governments, by which the heir, or legatee, is excluded from benefit under the testament if he has been convicted of killing, or attempting to kill, the testator. In the absence of such legislation here, the courts are not empowered to institute such a system of remedial justice. The deprivation of the heir of his testamentary succession by the Roman law, when guilty of such a crime, plainly was intended to be in the nature of a punishment imposed upon him. The succession, in such a case of guilt, escheated to the exchequer. See Dom. Civil Law, pt. 2, bk. 1, tit. 1, § 3. I concede that rules of law which annul testamentary provisions made for the benefit of those who have become unworthy of them may be based on principles of equity and of natural justice. It is quite reasonable to suppose that a testator would revoke or alter his will, where his mind has been so angered and changed as to make him unwilling to have his will executed as it stood. But these principles only suggest sufficient reasons for the enactment of laws to meet such cases.

The statutes of this state have prescribed various ways in which a will may be altered or revoked; but the very provision defining the modes of alteration and revocation implies a prohibition of alteration or revocation in any other way. The words of the section of the statute are: "No will in writing, except in the cases hereinafter mentioned, nor any part thereof, shall be revoked or altered otherwise," etc. Where, therefore, none of the cases mentioned are met by the facts, and the revocation is not in the way described in the section, the will of the testator is unalterable. I think that a valid will must continue as a will always, unless revoked in the manner provided by the statutes. Mere intention to revoke a will does not have the effect of revocation. The intention to revoke is necessary to constitute the effective revocation of a will, but it must be demonstrated by one of the acts contemplated by the statute. As WOODWORTH, J., said in Dan v. Brown, 4 Cow. 490: "Revocation is an act of the mind, which must be demonstrated by some outward and visible sign of revocation." The same learned judge said in that case: "The rule is that if the testator lets the will stand until he dies, it is his will; if he does not suffer it to do so, it is not his will." And see Goodright v. Glazier, 4 Burrows, 2512, 2514; Pemberton v. Pemberton, 13 Ves. 290. The finding of fact of the referee that presumably the testator would have altered his will had he known of his grandson's murderous intent cannot affect the question. We may concede it to the fullest extent; but still the cardinal objection is undisposed of,—that the making and the revocation of a will are purely matters of statutory regulation, by which the court is bound in the determination of questions relating to these acts.

Two cases,—in this state and in Kentucky,—at an early day, seem to me to be much in point. Gains v. Gains, 2 A. K. Marsh. 190, was decided by the Kentucky court of appeals in 1820. It was there urged that the testator intended to have destroyed his will, and that he was forcibly prevented from doing so by the defendant in error or devisee; and it was insisted that the will, though not expressly, was thereby virtually, revoked. The court held, as the act concerning wills prescribed the manner in which a will might be revoked, that, as none of the acts evidencing revocation were done, the intention could not be substituted for the act. In that case the will was snatched away, and forcibly retained. In 1854, SURROGATE BRADFORD, whose opinions are entitled to the highest consideration, decided the case of Leaycraft v. Simmons, 3 Bradf. Sur. 35. In that case the testator, a man of 89 years of age, desired to make a codicil to his will, in order to enlarge the provisions for his daughter. His son, having the custody of the instrument, and the one to be prejudiced by the change, refused to produce the will at testator's request, for the purpose of alteration. The learned surrogate refers to the provisions of the civil law for such and other cases of unworthy conduct in the heir or legatee, and says: "Our statute has undertaken to prescribe the mode in which wills can be revoked [citing the statutory provision]. This is the law by which I am governed in passing upon questions touching the revocation of wills. The whole of this subject is now regulated by statute; and a mere intention to revoke, however well authenticated, or however defeated, is not sufficient." And he held that the will must be admitted to probate. I may refer also to a case in the Pennsylvania courts. In that state the statute prescribed the mode for repealing or altering a will, and in Clingan v. Micheltree, 31 Pa. St. 25, the supreme court of the state held, where a will was kept from destruction by the fraud and misrepresentation of the devisee, that to declare it canceled as against the fraudulent party would be to enlarge the statute.

I cannot find any support for the argument that the respondent's succession to the property should be avoided because of his criminal act, when the laws are silent. Public policy does not demand it; for the demands of public policy are satisfied by the proper execution of the laws and the punishment of the crime. There has been no convention between the testator and his legatee; nor is there any such contractual element, in such a disposition of property by a testator, as to impose or imply conditions in the legatee. The appellants' argument practically amounts to this: that, as the legatee has been guilty of a crime, by the commission of which he is placed in a position to sooner receive the benefits of the testamentary provision, his rights to the property should be forfeited, and he should be divested of his estate. To allow their argument to prevail would involve the diversion by the court of the testator's estate into the hands of persons whom, possibly enough, for all we know, the testator might not have chosen or desired as its recipients. Practically the court is asked to make another will for the testator. The laws do not warrant this judicial action, and mere presumption would not be strong enough to sustain it. But, more than this, to concede the appellants' views would involve the imposition of an additional punishment or penalty upon the respondent. What power or warrant have the courts to add to the respondent's penalties by depriving him of property? The law has punished him for his crime, and we may not say that it was an insufficient punishment. In the trial and punishment of the respondent the law has vindicated itself for the outrage which he committed, and further judicial utterance upon the subject of punishment or deprivation of rights is barred. We may not, in the language of the court in People v. Thornton, 25 Hun. 456, "enhance the pains, penalties, and forfeitures provided by law for the punishment of crime." The judgment should be affirmed, with costs.

DANFORTH, J., concurs.

DUTY TO RESCUE

WAGNER V. INTERNATIONAL RY. CO.

COURT OF APPEALS OF NEW YORK, 1921
232 N.Y. 176, 133 N.E. 437

CARDOZO, J. The action is for personal injuries. The defendant operates an electric railway between Buffalo and Niagara Falls. There is a point on its line where an overhead crossing carries its tracks above those of the New York Central and the Erie. A gradual incline upwards over a trestle raises the tracks to a height of 25 feet. A turn is then made to the left at an angle of from 64 to 84 degrees. After making this turn, the line passes over a bridge, which is about 158 feet long from one abutment to the other. Then comes a turn to the right at about the same angle down the same kind of an incline to grade. Above the trestle, the tracks are laid on ties unguarded at the ends. There is thus an overhang of the cars, which is accentuated at curves. On the bridge, a narrow footpath runs between the tracks, and beyond the line of overhang there are tie rods and a protecting rail.

Plaintiff and his cousin Herbert boarded a car at a station near the bottom of one of the trestles. Other passengers, entering at the same time, filled the platform, and blocked admission to the aisle. The platform was provided with doors, but the conductor did not close them. Moving at from 6 to 8 miles an hour, the car, without slackening, turned the curve. There was a violent lurch, and Herbert Wagner was thrown out, near the point where the trestle changes to a bridge. The cry was raised, "Man overboard." The car went on across the bridge, and stopped near the foot of the incline. Night and darkness had come on. Plaintiff walked along the trestle, a distance of 445 feet, until he arrived at the bridge, where he thought to find his cousin's body. He says that he was asked to go there by the conductor. He says, too, that the conductor followed with a lantern. Both these statements the conductor denies. Several other persons, instead of ascending the trestle, went beneath it, and discovered under the bridge the body they were seeking. As they stood there, the plaintiff's body struck the ground beside them. Reaching the bridge, he had found upon a beam his cousin's hat, but nothing else. About him there was darkness. He missed his footing, and fell.

The trial judge held that negligence toward Herbert Wagner would not charge the defendant with liability for injuries suffered by the plaintiff unless two other facts were found: First, that the plaintiff had been invited by the conductor to go upon the bridge; and, second, that the conductor had followed with a light. Thus limited, the jury found in favor of the defendant. Whether the limitation may be upheld is the question to be answered.

Danger invites rescue. The cry of distress is the summons to relief. The law does not ignore these reactions of the mind in tracing conduct to its consequences. It recognizes them as normal. It places their effects within the range of the natural and probable. The wrong that imperils life is a wrong to the imperiled victim; it is wrong also to his rescuer. The state that leaves an opening in a bridge is liable to the child that falls into the stream, but liable also to the parent who plunges to its aid. . . . The railroad company whose train approaches without signal is a wrongdoer toward the traveler surprised between the rails, but a wrongdoer also to the bystander who drags him from the path. Eckert v. Long Island R.R. Co., 43 N.Y. 502, 3 Am. Rep. 721. . . . The rule is the same in other jurisdictions. . . . The risk of rescue, if only it be not wanton, is born of the occasion. The emergency begets the man. The wrongdoer may not have foreseen the coming of a deliverer. He is accountable as if he had. . . .

The defendant says that we must stop, in following the chain of causes, when action ceases to be "instinctive." By this is meant, it seems, that rescue is at the peril of the rescuer, unless spontaneous and immediate. If there has been time to deliberate, if impulse has given way to judgment, one cause, it is said, has spent its force, and another has intervened. In this case the plaintiff walked more than 400 feet in going to Herbert's aid. He had time to reflect and weigh; impulse had been followed by choice; and choice, in the defendant's view, intercepts and breaks the sequence. We find no warrant for thus shortening the chain of jural causes. We may assume, though we are not required to decide, that peril and rescue must be in substance one transaction; that the sight of the one must have aroused the impulse to the other; in short, that there must be unbroken continuity between the commission of the wrong and the effort to avert its consequences. If all this be assumed, the defendant is not aided. Continuity in such circumstances is not broken by the exercise of volition. . . . So sweeping an exception, if recognized, would leave little of the rule. "The human mind," as we have said (People v. Majone, 91 N.Y. 211, 212), "acts with celerity which it is sometimes impossible to measure." The law does not discriminate between the rescuer oblivious of peril and the one who counts the cost. It is enough that the act, whether impulsive or deliberate, is the child of the occasion.

The defendant finds another obstacle, however, in the futility of the plaintiff's sacrifice. He should have gone, it is said, below the trestle with the others; he should have known, in view of the overhang of the cars, that the body would not be found above; his conduct was not responsive to the call of the emergency; it was a wanton exposure to a danger that was useless. . . . We think the quality of his acts in the situation that confronted him was to be determined by the jury. Certainly he believed that good would come of his search upon the bridge. He was not going there to view the landscape. The law cannot say of his belief that a reasonable man would have been unable to share it. He could not know the precise point at which his cousin had fallen from the car. If the fall was from the bridge, there was no reason why the body, caught by some projection, might not be hanging on high, athwart the tie rods or the beams. Certainly no such reason was then apparent to the plaintiff, or so a jury might have found. Indeed, his judgment was confirmed by the finding of the hat. There was little time for delay, if the facts were as he states them. Another car was due, and the body, if not removed, might be ground beneath the wheels. The plaintiff had to choose at once, in agitation and with imperfect knowledge. He had seen his kinsman and companion thrown out into darkness. Rescue could not charge the company with liability if rescue was condemned by reason. "Errors of judgment," however, would not count against him if they resulted "from the excitement and confusion of the moment." . . . The reason that was exacted of him was not the reason of the morrow. It was reason fitted and proportioned to the time and the event.

Whether Herbert Wagner's fall was due to the defendant's negligence, and whether plaintiff, in going to the rescue, as he did, was foolhardy or reasonable in the light of the emergency confronting him, were questions for the jury.

The judgment of the Appellate Division and that of the Trial Term should be reversed, and a new trial granted, with costs to abide the event.

DUTY TO BE INTELLIGENT

Marengo v. Roy

SUPREME JUDICIAL COURT OF MASSACHUSETTS, 1945
318 MASS. 719, 63 N.E.2D 893

QUA, JUSTICE. This action is for conscious suffering and death of the plaintiff's intestate, a boy six years and three months of age, which resulted from his being burned on May 27, 1941, in a tar kettle containing hot tar located in the back yard of a tenement house in which his father, the plaintiff was a tenant at 52 West Street, Holyoke.

The jury found for the defendants on counts alleging wilful, wanton, and reckless conduct but returned verdicts for the plaintiff on counts alleging negligence. On leave reserved the judge entered verdicts for the defendants on the negligence counts as well. The only question presented is whether there was any evidence to warrant a finding that the injury and death were caused by the violation of any duty of care which the defendant owed to the deceased.

The premises were owned by one Perron. In the back yard was a garage, also owned by Perron, the brick wall of which was surmounted by a flat roof a little over six feet above the surface of the yard. The plaintiff himself testified that this garage was not included in the tenement rented to him, and that it was rented to others. The defendants were in the roofing business. Perron had engaged them to put a new tar roof upon the main building and had given them permission to place their tar kettle in the yard. They placed it about three feet from the garage wall. The tar kettle is described as "a sort of stove." It consisted of an outside shell of cylindrical form about three feet high, within

38

which the fire was built, and an inner pot of smaller dimensions, which contained the tar. On the day of the injury the defendants' men finished with the hot tar and put the fire out at about 11 or 11:30 in the forenoon. The top of the tar kettle was covered by a flat piece of sheet metal on which was placed a slab of wood. The injury occurred between 3:30 and 4:30 in the afternoon, while all the defendants' men were on the main roof. There were still from ten to twelve inches of tar in the pot, and although according to all the evidence on the point the fire had been out for several hours, the remaining tar appears to have been hot enough to cause burns. Not all of the evidence just recited seems to have come from sources by which the plaintiff is bound, but none of it was contradicted, and there was nothing from which inferences more favorable to the plaintiff could be drawn.

The only evidence as to how the deceased got into the tar kettle came from a ten year old boy who was an eyewitness, and in the form of declarations which the plaintiff testified the deceased made before his death. The ten year old boy testified that the deceased got up on the garage roof; that an older boy promised the deceased a penny, if the deceased could jump on the cover of the tar kettle; and that the deceased jumped from the roof to the cover, but hit the cover on the side, and "it slid and he fell right in." However, the alleged declarations by the deceased were to the effect that he "thought it was a box" and tried to jump over it, but went into it; and that he did not know there was tar in it. There was evidence that "after the accident" the cover of the tar kettle was bent and "one side was pushed in." There seems to be no question but that the deceased got into the tar kettle as a result of jumping from the garage roof. The plaintiff himself in his brief states this as a fact.

The defendants contend that they are not liable for negligence because the deceased was injured as the result of trespassing upon their tar kettle. . . . But this contention is disposed of by the evidence of the declarations of the deceased from which the jury could find that he did not come into contact with the tar kettle intentionally but that he landed upon it unintentionally while trying to jump over it. If the jury believed this, such an unintended and inadvertent contact with the defendants' personal property was not itself a trespass upon that property. United Electric Light Co. v. Deliso Const. Co., Inc., 325 Mass. 313, 318,

52 N.E.2d 553. Am. Law Inst. Restatement: Torts, s. 217, and comments, s. 218 comments a and b. Compare as to real estate, Am. Law Inst. Restatement: Torts, 389, Topic 2, scope note, and ss. 165 and 166, and comments.

But the entry of verdicts for the defendants on the negligence counts was right for another reason. We think there was no evidence that the defendants were negligent with respect to such an injury as that suffered by the deceased in the circumstances shown. Even if the deceased had been playing about on the surface of the yard, it is not clear that there would have been evidence for the jury of negligence in leaving the tar kettle where it was in the condition in which it was left. So far as appears there had been no fire in it for over four hours. So far as appears no one could be injured unless he got into the tar which was still hot in the inner pot. It is not easy to understand how a child too young to appreciate the danger could get into the inner pot from the surface of the yard or how an older child could get into it without deliberately intending to do so. But however this may be, and whatever duty the defendants may have owed to children in the yard, we think that the defendants were not bound to anticipate and to guard against the bare possibility of injury to some child jumping through the cover into the pot from an adjoining roof, where in all probability he would be a trespasser either as to Perron or as to the tenants of the garage, and where his presence could not reasonably be expected. . . . Although there was considerable evidence that children did at times climb upon the garage roof, if in the circumstances this is material, we can discover no evidence sufficient to warrant a finding that the defendants had such knowledge of this as required them to act with reference to it. . . . Due care does not require that special precautions be taken against that which is only remotely possible. . . . This case is distinguishable from Sample v. City of Melrose, 312 Mass. 170, 43 N.E.2d 665, where it could be found that the defendant should have anticipated that the excavation in the yard would be a source of danger to children who might be expected to play there.

We are of opinion that the defendants were not shown to be liable for this unfortunate occurrence.

Exceptions overruled.

Notes

1. In general the law expects a certain level of intelligent behavior from everyone. However, certain classes of persons, otherwise sane, present special problems: children, aged persons, blind people, etc. Children are notorious for their thoughtlessness and capacity to get into dangerous situations. In some states, but not in all, the law tries to take account of this by means of the so-called "attractive nuisance" doctrine. One has a duty to anticipate the behavior of trespassing children under certain circumstances. Since there are limits to what can be anticipated or known to be dangerous, the question arises, To what extent must society go in protecting youth to the disadvantage of adults? Cf. *Marengo v. Roy.*

Should a blind pedestrian be required to be more cautious and abide by a higher standard of care than a person with sight? Should a person of less than average intelligence be required to act in accordance with the same standard that applies to the average citizen?

2. According to Judge Cardozo in *Wagner v. International Ry. Co.,* "The cry of distress is the summons to relief." Are we always obliged to answer the summons? A long established legal rule states that there is no duty to assist or to rescue a mere stranger. If one does assist a fellow human in danger and does so negligently, he is liable for any consequent injuries. Lawyers themselves have been critical of this rule. Yet, it persists. Are there any sound moral reasons why it should persist?

3. The dissenting judge in *Riggs v. Palmer* denies that the case is one to be decided by "conscience," or on the basis of the probability that the testator would have altered his will had he known of his grandson's murderous intent. The court is bound, he says, to follow statutory regulation. Is the matter merely one of pure legality for him, or is he too seeking to prevent injustice in another way or in another sense?

4. Certain moral philosophers (Cf. J. S. Mill, *Utilitarianism,* Ch. V; Kant, *Fundamental Principles of the Metaphysics of Morals,* Second Section) make a distinction between "duties of perfect obligation" and "duties of imperfect obligation." The former confers a right on some particular individual which he can claim against the one having the duty, e.g., the right of a promisee. The latter type of duty confers no such right. A common illustration of the latter is the duty to be charitable. Perhaps one ought to be charitable, but no one in particular has

41

a "right" to demand it of us. The duty to be grateful would seem to fall into the second category. Examine this distinction in the light of *Webb v. McGowin.*

5. The term "responsible" has many meanings. One sense is "liable to punishment, payment, or blame." Another is "conscientious" or "dependable," as in the expression "a responsible person," for example. A third sense is roughly equivalent to "is the cause of." Occasionally we make statements such as "The earthquake was responsible for the destruction" in this latter sense. When used of persons, "He was responsible for the injury" sometimes means only that he caused it. In the case of *Mitchell v. Rochester Ry. Co.,* the defendant was found responsible in the sense of being the "actual cause" of the injury, but he was not found legally liable for it. Are there occasions when being the actual cause of an injury ought to be enough to hold legally liable the person causing the injury? If so, what occasions? If not, what additional factors must be taken into account in assigning responsibility, in one of the other senses, in such cases?

6. In *Swinton v. Whitinsville Savings Bank* the problem in whether non-disclosure of the truth is a basis for liability. It is settled in part by inquiring whether any special relationship of trust is involved, e.g., that between an executor and a beneficiary or a guardian and child. In determining moral responsibility, is not the determination of the personal relations of those involved of considerable importance also? Do we have a responsibility to tell the whole truth and nothing but the truth to some persons (a jury, for example) but not to others (a door-to-door salesman)?

7. Just as the law recognizes oral as well as written contracts, it also recognizes "implied" as well as "express" contracts. In *Britton v. Turner,* an implied promise to receive day to day performance of the express contract for labor was found as a basis for an implied contract upon which the plaintiff could recover. What is the basis of the implication? Does the distinction between express and implied apply also to moral promises? Would it make sense to hold a person morally responsible for an "unexpressed" promise, or one which he himself was unaware of making?

2

WRONGS: EXCUSES

The term "wrongs" is used in this and the following chapter in a deliberately broad sense. It includes injurious actions which are excusable or justifiable as well as those which are inexcusable or unjustifiable. In short, it covers "injuries" as well as "injustices."

The need for such a term is apparent. It does not necessarily follow that a person who inflicts an injury upon another is either legally or morally responsible for it. Yet, in a larger conception of value, the injury itself is "bad," and so the negative connotation of the term "wrong" seems appropriate. Furthermore, when an injury occurs, there usually exists a prima facie case for ascribing responsibility, the basis of which being in many instances, what Ross calls the "duty not to harm others." To escape blame for the "wrong," it is incumbent upon the moral or legal defendant to come forward with an excuse or justification.

The distinction between excuses and justifications is not an easy one to draw. However, it is a familiar one to lawyers especially in connection with criminal law. Penal codes, for example, carefully stipulate the difference between excusable homicide and justifiable homicide, the former covering homicide committed by "accident or misfortune," and the latter homicide in self-defense or by public officers in the performance of their duties. Although the primary employment of the distinction is perhaps in the area of criminal law, it is by no means restricted to it, and this has justified our use of it as a way of classifying noncriminal cases as well. A more customary legal classification of civil cases of this type is by means of the less discriminating rubric of "defenses." But for our purposes, it is useful to make the distinction apply generally.

The notion underlying the distinction, in criminal law as well as outside it, is that there is a difference between wrongs or injuries which, if done under normal circumstances or by normal people, would be

43

clearly indefensible actions deserving punishment, blame, or enforced payment, and those wrongs or injuries which the agent may have had a right to do, but which are unfortunate occurrences nonetheless. Another way of expressing the distinction is by saying that excuses are appropriate only when the injurious act is unintentional, and justifications only when the act is intentional. This basis for the distinction unfortunately does not always coincide with the language of jurists, who sometimes speak of self-defense, for example, as an excuse. From the standpoint of a moral, as contrasted with a purely legal classification, it is better to regard cases of excusability as involving either inadvertence or incontinence, and cases of justifiability as involving conflict of duty situations. This rather clearly demarcates the two sets of cases, and in addition brings to light two new problems connected with the assignment of responsibility.

The first of these problems, which is the topic of this chapter, concerns the evaluation of inadvertence and incontinence as reasons for not holding a person responsible for his wrongs. The same reason may prove to be a legitimate excuse in one set of circumstances, but not in others. In the case of *Watson v. Kentucky & Indiana Bridge & R. R. Co.*, the connection between a negligent act and another's injuries was such that not even an intervening cause served as an excuse. As the judge himself suggests, however, the intervention of another agent or natural circumstance, under slightly different conditions, might be an excuse. It makes a difference, for instance, whether the act was inadvertent or intentional, or whether the intervening event or act was foreseeable.

Insanity is usually regarded as a moral as well as a legal excuse for one's wrongs. What states of mind are to be considered "insane" has always been a problem, and where the test is whether a person knows the difference between "right" and "wrong," as it is in the law, the problem is further complicated. What exactly is meant by these terms, "right" and "wrong," in this particular legal context? Jurists themselves have not always been in agreement about the answer to this question.

It is also instructive to discover that the law recognizes insanity as an excuse in connection with criminal acts, but not in connection with civil injuries, i.e., injuries for which compensation rather than punishment is demanded. In the latter type of case the insane person, or more accurately, the guardians of his estate, are held liable. This sort of vicarious responsibility, or responsibility for another's behavior, is not altogether unfamiliar in morals. Parents are sometimes held morally responsible for their children's conduct, for example, or a whole nation for the acts of its leaders. The moral legitimacy of such ascriptions of responsibility, however, has often been questioned.

The problem whether drunkenness is an excuse for wrong-doing is not a particularly new problem to philosophers. Aristotle dealt with the notion of "incontinence" in quite some detail. Though we cannot, he said, hold the person responsible for his incapacity to act otherwise at the time of the act, we can assign responsibility to him for his earlier choice by which he became drunk, and thus for the consequences of his drunken behavior. This solution to the problem is widely accepted by both philosophers and lawyers.

But the problem is not quite so simple. Neither in law nor in morals is it simply one of assigning responsibility, but also one of determining how much blame and how much responsibility. Lest we wish to rank all immoral acts equally, surely such considerations as those taken account of in *People v. Koerber* must have some analogue in moral reasoning as well.

The last two cases raise particularly challenging questions for the philosopher. Both involve legal questions about "strict liability," i.e., the holding of a person legally responsible despite the fact that he is judged to be "without fault," which, in legal terms, means that he neither conducted himself negligently nor intentionally committed an unlawful act. Such placement of responsibility is practically unheard of in morals, although there are overtones of it in the utilitarian mode of thinking, particularly in what is called "rule utilitarianism."

Ordinary or "case" utilitarians argue that an act is right if its consequences tend to promote more benefit than detriment in the world. Rule utilitarians prefer not to determine the morality of an act by the direct application of the principle of utility, but rather to argue from certain rules, the general observance of which tends to promote the greatest social benefit.

Rule utilitarianism seems to have been invented in order to avoid certain conflicts with the general moral consensus which case utilitarianism occasionally encounters. For example, on the latter position, there might be cases when a direct application of the principle of utility would condone murder, say, the killing of a man like Hitler. Rule utilitarians can admit the possible beneficial consequences of such an act, and yet condemn it, since murder "as a rule" is wrong, i.e., the general observance of the law against murder has greater beneficial consequences.

It is by no means evident, however, that rule utilitarians can always be consistent with the general moral consensus. For suppose the total social consequences of holding a person morally responsible for any death he causes, regardless of any excuse or justification he might offer, are found on the whole to be beneficial. This would, no doubt, incite considerable social indignation, but were one seriously to maintain this view, and argue for it on the ground that "as a rule" it tends to maximize the good, the result would be an extension of the doctrine of "strict liability" to morals.

Needless to say, modern Anglo-American law has never gone as far as the above hypothetical illustration suggests. The criminal law, in particular, has opposed all attempts to introduce the notion of absolute or strict liability. On the other hand, the case of *People v. Werner* clearly indicates that strict liability is not entirely absent from the criminal law. This type of legal responsibility, however, is most commonly found in certain classes of civil cases where it finds its best illustration. *Luthringer v. Moore* is such a case.

INTERVENING CAUSE

WATSON V. KENTUCKY & INDIANA BRIDGE
& R.R. Co.

COURT OF APPEALS OF KENTUCKY, 1910
137 KY. 619, 126 S.W. 146

SETTLE, J. This action was instituted by the appellant, John Watson, in the court below against the appellees, Kentucky & Indiana Bridge & Railroad Company, hereinafter called the Bridge & Railroad Company, the Southern Railway Company, the Southern Railway Company in Kentucky, and the Union Tank Line Company, to recover $20,000 damages for injuries sustained to his person on the night of June 14, 1907, from an explosion of gas caused, as alleged, by the negligence of the appellees. It was, in substance, alleged in the petition as amended that while a tank car, owned by the appellee Union Tank Line Company, and filled with a highly explosive substance known as gasoline, was being transported through a populous section of the city of Louisville over the roadbed of the appellee Bridge & Railroad Company, it was derailed and its valve broken, thereby causing all the gasoline to escape and flow in large quantities on the street and into the gutters; that from the gasoline thus flowing and standing in pools upon the street and gutters there arose and spread over the neighborhood of the place of derailment and into the houses of the residents thereof, great quantities of highly explosive and combustible gas which, three hours after the derailment of the tank car, exploded with force from contact with a lighted match thrown on the street by one Chas. Duerr, who

47

claimed to have used it in igniting a cigar; that the explosion threw appellant from his bed and almost demolished his house, from the ruins of which he was taken unconscious and bleeding with a fractured jaw and one cheek nearly torn from his face. It was further charged in the petition that the explosion and appellant's consequent injuries resulted from the negligence of all the appellees; the negligence of the Union Tank Line Company lying, as alleged, in its failure to provide the tank car with proper trucks and main valve; that of the Bridge & Railroad Company in failing to maintain in a safe condition the roadbed and track at the point of derailment; in permitting the tank car to remain at the place of derailment in its wrecked condition an unreasonable time, and in allowing ignorant and careless meddling on the part of their servants with the main valve of the tank after it was broken, whereby the flow of the gasoline from the tank was increased instead of diminished. All the material averments of the petition were specifically denied by the answer of the appellees. As on the trial the proof failed to show that either the Southern Railway Company, or the Southern Railway Company in Kentucky, was charged with the duty of maintaining the roadbed or tracks at the place of derailment or that they had handled or had anything to do with the tank car in question, appellant, at the conclusion of all the evidence, dismissed the action without prejudice as to those two appellees. At the conclusion of appellant's evidence, the appellees Bridge & Railroad Company and Union Tank Company moved the court peremptorily to instruct the jury to find for them. The motion was overruled, but being renewed by appellees after the introduction of all the evidence, it was sustained, and the jury, in obedience to the peremptory instruction then given by the court, returned a verdict in behalf of appellees, upon which judgment was entered in their favor for costs. Appellant being dissatisfied with that judgment and the refusal of the circuit court to grant him a new trial, has appealed.

The main question involved in this appeal is, whether or not the trial court erred in giving the peremptory instruction. Its decision will require consideration of the evidence. It is conceded that the tank car belonged to appellee Union Tank Line Company, and the evidence conclusively shows that it was loaded at Franklin, Pa., with gasoline. In reaching the consignee at Louisville it passed over several lines of railroad, but was delivered by the Baltimore, Ohio & Southwestern Railroad to the appellee Bridge & Railroad Company, in the city of Louisville at what is known as the Youngtown yards. The latter company was at the time of the accident hauling the tank car, attached to one of its trains, from which its railroad yards near the Ohio river to the place of business of the consignee in the southern part of the city. The derailment of the car occurred about 7:30 o'clock in the evening between Walnut and Madison streets. The gasoline began at once to escape from the tank and continued to do so for several hours until the tank was emptied. By the derailing of the car the discharge pipe beneath the tank provided for emptying it of its contents, was broken, as were the appliances for opening and closing the valves by which the contents were allowed to leave, or prevented from leaving, the tank. The gasoline in escaping from the tank ran down a gutter or drain in the street and along appellee Bridge & Railroad Company's right of way several hundred feet to a sewer into which it flowed. The employees of appellee Bridge & Railroad Company connected with the train in question, and later the wrecking crew called to their assistance, seemed to be unable to stop the escape of gasoline from the tank, or at any rate did not do so. From the gasoline vapor or gas of a highly combustible character arose and permeated the atmosphere a distance of 500 or 600 feet from the place of derailment. About 11:30 o'clock, Charles Duerr, who with Charles Miller and two young women, designated in the record as the Warner girls, was standing in front of the Warner residence on Madison street, a square west of the place of the accident, struck a match which he threw to the ground, and this match in its descent came in contact with the gas generated by the flowing gasoline, thereby causing the explosion by which appellant was injured.

There is no disagreement between the parties as to the facts thus far stated, but there are several issues of fact yet to be considered with respect to which there is sharp controversy. One of the points of difference is as to the condition of the railroad track where the tank car was derailed. The evidence of appellant conduced to prove that it was defective and unsafe. Indeed several witnesses introduced by him testified that the derailment of the car was caused by a low or loose joint in the rails which sank under the wheels of the car to such an extent as to throw it from the track, in leaving which it broke one of the rails; that the low joint was produced by the rottenness of the ties supporting it, want of ballast between the ties, and the flat or swampy condition of the roadbed at the place of derailment. According to the further statements of the witnesses in question the bad condition of the roadbed and track, as described, had continued a long time, and must have been known to those charged with the duty of keeping it in repair. On the other hand, a number of witnesses introduced by appellees were of opinion that the roadbed and track were in a reasonably safe condition and the testimony of some of them conduced to prove that there was no low joint in the rail and that the car left the track 26 feet before reaching what appellant's witnesses called the low joint, and that the derailment of the car was an unavoidable casualty or accident which could not, by the exercise of ordinary care, have been prevented. But considering the evidence as a whole it cannot be denied that much of it was to the effect that the derailment was caused by the negligence of the appellee Bridge & Railroad Company in failing to keep its roadbed and track in repair. We find a much greater contrariety of evidence as to appellant's contention that the employes of the appellee Bridge & Railroad Company were negligent in handling the tank car after the derailment. It is apparent from the testimony of all the witnesses that the discharge pipe under the tank and the appliances for operating the tank valve were broken by the derailment of the car, and that the gasoline immediately began to escape. It was, however, stated by appellant's witnesses that the escaping gasoline was at first but a small stream, but that appellee Bridge & Railroad Company's servants in charge of the derailed car by their negligence in handling it increased the flow of gasoline therefrom. This they stated was done by their opening a manhole on top of the tank and also by completely opening the valve at the bottom thereof in the effort to close it; that by thus opening the valve below and thereby removing the partial obstruction to the escape of the gasoline, the pressure of the air coming through the manhole above facilitated its flow, and such increase of the flow created the greater quantity of gas in the surrounding atmosphere, which,

in turn, increased the probability of an explosion, and added to the danger of all persons within the radius of its influence.

As already intimated, the testimony of appellee's witnesses radically differed from that of appellant's as to what was done to stop the escape of the gasoline after the derailment of the car. They all denied that they caused, or that there was, any increase in the flow of the gasoline from the tank, and claimed that they did everything in their power to stop the leak; using for that purpose waste, mud, and other appliances, after they discovered that the discharge pipe was broken, the valves open, and that the appliances for closing the valve would not perform their work. They further testified that their attempts to stop the leak were attended by great risk and danger to their lives; that the bad odor of the gasoline was nauseating, the darkness interfered with their vision and movements, and the use of lanterns or torches near enough to the car to obtain a good view of the situation, would inevitably have resulted in an explosion of the gas escaping in great volume from the flowing gasoline. Whether the jury, if the case had been submitted to them, would have decided this issue of fact in accordance with the testimony of appellant's witnesses, or that of appellee's witnesses, cannot be known, but it is manifest that the issue was one to be determined by the jury if the case should have gone to them at all. Another issue of fact was as to whether the servants of appellee Bridge & Railroad Company gave residents near the place of the accident and persons traveling Madison street at that point warning against the dangers from the gas.

Appellant, and at least five other witnesses introduced in his behalf, testified that they lived, or happened to be near the place of the accident and saw or felt the force of the explosion, but that they received neither notice nor warning of the presence of gas or that there was danger of an explosion. Mrs. Kern, one of the witnesses, testified that she had lights in her house down to the time of the explosion, but that she was not warned to put them out. Appellees' testimony tended to show that the railroad employes in charge of the wrecked car sent word to the train dispatcher to keep trains away from the place of the accident; that they stationed guards around the place to keep spectators at a safe distance and to prevent lights from being brought into the gaseous atmosphere, and that many people who went to the place of the accident were warned generally of the danger to be apprehended from the presence of the gas. It will readily be seen that the testimony upon this issue was also conflicting.

There is no contrariety of proof as to the fact that Charles Duerr lighted the match that caused the explosion. Indeed, the act was admitted by him, but he testified that when it was done he and Miller, a companion, were standing on Madison street in front of the Warner residence a square from the derailed car, talking with the two Warner girls, the four having just returned from Shawnee Park; that he took a cigar and match from his pockets, struck a light from the match, and ignited the cigar; that the explosion followed before the match reached the ground; and that he was knocked down by the explosion. He further testified that at the time of lighting the match he had just returned from Shawnee Park and knew nothing of the derailment of the tank car, or of the existence of the gas arising from the escaping gasoline, and that he did not intend to cause the explosion, nor did he know that the lighting of the match would cause it. Duerr was corroborated by Miller and one of the Warner girls, and Mrs. Kern testified that she saw the two young men standing on Madison street and talking with the Warner girls, she being at her gate near them; that although she saw Duerr when he struck the match, she did not see him drop it, but saw that the explosion immediately followed the lighting of the match. W. G. Schnepp who was near Duerr and his companions said he did not see the match thrown, but heard a woman call out at that time for everybody to run as some one had thrown a match. R. W. Polly, a witness for appellees, testified that he was across the street and within 60 feet of Duerr, Miller, and the Warner girls at the time of the explosion; that there was an electric light burning just above where they were standing and he could see them plainly; that neither of the young men had a cigar or pipe; that he saw Duerr strike a match against the fence and throw it into the plainly visible vapor arising from the gasoline and that the explosion immediately followed.

Appellees were permitted to prove that Duerr, who had been a telegraph operator in the employ of the appellee Bridge &

Railroad Company, was on the morning of the day of the explosion discharged from its service, and that 20 minutes before the explosion Duerr remarked to his companion, in the hearing of Giacometti and Darnall, "Let us go and set the damn thing on fire." The foundation for the introduction of the testimony of Giacometti and Darnall was laid by first obtaining from Duerr a denial that he had made the statement. Appellees introduced and had read to the jury, an indictment against Duerr for feloniously burning a stable, and also a judgment showing that he was allowed, after waiving a trial by jury, to plead guilty to a misdemeanor, viz., the offense of unlawfully destroying the property of another, for which he was fined by the court $350. The peremptory instruction was granted by the trial court upon the theory that though the Bridge & Railroad Company may have been guilty of negligence in permitting the tank car to be derailed, such negligence was not the proximate cause of the appellant's injuries, but that the act of Duerr in lighting and throwing the match, which the court declared was done purposely and in a spirit of wantonness, malice, or mischief, was the proximate cause thereof. We are clearly of opinion that the peremptory instruction, in so far as it required the jury to find for the appellee Bridge & Railroad Company was unauthorized.

There was, as previously indicated, evidence from which the jury might have found the appellee Bridge & Railroad Company guilty of negligence in failing to keep in proper repair and condition its roadbed and track at the place where the tank car was derailed, and that such failure caused the derailment resulting in the escape from the tank of the gasoline, contact of the gas from which with the match lighted by Duerr caused the explosion. There was also some evidence, very slight, it is true, tending to support appellant's contentions that the employes of the appellee Bridge & Railroad Company were negligent in handling the car after its derailment, and in failing to sufficiently warn residents and others near the place of the accident against the dangers to be apprehended from the presence of the gas produced by the escaping gasoline.

The lighting of the match by Duerr having resulted in the explosion, the question is, was that act merely a contributing cause, or the efficient and, therefore, proximate cause of appellant's injuries? The question of proximate cause is a question for the jury. In holding that Duerr in lighting or throwing the match acted maliciously or with intent to cause the explosion, the trial court invaded the province of the jury. There was, it is true, evidence tending to prove that the act was wanton or malicious, but also evidence conducing to prove that it was inadvertently or negligently done by Duerr. It was therefore for the jury and not the court to determine from all the evidence whether the lighting of the match was done by Duerr inadvertently or negligently, or whether it was a wanton and malicious act. As said in Milwaukee Railroad Co. v. Kellogg, 94 U.S. 469, 24 L. Ed. 256: "The true rule is that what is the proximate cause of the injury is ordinarily a question for the jury. It is not a question of science or legal knowledge. It is to be determined as a fact in view of the circumstances of fact attending it." Snydor v. Arnold, 122 Ky. 557, 92 S.W. 289, 28 Ky. Law Rep. 1252. In Thompson on Negligence, §161, it is said: "On principle, the rule must be here, as in other cases, that, before the judge can take the question away from the jury and determine it himself, the facts must not only be undisputed, but the inference to be drawn from those facts must be such that fair-minded men ought not to differ about them. It must be concluded that this is so when it is considered that proximate cause is a cause which would probably, according to the experience of mankind, lead to the event which happened, and that remote cause is a cause which would not, according to such experience, lead to such an event. Now, whether a given cause will probably lead to a given result is plainly to be determined by the average experience of mankind; that is, by a jury rather than by a legal scholar on the bench." No better statement of the law of proximate cause can be given than is found in 21 Am. & Eng. Ency. of Law (2d Ed.) 490 A. (N.S.) 548: "It is well settled that the mere fact that there have been intervening causes between the defendant's negligence and the plaintiff's injuries is not sufficient in law to relieve the former from liability; that is to say, the plaintiff's injuries may yet be natural and proximate in law, although between the defendant's negligence and the injuries other causes or conditions, or agencies, may have operated, and, when this is the case, the defendant is liable. So the defendant is clearly responsible where the intervening causes, acts, or conditions were set in motion by his earlier negligence, or naturally induced by such wrongful act or omission, or even, it is generally held, if the intervening acts or conditions were of a nature the happening of which was reasonably to have been anticipated, though they may have been acts of the plaintiff himself. An act or omission may yet be negligent and of a nature to charge a defendant with liability, although no injuries would have been sustained but for some intervening cause, if the occurrence of the latter might have been anticipated. . . . A proximate cause is that cause which naturally led to and which might have been expected to produce the result. . . . The connection of cause and effect must be established. It is also a principle well settled that when an injury is caused by two causes concurring to produce the result, for one of which the defendant is responsible, and not for the other, the defendant cannot escape responsibility. One is liable for an injury caused by the concurring negligence of himself and another to the same extent as for one caused entirely by his own negligence." Black's Law & Practice, §21; Thompson on Negligence, §§47-52; Whitaker's Smith on Negligence, 27; 29 Cyc. 488-502.

If the presence on Madison street in the city of Louisville of the great volume of loose gas that arose from the escaping gasoline was caused by the negligence of the appellee Bridge & Railroad Company, it seems to us that the probable consequences of its coming into contact with fire and causing an explosion was too plain a proposition to admit of doubt. Indeed, it was most probable that some one would strike a match to light a cigar or for other purposes in the midst of the gas. In our opinion, therefore, the act of one lighting and throwing a match under such circumstances cannot be said to be the efficient cause of the explosion. It did not of itself produce the explosion, nor could it have done so without the assistance and contribution resulting from the primary negligence, if there was such negligence, on the part of the appellee Bridge & Railroad Company in furnishing the presence of the gas in the street. This conclusion, however, rests upon the theory that Duerr inadvertently or negligently lighted and threw the match in the gas. This view of the case is sustained by the following leading cases, all decided by this court: Snydor v. Arnold, 122 Ky. 557, 92 S.W. 289, 28 Ky. Law Rep. 1252; Louisville Gas Co. v. Gutenkuntz, 82 Ky. 432; Whitman-

McNamara Tobacco Co. v. Warren, 66 S.W. 609, 23 Ky. Law Rep. 2120; Louisville Home Telephone Co. v. Gasper, 123 Ky. 128, 93 S.W. 1057, 29 Ky. Law Rep. 578, 9 L.R.A. (N.S.) 548. The cases supra are, indeed, in point of fact and principle so analogous to the case under consideration as to completely control its determination, and to render further discussion of it unnecessary.

If, however, the act of Duerr in lighting the match and throwing it into the vapor or gas arising from the gasoline was malicious, and done for the purpose of causing the explosion, we do not think appellees would be responsible, for while the appellee Bridge & Railroad Company's negligence may have been the efficient cause of the presence of the gas in the street, and it should have understood enough of the consequences thereof to have foreseen that an explosion was likely to result from the inadvertent or negligent lighting of a match by some person who was ignorant of the presence of the gas or of the effect of lighting or throwing a match in it, it could not have foreseen or deemed it probable that one would maliciously or wantonly do such an act for the evil purpose of producing the explosion. Therefore, if the act of Duerr was malicious, we quite agree with the trial court that it was one which the appellees could not reasonably have anticipated or guarded against, and in such case the act of Duerr, and not the primary negligence of the appellee Bridge & Railroad Company, in any of the particulars charged, was the efficient or proximate cause of appellant's injuries. The mere fact that the concurrent cause or intervening act was unforeseen will not relieve the defendant guilty of the primary negligence from liability, but if the intervening agency is something so unexpected or extraordinary as that he could not or ought not to have anticipated it, he will not be liable, and certainly he is not bound to anticipate the criminal acts of others by which damage is inflicted and hence is not liable therefor. 29 Cyc. 501-512; Sofield v. Sommers, 9 Ben. 526, 22 Fed. Cas. 769, Cas. No. 13,157; Andrews v. Kinsel, 114 Ga. 390, 40 S.E. 300, 88 Am. St. Rep. 25.

The record shows no cause of action whatever against the Union Tank Line Company. The only complaint against it is that the tank car was defective. The testimony conclusively shows that the car was inspected at Franklin, Pa., before its delivery to the railroad company there for transportation to Louisville, and was found to be in good condition; that it remained in such condition on the way to Louisville, and such was its condition when delivered to appellee Bridge & Railroad Company, at Louisville. On the other hand the appellant introduced no evidence to show that the car was not properly constructed, that any of its appliances were defective, or that it was leaking prior to the time of the accident. This being true, it is patent that the derailment of the car broke or injured it to such an extent as to cause the escape of the oil, and with that accident the appellee, Union Tank Line Company, had nothing to do and was in no sense responsible therefor. The peremptory instruction, therefore, so far as the appellee, Union Tank Line, was concerned, was proper.

We do not think the court erred in allowing the indictment against Duerr for burning the stable, or the judgment showing what disposition was made of the case, to be read to the jury. The stable was destroyed by the gas explosion. The plea of Duerr to the indictment was a confession that he unlawfully caused it to be burned, although its destruction resulted from the lighting of the match. The record, therefore, tended to contradict his testimony in this case that his act in producing the explosion was not malicious. We are of opinion, however, that the trial court erred in refusing to permit Duerr to testify as to the circumstances under which the plea was made and the trial had, and that in entering the plea of guilty as indicated, and submitting to the imposition of the fine, he acted upon the advice of his counsel. We also think the testimony of Giacometti and Darnall showing the threat of Duerr to cause the explosion was properly admitted for the purpose of contradicting Duerr, who had previously denied making the threat. But the testimony as well as that furnished by the indictment and judgment should have been considered by the jury only for the purpose of affecting Duerr's credibility as a witness, and the court should have so told the jury.

For the reasons indicated, the judgment is affirmed as to the Union Tank Line Company, but reversed as to the Bridge & Railroad Company, and cause remanded for a new trial consistent with the opinion.

INSANITY (CRIME)

PEOPLE V. SCHMIDT

COURT OF APPEALS OF NEW YORK, 1915
216 N.Y. 324, 110 N.E. 945

CARDOZO, J. In September, 1913, the dismembered body of Anna Aumuller was found in the Hudson river. Suspicion pointed to the defendant. He was arrested, and confessed that he had killed the woman by cutting her throat with a knife. He repeated this confession again and again. He attempted, however, to escape the penalty for murder by the plea that he was insane. He told the physicians who examined him that he had heard the voice of God calling upon him to kill the woman as a sacrifice and atonement. He confessed to a life of unspeakable excesses and hideous crimes, broken, he said, by spells of religious ecstasy and exaltation. In one of these moments, believing himself, he tells us, in the visible presence of God, he committed this fearful crime. Two physicians of experience, accepting as true his statement that he was overpowered by this delusion, expressed the opinion that he was insane. Other physicians of experience held the view that his delusion was feigned, and his insanity a sham. The jury accepted the latter view, and by their verdict found him guilty of murder in the first degree.

The defendant was condemned to death in February, 1914. In July, 1914, he made a motion for a new trial on the ground of newly-discovered evidence. In his affidavit, upon that motion, he tells a most extraordinary tale. He now says that he did not murder Anna Aumuller, and that his confession of guilt was false. He says that she died from a criminal operation, and that to con-

ceal the abortion, to which he and others were parties, he hacked
the dead body to pieces, and cast the fragments in the river. His
crime, he now says, was not murder, but manslaughter. He tells
us why he chose to charge himself with the graver offense. He believed that he could feign insanity successfully, and that after a
brief term in an asylum he would again be set at large. To confess to the abortion would implicate his confederates, and bring
certain punishment to every one. To confess to murder, but at
the same time feign insanity, might permit every one to go free.
The compact was then made, he says, between himself and his
confederates, that he would protect them from suspicion, and
play the madman himself. The men and the woman who are said
to have been confederates, deny that such a compact was made.
Whether they were parties or not to the fraud upon the court is
of little moment at this time; in any event, the defendant now
tells us that he was sane; that the tale which he told the physicians was false; and that he did not hear the divine voice calling
him to sacrifice and to slay. He asks that he be given another opportunity to put before a jury the true narrative of the crime.

There is no power in any court to grant a new trial upon
that ground. The statute says that a new trial may be granted
"when it is made to appear, by affidavit, that upon another trial,
the defendant can produce evidence such as if before received
would probably have changed the verdict; if such evidence has
been discovered since the trial, is not cumulative; and the failure
to produce it on the trial was not owing to want of diligence"
(Code Crim. Pro. §465, subd. 7). The power to order a new trial
in criminal causes is created and measured by the statute. The
defense now offered by the defendant was not "discovered since
the trial." It was known to him, on his own showing, from the
beginning. He chose to withhold it, because he had faith in his
ability to deceive the courts of justice. We do not attempt to determine how much of his present tale is true. Even if the entire
tale is true, the courts are powerless to help him. A criminal may
not experiment with one defense, and then when it fails him, in-
voke the aid of the law which he has flouted, to experiment with
another defense, held in reserve for that emergency. It would be
strange if any system of law were thus to invite contempt of its
authority. . . . The remedy and the one remedy available to a

criminal who finds himself thus enmeshed in a trap of his own making, is not in the processes of courts or the machinery of law; it is by appeal to the clemency of the Governor. Strange to say, with all its incongruous features, the defendant's tale supplies a plausible explanation of some of the mysteries of this tragedy. We do not mean to express a belief that the tale is true. All that we say is that in an appropriate proceeding it would merit earnest scrutiny. We do not doubt that such scrutiny will be given to it, and that right will be done, if hereafter an appeal for clemency is made to the Executive.

The defendant shifts his ground, however, and insists that even though his motion for a new trial was properly denied, we must none the less reverse the judgment for error in the charge. The error is said to have been committed in the definition of the degree of insanity that relieves from responsibility for crime. . . . The learned trial judge said to the jury that "wrong" in this [statutory] definition means "contrary to the law of the state." The jury was instructed in pointed and impressive terms, that even if the defendant believed in good faith that God had appeared to him and commanded the sacrifice of Anna Aumuller, and this belief was a delusion, the result of a defect of reason, the defendant must none the less answer to the law if he knew the nature and quality of the act, and knew that it was wrong, in the sense that it was forbidden by the law of the state. We think that is the fair meaning of the whole charge as the jury must have understood it. For brevity, we quote its substance rather than its exact language. It is true that adopting with a proviso a request of the defendant's counsel, the court did say that "if the jury believe that at the time of the commission of the act, the defendant was completely obsessed by the delusion that he was acting under a divine command and that every other thought was excluded from his mind at the time, they must acquit the defendant, provided that the jury are satisfied that at the time he committed that act he was laboring under such a defect of reason as either not to know the nature and quality of the act he was committing or that it was wrong." This left the meaning of the word "wrong" still obscure, and the judge had already told the jury that it meant an offense against the law of the state. If, however, the jury could have supposed that he intended to modify his previous instructions, that belief must have been dispelled by the instructions that immediately followed. The counsel for the People said: "The only matter I would ask your Honor to charge again to the jury is based on the last request of the defendant, that the term 'wrong' as used in your Honor's charge, means 'wrong according to the law of the state of New York,'" and to this the court responded: "I so charge you, gentlemen." The defendant saved his rights by appropriate exceptions.

We are unable to accept the view that the word "wrong" in the statutory definition is to receive so narrow a construction. We must interpret the rule in the light of its history. That history has been often sketched. In the beginning of our law the madman charged with murder was not acquitted. A special verdict was given that he was mad, and then the king pardoned him. There was the same need of the royal pardon for homicide by misadventure or in self-defense. . . . Then came the age of what has become known as the "wild beast test." . . . As late as 1800, in Hadfield's case (27 St. Tr. 1288), that test was announced as law. The first departure from the ancient rule came in 1812. The capacity to distinguish right from wrong was then put forward as another test. As propounded in these cases, it meant a capacity to distinguish right from wrong, not with reference to the particular act, but generally or in the abstract. Sometimes it was spoken of as a capacity to distinguish between "good and evil." Wrong was conceived of as synonymous not with legal but rather with moral wrong. Lord Mansfield told the jury in Bellingham's case (Collinson on Lunacy, p. 636): "It must be proved beyond all doubt that at the time he committed the atrocious act, he did not consider that murder was a crime against the laws of God and nature." That became for many years the classic definition. . . . Its phraseology, as we shall see, has survived with little variation in charges and opinions of our own day.

Then in 1843 came the famous decision of the House of Lords in M'Naghten's case. It is idle to look to this decision for precise and scientific statement. The judges passed, not on a concrete case, but on hypothetical questions addressed to them by the lords. Five questions were answered, of which three only are material for present purposes. The second and third questions, which were answered together, were:

"What are the proper questions to be submitted to the jury, where a person alleged to be afflicted with insane delusion, respecting one or more particular subjects or persons, is charged with the commission of a crime (murder, for example), and insanity is set up as a defense?" and

"In what terms ought the question to be left to the jury, as to the prisoner's state of mind at the time when the act was committed?"

To this the judges responded "that the jurors ought to be told in all cases that every man is to be presumed to be sane, and to possess a sufficient degree of reason to be responsible for his crimes, until the contrary be proved to their satisfaction; and that to establish a defense on the ground of insanity, it must be clearly proved that, at the time of committing the act, the accused was laboring under such a defect of reason, from disease of the mind, as not to know the nature and quality of the act he was doing, or, if he did know it, that he did not know he was doing what was wrong. The mode of putting the latter part of the question to the jury on these occasions has generally been, whether the accused at the time of doing the act knew the difference between right and wrong; which mode, though rarely, if ever, leading to any mistake with the jury, is not, as we conceive, so accurate when put generally and in the abstract, as when put with reference to the party's knowledge of right and wrong, in respect to the very act with which he is charged. If the question were to be put as to the knowledge of the accused solely and exclusively with reference to the law of the land, it might tend to confound the jury, by inducing them to believe that an actual knowledge of the law of the land was essential in order to lead to a conviction; whereas, the law is administered upon the principle that everyone must be taken conclusively to know it, without proof that he does know it. If the accused was conscious that the act was one that he ought not to do, and if that act was at the same time contrary to the law of the land, he is punishable; and the usual course, therefore, has been to leave the question to the jury, whether the party accused had a sufficient degree of reason to know that he was doing an act that was wrong; and this course we think is correct, accompanied with such observations and explanations as the circumstances of each particular case may require."

The definition here propounded is the one that has been carried forward into our statute. The judges expressly held that a defendant who knew nothing of the law would none the less be responsible if he knew that the act was wrong, by which, therefore, they must have meant, if he knew that it was morally wrong. Whether he would also be responsible if he knew that it was against the law, but did not know it to be morally wrong, is a question that was not considered. In most cases, of course, knowledge that an act is illegal will justify the inference of knowledge that it is wrong. But none the less it is the knowledge of wrong, conceived of as moral wrong, that seems to have been established by that decision as the controlling test. That must certainly have been the test under the older law when the capacity to distinguish between right and wrong imported a capacity to distinguish between good and evil as abstract qualities. There is nothing to justify the belief that the words right and wrong, when they became limited by M'Naghten's case to the right and wrong of the particular act, cast off their meaning as terms of morals, and became terms of pure legality.

Another answer in M'Naghten's case, the answer to the first question, is yet to be considered. That question was:

"What is the law respecting alleged crimes committed by persons afflicted with insane delusion in respect of one or more particular subjects or persons; as, for instance, where, at the time of the commission of the alleged crime, the accused knew he was acting contrary to law, but did the act complained of with a view, under the influence of insane delusion, of redressing or revenging some supposed grievance or injury, or producing some supposed public benefit?"

And to this the answer was:

"Assuming that your Lordships' inquiries are confined to those persons who labour under such partial delusions only, and are not in other respects insane, we are of opinion that notwithstanding the accused did the act complained of with a view, under the influence of insane delusion, of redressing or revenging some supposed grievance or injury, or of producing some public benefit, he is nevertheless punishable, according to the nature of the crime committed, if he knew at the time of committing such crime that he was acting contrary to law, by which expression we understand your Lordships to mean the law of the land."

Many judges have pointed out that this answer introduces "an entirely new element" (Ladd, J., in State v. Jones, [50 N.H. 369]). "How," it is asked "are these two rules to be reconciled? It would seem to be plain that they are in hopeless conflict and cannot both stand." It is not the answer to the first question, but the answer to the second and third, that has become embodied in our statute. In case of conflict, therefore, the first answer must give way. But the truth, we think, is that the conflict is more apparent than real. The answer to the first question, though it seems to make the knowledge of the law a test, presupposes the offender's capacity to understand that violation of the law is wrong. It applies only to persons who "are not in other respects insane." We must interpret the answer in the light of the assumptions of the question. A delusion that some supposed grievance or injury will be redressed, or some public benefit attained, has no such effect in obscuring moral distinctions as a delusion that God himself has issued a command. The one delusion is consistent with knowledge that the act is a moral wrong, the other is not.

"The questions are so general in their terms, and the answers follow the words of the questions so closely, that they leave untouched every state of facts which, though included under the general words of the question, can nevertheless be distinguished from them by circumstances which the House of Lords did not take into account in framing the questions" (2 Stephen, History Criminal Law, p. 154). The real point of the inquiry was whether a defendant who knew that the act was wrong, was excused because he had an insane belief that either personal or public good would be promoted by the deed. There was no thought of any conflict between the commands of law and morals.

We have still another guide to help us to a sound construction of M'Naghten's case and of the statutory rule derived from it. That guide is found in the practice of judges by whom the decision has been applied. We refer to a few instances among many. In R. v. Townley (3 F. & F. 839) Martin, B., left it to the jury to say whether the prisoner knew that the act was "contrary to the law of God and punishable by the law of the land." In R. v. Lay-ton (4 Cox C.C. 149) Rolfe, B., said that the jury must determine whether the prisoner's delusion "had the effect of making him incapable of understanding the wickedness of murdering his wife." In many cases, both in our own courts and in those of sister states, the language of Lord Mansfield in Bellingham's case is adopted with trifling changes, and the test is said to be whether the defendant understood that the act was forbidden "by the laws of God and man." In Comm. v. Rogers (7 Metc. 500) Shaw, Ch. J., in expounding the rule, assumed for illustration an insane delusion that God had commanded a crime. He told the jury that a defendant, to be responsible, "must have sufficient power of memory to recollect the relation in which he stands to others, and in which others stand to him; that the act he is doing is contrary to the plain dictates of justice and right, injurious to others, and a violation of the dictates of duty"; and then to explain the delusions that will relieve a man from criminal liability, he said: "A common instance is where he fully believes that the act he is doing is done with the immediate command of God, and he acts under the delusive but sincere belief that what he is doing is by the command of a superior power, which supersedes all human laws, and the laws of nature." In Guiteau's case (10 Fed. Rep. 161) these words were quoted approvingly, and supplemented by other illustrations. The court instanced the case of a man known to be an affectionate father, who "insists that the Almighty has appeared to him, and commanded him to sacrifice his child." Of these and like cases, the court said (p. 182): "If a man insanely believes that he has a command from the Almighty to kill, it is difficult to understand how such a man can know that it is wrong for him to do it." Such a man is no less insane because he knows that murder is prohibited by human law. Indeed, it may emphasize his insanity that, knowing the human law, he believes that he is acting under the direct command of God.

Cases may be found where, in explaining what is meant by knowledge that an act is wrong, the courts have blended the elements of legal and moral wrong, but none, we believe, can be found in which the element of moral wrong has been excluded. . . . To the reported cases in which the word "wrong" in the statutory definition has been used as importing a moral wrong, there may be added a multitude of unreported cases. As an illustration we may refer to a case recently decided by this court (People v. Purcell, 214 N.Y. 693). There the trial judge (Nott, J.) in a careful and able charge told the jury that knowledge of the nature and quality of the act has reference to its physical nature and quality, and that knowledge that it is wrong refers to its moral side; that to know that the act is wrong, the defendant must know that it is "contrary to law, and contrary to the accepted standards of morality": and then he added, with a slight variation of the words of Lord Mansfield, that it must be known to be "contrary to the laws of God and man."

In the light of all these precedents, it is impossible, we think, to say that there is any decisive adjudication which limits the word "wrong" in the statutory definition to legal as opposed to moral wrong. The trend of the decisions is indeed the other way. The utmost that can be said is that the question is still an open one. We must, therefore, give that construction to the statute which seems to us most consonant with reason and justice. The definition of insanity established by the statute as sufficient to relieve from criminal liability has been often and harshly criticized. Some states reject it altogether. A recent case in Massachusetts (Comm. v. Cooper, 219 Mass. 1, 5) says that an offender is not responsible if he was "so mentally diseased that he felt impelled to act by a power which overcame his reason and judgment and to him was irresistible." That is not the test with us. Whatever the views of alienists and jurists may be, the test in this state is prescribed by statute, and there can be no other. We must not, however, exaggerate the rigor of the rule by giving the word "wrong" a strained interpretation, at war with its broad and primary meaning, and least of all, if in so doing, we rob the rule of all relation to the mental health and true capacity of the criminal. The interpretation placed upon the statute by the trial judge may be tested by its consequences. A mother kills her infant child to whom she has been devotedly attached. She knows the nature and quality of the act; she knows that the law condemns it; but she is inspired by an insane delusion that God has appeared to her and ordained the sacrifice. It seems a mockery to say that, within the meaning of the statute, she knows that the act is wrong. If the definition propounded by the trial judge is right, it would be the duty of a jury to hold her responsible for the crime. We find nothing either in the history of the rule, or in its reason and purpose, or in judicial exposition of its meaning, to justify a conclusion so abhorrent. No jury would be likely to find a defendant responsible in such a case, whatever a judge might tell them. But we cannot bring ourselves to believe that in declining to yield to such a construction of the statute, they would violate the law.

We hold, therefore, that there are times and circumstances in which the word "wrong" as used in the statutory test of responsibility ought not to be limited to legal wrong. A great master of the theory and practice of the criminal law, Sir James Fitz-James Stephen, in his *General View of the Criminal Law of England* (pages 79, 80), casts the weight of his learning and experience in favor of that view. Knowledge that an act is forbidden by law will in most cases permit the inference of knowledge that, according to the accepted standards of mankind, it is also condemned as an offense against good morals. Obedience to the law is itself a moral duty. If, however, there is an insane delusion that God has appeared to the defendant and ordained the commission of a crime, we think it cannot be said of the offender, that he knows the act to be wrong. It is not enough, to relieve from criminal liability, that the prisoner is morally depraved. It is not enough that he has views of right and wrong at variance with those that find expression in the law. The variance must have its origin in some disease of the mind. The anarchist is not at liberty to break the law because he reasons that all government is wrong. The devotee of a religious cult that enjoins polygamy or human sacrifice as a duty is not thereby relieved from responsibility before the law. In such cases the belief, however false according to our own standards, is not the product of disease. Cases will doubtless arise where criminals will take shelter behind a professed belief that their crime was ordained by God, just as this defendant attempted to shelter himself behind that belief. We can safely leave such fabrications to the common sense of juries.

We have considered the charge of the trial judge upon the subject of insanity, because the question is in the case, and the true rule on a subject so important ought not to be left in doubt. But even though we hold that there was error in the charge, we think the error does not require us to disturb the judgment of conviction. It is of no importance now whether the trial judge charged the jury correctly upon the question of insanity, because in the record before us the defendant himself concedes that he is sane, and that everything which he said to the contrary was a fraud upon the court. It is of no importance now whether the defendant would be relieved of guilt if his diseased mind had revealed the divine presence to his eyes and the divine command to his ears, because he tells us that he never saw the vision and never heard the command. He concedes, therefore, that the issue of his sanity was correctly determined by the jury; he concedes that even if there was error in the definition of insanity no injustice has resulted; and his position is that having fabricated a defense of insanity in order to deceive the trial court, it is now the duty of another court to give him a new trial because his fabricated defense was imperfectly expounded.

. . . [W]e will not aid the defendant in his effort to gain the benefit of a fraudulent defense.

The judgment of conviction should be affirmed.

INSANITY (TORT)

McGuire v. Almy

SUPREME JUDICIAL COURT OF MASSACHUSETTS, 1937
297 MASS. 323, 8 N.E.2D 760

QUA, JUSTICE. This is an action of tort for assault and battery. The only question of law reported is whether the judge should have directed a verdict for the defendant.

The following facts are established by the plaintiff's own evidence: In August, 1930, the plaintiff was employed to take care of the defendant. The plaintiff was a registered nurse and was a graduate of a training school for nurses. The defendant was an insane person. Before the plaintiff was hired she learned that the defendant was a "mental case and was in good physical condition," and that for some time two nurses had been taking care of her. The plaintiff was on "24 hour duty." The plaintiff slept in the room next to the defendant's room. Except when the plaintiff was with the defendant, the plaintiff kept the defendant locked in the defendant's room. There was a wire grating over the outside of the window of that room. . . .

On April 19, 1932, the defendant, while locked in her room, had a violent attack. The plaintiff heard a crashing of furniture and then knew that the defendant was ugly, violent and dangerous. The defendant told the plaintiff and a Miss Maroney, "the maid," who was with the plaintiff in the adjoining room, that if they came into the defendant's room, she would kill them. The plaintiff and Miss Maroney looked into the defendant's room, "saw what the defendant had done," and "thought it best to take the broken stuff away before she did any harm to herself with it."

They sent for a Mr. Emerton, the defendant's brother-in-law. When he arrived the defendant was in the middle of her room about ten feet from the door, holding upraised the leg of a low-boy as if she were going to strike. The plaintiff stepped into the room and walked toward the defendant, while Mr. Emerton and Miss Maroney remained in the doorway. As the plaintiff approached the defendant and tried to take hold of the defendant's hand which held the leg, the defendant struck the plaintiff's head with it, causing the injuries for which the action was brought.

The extent to which an insane person is liable for torts has not been fully defined in this Commonwealth. . . .

Turning to authorities elsewhere, we find that courts in this country almost invariably say in the broadest terms that an insane person is liable for his torts. As a rule no distinction is made between those torts which would ordinarily be classed as intentional and those which would ordinarily be classed as negligent, nor do the courts discuss the effect of different kinds of insanity or of varying degrees of capacity as bearing upon the ability of the defendant to understand the particular act in question or to make a reasoned decision with respect to it, although it is sometimes said that an insane person is not liable for torts requiring malice of which he is incapable. Defamation and malicious prosecution are the torts more commonly mentioned in this connection. . . . Those decisions are rested more upon grounds of public policy and upon what might be called a popular view of the requirements of essential justice than upon any attempt to apply logically the underlying principles of civil liability to the special instance of the mentally deranged. Thus it is said that a rule imposing liability tends to make more watchful those persons who have charge of the defendant and who may be supposed to have some interest in preserving his property; that as an insane person must pay for his support, if he is financially able, so he ought also to pay for the damage which he does; that an insane person with abundant wealth ought not to continue in unimpaired enjoyment of the comfort which it brings while his victim bears the burden unaided; and there is also a suggestion that courts are loath to introduce into the great body of civil litigation the difficulties in determining mental capacity which it has been found impossible to avoid in the criminal field.

The rule established in these cases has been criticized severely by certain eminent text writers both in this country and in England, principally on the ground that it is an archaic survival of the rigid and formal mediaeval conception of liability for acts done, without regard to fault, as opposed to what is said to be the general modern theory that liability in tort should rest upon fault. Notwithstanding these criticisms, we think, that as a practical matter, there is strong force in the reasons underlying these decisions. They are consistent with the general statements found in the cases dealing with the liability of infants for torts . . . including a few cases in which the child was so young as to render his capacity for fault comparable to that of many insane persons . . . Fault is by no means at the present day a universal prerequisite to liability, and the theory that it should be such has been obliged very recently to yield at several points to what has been thought to be paramount considerations of public good. Finally, it would be difficult not to recognize the persuasive weight of so much authority so widely extended.

But the present occasion does not require us either to accept or to reject the prevailing doctrine in its entirety. For this case it is enough to say that where an insane person by his act does intentional damage to the person or property of another he is liable for that damage in the same circumstances in which a normal person would be liable. This means that in so far as a particular intent would be necessary in order to render a normal person liable, the insane person, in order to be liable, must have been capable of entertaining that same intent and must have entertained it in fact. But the law will not inquire further into his peculiar mental condition with a view to excusing him if it should appear that delusion or other consequence of his affliction has caused him to entertain that intent or that a normal person would not have entertained it.

We do not suggest that this is necessarily a logical stopping point. If public policy demands that a mentally affected person be subjected to the external standard for intentional wrongs, it may well be that public policy also demands that he should be subjected to the external standard for wrongs which are commonly classified as negligent, in accordance with what now seems to be the prevailing view. We stop here for the present, because we are not required to go further in order to decide this case, because of deference to the difficulty of the subject, because full and adequate discussion is lacking in most of the cases decided up to the present time, and because by far the greater number of those cases, however broad their statement of the principle, are in fact cases of intentional rather than of negligent injury.

Coming now to the application of the rule to the facts of this case, it is apparent that the jury could find that the defendant was capable of entertaining and that she did entertain an intent to strike and to injure the plaintiff and that she acted upon that intent. See American Law Institute Restatement, Torts, §§ 13, 14. We think this was enough. . . .

Judgment for the plaintiff on the verdict.

DRUNKENNESS

PEOPLE V. KOERBER

COURT OF APPEALS OF NEW YORK, 1926
244 N.Y. 147, 155 N.E. 79

POUND, J. Defendant was convicted of murder in the first degree for killing one Mahairas when engaged in the commission of a felony, to wit, the crime of robbery, upon the person killed. The homicide occurred about five o'clock in the morning of Sunday, March 21, 1926. Defendant testified in his own behalf in substance that he had been drinking heavily and that he was intoxicated at the time so that he did not know what he was doing. He narrated with considerable detail the occurrences of the night, both before and after the homicide, and the jury might properly have found that his intoxication was not such as to affect his responsibility for his acts had it been permitted to pass on the question. It was, however, instructed merely that voluntary intoxication would not excuse a criminal act committed while under the influence of intoxication. A request to charge the jury as to the different degrees of homicide and the rule of reasonable doubt as applied to lower degrees of crime was refused and also a request to instruct the jury as to intoxication as a defense substantially in the language of section 1220 of the Penal Law. The question of voluntary intoxication as defense for crime is thus fairly, although not with any great degree of precision, presented on the record, both on the facts and the law.

On the question of murder in the first degree where the killing is committed from a deliberate and premeditated design to effect the death of the person killed, it has been held that, when the case contains testimony which if believed might have led the jury to conclude that at the time of the shooting defendant was intoxicated to a greater or less degree, the question of intoxication should be presented and explained to the jury and, if the question is a serious one and such instructions are omitted, a judgment of conviction should be reversed even in the absence of a proper request by the counsel for the defendant.

The view is expressed that in felony murder the rule is different; that a refusal to instruct the jury as to the lower degrees of homicide is proper and that the jury should be instructed to find the defendant guilty of murder in the first degree or to acquit. Such is the rule only "where . . . no possible view of the facts would justify any other verdict except a conviction of the crime charged or an acquittal." We are, therefore, free to enter upon a consideration of voluntary intoxication as a fact for the consideration of the jury in such cases.

The effect of this section [Penal Law, section 1220] is discussed in People v. Leonardi (143 N.Y. 360) where the indictment was for a deliberate and premeditated killing. At common law, said the court, if a man made himself voluntarily drunk it was no excuse for any crime he might commit when he was in that condition, and he had to take the responsibility of his own voluntary act in becoming intoxicated. The fact was not to be considered even on the question of premeditation. Under the section, however, while no act of a person in a state of voluntary intoxication shall be deemed less criminal by reason of his having been in such condition, the judge should, whenever the actual existence of any particular purpose, motive or intent is a necessary element to constitute a particular species or degree of crime, allow the jury to take into consideration the question of intoxication in determining the existence of such particular intent and, if it should be of the opinion that the deliberation or premeditation necessary to constitute murder in the first degree did not exist, the crime might be reduced to a lower degree of murder or, in the absence of any intent to kill, then to manslaughter in some of its degrees. That is, the law does not, as in the case of insanity, deem the act less criminal by reason of the voluntary intoxication of the accused, but the jury may take into consideration the fact of intoxication in determining the element of the crime charged, not as calling for an acquittal, where the act charged, minus the particular intent, remains a criminal act, but as tending to reduce the character or grade of the offense in a proper case.

In a recent English case (Director of Public Prosecutions v. Beard, [1920] A.C. 479) the subject is fully considered. The learned lords agreed that at common law voluntary intoxication was regarded as an aggravation of the offense but held that the rule had been relaxed and that, while voluntary intoxication cannot excuse the commission of a crime, it may be taken into consideration where a specific intent is an essential element of the offense charged in order to determine whether the defendant had in fact formed the specific intent necessary to constitute the particular crime. The court pointed out, as did this court in the Leonardi Case (supra), that in the case of drunkenness the test of criminal responsibility is not the same as in the case of insanity, to be considered by the jury only if so extreme as to obliterate knowledge on the part of the defendant as to what he was doing or that he was doing wrong.

In brief then, the rule may be thus stated: When criminal intent in general is all that need be established the drunken defendant is treated as if he knew the consequence of his acts; but where a particular or specific intent must be established, if the jury find that the mind of the defendant was so obscured by drink that he was incapable of forming that intent, it may justify itself in the reduction of a charge.

Generally speaking murder in the first or second degree connotes the specific or particular intent to kill, while manslaughter in the first or second degree is felonious homicide when the intent to kill is absent. But when one engaged in the commission of a felony, his mind being fatally bent on mischief but without a design to effect death, kills a human being, at common law, the killing is said to be with malice aforethought and so murder, and the Penal Law attaches to the act the consequences of murder in the first degree. The People on an indictment for felony murder may fail to establish that defendant was engaged in the commission of a felony, but may offer evidence tending to show that the homicide was committed by him when engaged in a misdemeanor, which would reduce the offense to manslaughter in the first degree, or in the commission of a trespass or other invasion of a private right, which would reduce it to manslaughter in the second degree. Where the facts would justify a verdict based on such a theory, the degrees of manslaughter should be submitted to the jury. Thus, where the felony charged in the indictment is burglary and the entry is under circumstances or in a manner not amounting to a burglary, the offense is unlawfully entering a building, which is a misdemeanor. Could it be said with reason that on an indictment for murder in the first degree for killing when engaged in the commission of burglary, the offense might not thus be reduced to manslaughter in the first degree? Or, if it were shown that the killing took place before a building was entered while defendant was engaged in a trespass or other invasion of a private right, that the offense might not be thus reduced to manslaughter in the second degree? . . .

We now come to consider the charge against defendant as affected by his intoxication. Disregarding for the moment the statutory modification of common-law rules and principles and the fine distinctions not applicable hereto, we find that the gist of robbery is larceny by force from the person, and that the gist of larceny is the taking and carrying away of personal property of another with the specific intent to steal such property. If on an indictment for larceny or robbery the testimony leaves uncertain the intent with which the accused took the property, the jury should be instructed to give the defendant the benefit of the doubt. That the intent is usually to be inferred from the act does not change the rule that a taking without intent to steal is not larceny at common law. No statutory larceny is involved in the consideration of the instant case.

Robbery, as thus defined, is "a particular species . . . of crime" of which "the actual existence of any particular . . . intent is a necessary element" within the meaning of Penal Law, section 1220. It follows that the jury should have been instructed "to take into consideration the fact that the accused was intoxicated at the time, in determining the . . . intent with which he committed the act." The fact that the accused did not have the intent to rob would not mean that an acquittal should follow. It is conceivable, for example, that a youth whose mind was befuddled by drink might intend merely to stage a hold-up and yet be guilty of some degree of homicide. He might be so frightened by resistance as to shoot in the heat of passion, the emotion of fright, and thus be guilty of manslaughter in the first degree, or conceivably, even of murder in the second degree. The jury would have to say under proper instructions as to the degrees of crime.

It is common knowledge that intoxicated men, although not in normal control of their faculties, do deliberate and premeditate and form a particular intent and commit criminal acts as they might not do if they were sober. Intoxication as such does not mitigate the offense. The question is not whether the accused was drunk but whether his intoxication was of such a character that it destroyed the power to form the particular intent which is a necessary element of the crime charged. The jury should, therefore, proceed with the utmost caution before arriving at the conclusion that the voluntary intoxication of an accused person has in any way altered the character or grade of his criminal act. His own evidence on the point need not be accepted as true even if uncontradicted. We may doubt whether the evidence of intoxication adduced by this defendant would carry sufficient weight with an intelligent jury to affect its verdict. It presented, however, a serious question affecting a substantial right which should not have been withheld from the consideration of triers of fact. We cannot say that, with proper instructions, "but one decision and that adverse to the defendant could reasonably have been reached." When the alternative presented was conviction of murder in the first degree or acquittal, a conscientious jury would scarcely bring itself to a verdict of not guilty in this case. If they had been instructed that other verdicts were permissible, they might or might not have found the defendant guilty of a lesser degree of felonious homicide. We, therefore, cannot overlook the failure of the court to give proper instructions . . . , as we might if we could reach the conclusion that there was a lack of sufficient evidence to go to the jury that defendant was, in the only relevant sense, too drunk to form the specific intent of committing robbery.

The judgment of conviction should be reversed and a new trial ordered.

ANDREWS, J. (dissenting). Under the charge of the court we are here concerned solely with robbery. If guilty of that crime the defendant was guilty of murder in the first degree. He could be guilty of nothing else. If not guilty of robbery the jury was told that they must acquit him. Surely he may not complain because in that case they were not permitted to convict him of some lesser degree of homicide.

To be guilty of robbery it is essential that the defendant should have acted with a general criminal intent. I assume that means the intent to take the property of the deceased in his presence, against his will, by means of force or fear. Ordinarily from the occurrence itself the jury might and should have inferred this intent. He may, however, negative this presumption. He may give evidence tending to show that he was insane at the time. Or that he was playing a joke on a friend. Or that he was so drunk that he could not and did not form any such intent. Thus a question of fact may be presented, and if the jury have a reasonable doubt caused by this explanation he should be acquitted.

The issue is as to the existence of this intent, and the testimony offered by the defendant must be relevant to this precise issue. If it does not tend to show that the accused failed to know the nature and quality of his act or to show that he did not know that it was wrong, there is no question of insanity to be submitted to the jury. If it does not tend to show that he was so intoxicated that he did not and could not form an intent to rob, again there is no question for them.

In my judgment testimony of intoxication to the extent that would make the defendant's intent a question of fact is wholly absent from this case. It should, at least, tend to show at the time of the robbery a complete absence of conscious volition—an ignorance of his acts and purposes. Therefore, the trial court was right in refusing to submit any such question to the jury. The general rule that "no act committed by a person while in a state of voluntary intoxication, shall be deemed less criminal by reason of his having been in such a condition" is applicable.

It is quite true that in a limited number of cases another rule applies. Now and then crimes are divided into degrees or species dependent upon the motive, purpose, or intent of the criminal. His legal as well as his moral guilt varies with his mental attitude. Such a division is made as regards some kinds of homicide. So as to assault. Ordinarily, however, while other crimes may be divided into degrees, these degrees are not made dependent on any such purpose, motive or intent. There are degrees in arson, in burglary, in larceny, in forgery, in robbery itself; but no such test of guilt applies. The degree depends upon other circumstances. To convict there must be merely the usual general intent to commit the crime.

It is only in the exceptional cases of the first class that the jury may take into consideration the fact that the accused was to some extent intoxicated at the time in determining the question of the degree of guilt.

In my opinion the judgment of conviction should be affirmed.

CRANE, J. (dissenting). I concur with JUDGE ANDREWS, but desire to add the following:

That the defendant shot and killed the deceased has been proved beyond any reasonable doubt. The evidence shows that the killing happened while the defendant was committing the crime of robbery—it was a holdup case—in which the defendant at the point of a pistol attempted to rob the deceased. The attempted defense was that the deceased attacked the defendant leaving the store, and in the mixup the defendant's pistol went off accidentally. No one takes any stock in this defense, not even the defendant's counsel, who admitted on the argument that the defendant was guilty of a crime.

A discussion has arisen over the effect of liquor upon the defendant and whether the judge fully covered the law regarding intoxication as affecting crime and the degrees of crime. In my judgment the discussion is immaterial to this case, as the evidence clearly shows that the defendant, if he had been drinking, was not so intoxicated as to lessen the crime, but rather to aggravate the seriousness of it. In the first place, he is the only one who states that he had been drinking, and then on the stand as a witness remembers every detail of his conduct and actions on the night in question. He boldly states how a few hours previous to killing the deceased, he had held up a restaurant keeper at the point of a pistol—pointed a gun at him and told him to hold up his hands. The money he took he says he did not intend to steal, that it was a kind of joke—the kind that the people of this state do not appreciate. It was no joke to the restaurant keeper. Later, the defendant details how he entered the place of the deceased and what happened there. Surely the defendant, when he had sufficient mind and intelligence to recollect months afterwards all that happened on the night of the shooting, was not under such influence from liquor as to lessen in any way his criminal acts, or deprive him of criminal intent. His intoxication may have excited him and weakened his judgment, but it did not absolve him from the responsibility which the law attaches to one who kills another in an attempt to take his property.

I am for affirmance for these reasons.

CARDOZO, McLAUGHLIN, and LEHMAN, JJ., concur with POUND, J.

ANDREWS, J., dissents in opinion, in which HISCOCK, C.J., concurs and in which CRANE, J., concurs in memorandum.

Judgment reversed, etc.

IGNORANCE OF FACT

PEOPLE V. WERNER

COURT OF APPEALS OF NEW YORK, 1903
174 N.Y. 132, 66 N.E. 667

O'Brien, J. The defendant kept a hotel or tavern and was authorized to traffic in liquors. He was convicted of a violation of the act in that he sold and delivered liquor to a minor under the age of eighteen years, contrary to the provisions of section thirty of the statute. The jury would have been justified in finding that the defendant acted in good faith, supposing from what the boy and his father had told him that he was over eighteen years of age, but the absence of any criminal intent and the circumstance that the defendant acted in good faith would seem to be immaterial. The law on that subject seems to be that an act malum prohibitum is not excused by ignorance, or a mistake of fact when a specific act is made by the law indictable irrespective of the defendant's motive or intent. His belief that he was right in what he did based on a mistake of fact is no defense.

The general rule that the criminal intention is the essence of the crime does not apply to such prohibited acts; but while that is so, such statutes ought to be strictly construed and the People required to give strict proof of the commission of the offense. On the trial of this case the defendant was entitled to give all the proof that he had that had any bearing upon the issues involved or upon the credibility of the witnesses against him. We think this principle was violated upon the trial. The only proof given in support of the charge, so far as it was based upon the age of the boy to whom the liquor was sold, was given by his father, who testified to the date of his birth. On cross-examination this witness was asked whether he had not stated to the defendant, at a time and place mentioned and in the presence of certain persons named, that his son was over eighteen years of age at the time of the transaction. His answer was, in substance, that he did not recollect anything of that kind. After the People had rested the defendant was sworn as a witness in his own behalf, and was asked whether the father had not stated to him, in the presence of the persons named and at the time stated, that his son was over eighteen years of age. This question was objected to by the district attorney. The objection was sustained and the defendant excepted. We think that the defendant was entitled to give this testimony. The age of the boy was a material issue in the case, and although the father had testified in general terms to his age; yet the defendant had the right to contradict or impeach the father by showing that he had made a contrary statement out of court. The testimony of the father to prove that the boy was a minor under eighteen years of age could be impeached or contradicted by proof that he had stated otherwise out of court.

At a subsequent stage of the trial the defendant called the witnesses that he stated were present at the time and place when these declarations of the father as to the age of his son were made in the presence of the defendant. This testimony was objected to by the district attorney, and the objection was sustained by the court. We think that this testimony was admissible, for the reason already stated. . . . Judgment reversed, etc.

FAULTLESSNESS

LUTHRINGER V. MOORE

SUPREME COURT OF CALIFORNIA, 1948
31 CAL.2D 489, 190 P.2D 1

CARTER, JUSTICE. Plaintiff recovered a judgment on a
verdict for damages for personal injuries against defendant, R. L.
Moore. Plaintiff stated his action in two counts, the first predicated upon an absolute liability or liability without fault, and
the second, alleged negligence of defendants. The defendants are
Bedell, the tenant of the restaurant building hereafter mentioned
and the operator of the restaurant therein, Sacramento Medico-
Dental Building Company, a corporation, the owner of the office
and restaurant buildings, and Moore, an individual engaged in
the pest eradication business. A nonsuit was granted as to all defendants as to the second count in the complaint. Bedell and
Medico-Dental Building Company were exonerated. Plaintiff appeals from the unfavorable result as to those defendants but ad-
vises this court that he urges that appeal only in the event the
judgment is reversed as to Moore who is the only appealing defendant. In view of the result (affirmance of the judgment)
reached herein we will treat plaintiff's position as an abandonment of his appeal, and accordingly, it is dismissed.

From the foregoing it is apparent that we have presented,
the question of whether Moore was absolutely liable for the injury—was liable without fault—whether the doctrine of strict liability is applicable.

The locale of the accident giving rise to the action is commercial buildings in the business district of the City of Sacra-

mento. Defendant, Sacramento Medico-Dental Building Company, is the owner of two contiguous buildings, one a ten story concrete office building and the other a restaurant building. Tenants of that defendant occupy the buildings. Beneath the first floor of both buildings are basement rooms. They are connected by passageways. A room on the street level floor of the office building was occupied by a tenant Flynn in which he conducted a pharmacy. There was also a dress shop on that floor. A restaurant occupied the restaurant building. Flynn's store was adjacent to the main entrance lobby of the office building.

Defendant Moore was engaged to exterminate cockroaches and other vermin in the basement under the restaurant and that part under the dress shop. He made his preparations and released hydrocyanic acid gas in those rooms about midnight on November 16, 1943. Plaintiff, an employee of Flynn in the latter's pharmacy, in the course of his employment, arrived at the pharmacy about 8:45 a.m. on November 17, 1943, with the purpose of opening the store. Although there is a conflict in the evidence, there is testimony that none of the three entrances to the drug store bore any signs or notices warning of the presence or danger of the above mentioned gas. The evidence is clear that there was none on the door used by plaintiff. He entered by a door from the office building lobby. He was suffering from a cold. After entering the store he proceeded to a small mezzanine floor to put on his working clothes. Feeling ill he returned to the main floor and lost consciousness. He was discovered in that condition by Flynn's bookkeeper who arrived at the pharmacy between 9:15 and 9:30 a.m. Plaintiff was removed from the store, treated by the firemen of the city with a resuscitator and taken to the hospital where he received medical attention. He was found suffering from hydrocyanic acid gas poisoning and his injuries are from that source. . . .

Moore alleges error in the giving of the instruction reading: "I instruct you that any person engaging in an ultra-hazardous activity, who knew, or in the exercise of reasonable care, should have known its ultra-hazardous character, and thereby proximately causes injury to another by a miscarriage of such activity, is liable to the person harmed, unless the latter knew or in the exercise of reasonable care should have known its ultra-hazardous nature and failed to exercise reasonable care for his own safety, or unless he knowingly and voluntarily invited the injury, and brought it upon himself.

"Likewise, any person, firm or corporation who brings, or permits to be brought upon its premises that which is of an ultra-hazardous nature, and who knew, or in the exercise of reasonable care should have known its ultra-hazardous nature, is liable for any injury proximately caused another, by its miscarriage, unless the person so harmed knew, or in the exercise of reasonable care should have known of its ultra-hazardous nature and failed to exercise reasonable care for his own safety or unless he knowingly and voluntarily invited the injury, and brought it upon himself.

"This principle of law does not require a finding of negligence upon those so engaging in such activity, or upon those bringing or permitting it to be brought upon the premises.

"I instruct you as a matter of law that under all the facts and circumstances of this case, the use and release of hydrocyanic acid gas by the defendant Moore, in the premises of defendant Bedell and Sacramento Medico-Dental Building, a corporation, all as appears in the evidence, constituted an ultra-hazardous activity. . . ."

In connection with the foregoing it is urged that the instructions declare as a matter of law that the release of such gas on the premises constitutes an ultra-hazardous activity. It appears to be settled that the question of whether the case is a proper one for imposing absolute or strict liability is one of law for the Court. See, Green v. General Petroleum Corp., 205 Cal. 328, 270 P. 952, 60 A.L.R. 475. . . .

Turning to the question of whether absolute or strict liability is appropriate in the instant case, we find that according to witness Bell (a man engaged in the pest control business), there are only three operators licensed to use lethal gas in pest control in Sacramento. And in regard to the nature of hydrocyanic acid gas he testified:

"Q. Do you know whether hydrocyanic acid gas is a poisonous gas or a lethal gas? A. It definitely is.

"Q. By lethal, you mean it is deadly, or causes death? A. That's right. . . .

"Q. How about the quantities of it that are required to

cause death to animals or human beings? A. Minimum amount would be about 300 parts per million, would be a lethal dosage.

"Q. The amount to 300 parts by volume. A. Yes, sir.

"Q. Per volume of air? A. Yes, sir.

"Q. That amount would be lethal to human beings? A. That is correct.

"Q. Do you know how long a time would be required? A. It would take very little time with that amount.

"Q. Can you tell us what the physical characteristics of hydrocyanic acid gas are? A. It is a little lighter-than-air gas; a very highly penetrative gas; susceptible to moisture quite a bit, it will follow moisture; it is noninflammable; the flash point is very low so that it can be used without very much hazard of fire.

"Q. It is lighter than air? A. Yes, sir.

"Q. What about the diffusion quality of it? If you put it in a room with air, does it diffuse? A. If the air is warm, it will very rapidly. If the temperature is low, it will not diffuse so rapidly.

"Q. I think you said the gas was very penetrative? A. Definitely.

"Q. What do you mean by that? A. That is one of the advantages of the gas; why they use it in fumigation. It will penetrate behind baseboards, cracks and crevises that we couldn't get at with any type of liquid insecticide. It will go through mattresses, chesterfields, furniture, some types of porous walls.

"Q. It does a good job of fumigating? A. That's right.

"Q. Because it can get into small cracks and apertures? A. That's right.

"Q. Is it difficult to keep that gas confined? A. Yes, because of the fact it will penetrate, you have to be careful to keep it in a definite area.

"Q. In fumigation, what is your practice? You prepare a room so as to keep the gas confined as far as possible? A. You have to seal all the cracks around doors and windows; any holes around plumbing outlets; pack up the trim on the sinks, tape them off; on a regular fumigation they make a paste for that that is used. Sometimes we will use patching plaster; mostly through the use of a tape, because you tear it off in strips; depending on the width of the crack; pack the ventilator openings; wires; anything with any kind of a crack at all should be sealed.

"Q. In the ordinary operation, if you go in and seal up so that you consider it is adequately sealed, you still have some leakage of gas, or not? A. You will have some, yes, sir, unless it is a very well built building.

"Q. I see. What is your practice with reference to adjoining premises or adjoining parts of the same building? A. In fumigating the building, the tenants from an individual building, when you are fumigating any part of it, should be vacated.

"Q. All parts of the building? A. Yes, sir.

"Q. What is the reason for vacating other parts of the building that you do not fumigate? A. The operator going into a building isn't too familiar with the construction of the building. There might be a hidden flue and cracks some place you might miss. If you did miss that, the people above the area would be fumigated. That gas might leak up there. They would be subject to being gassed that way. The safest way is to vacate the building, no matter how careful you are to always be careful of every piece of construction of the building." Hydrocyanic acid gas is defined as a "dangerous or lethal chemical" in the statutes dealing with licensing of those engaged in the pest control business (Business & Professions Code, sec. 8513.) Bell testified on cross examination that the gas was generally used in the community, and that it is used for fumigating railroad cars, homes, apartments, and fruit trees, but as seen there are only three licensed operators in Sacramento.

Defendant Moore introduced a written notice which he claims was attached to the door of the pharmacy directing that he be contacted before entering the building because of possible gas leakage, indicating that he believed a leakage possible although he testified that he took every precaution to seal the basement before he released the gas. This evidence, as above discussed, clearly points to the conclusion that the gas escaped from the basement into the pharmacy although great care to prevent it was exercised by Moore. As before seen, the activity in releasing the gas was carried on in the basement of commercial buildings where there are a great many tenants. Under these circumstances we have a case which calls for liability without fault—a case falling within the category of what has been defined as the miscarriage of an ultra-hazardous activity. It has been said: "One who carries on an ultra-hazardous activity is liable to another whose person, land, or chattels the actor should recognize as likely to be harmed by the unpreventable miscarriage of the activity for harm resulting thereto from that which makes the activity ultra-hazardous, although the utmost care is exercised to prevent the harm. . . . An activity is ultra-hazardous if it (a) necessarily involves a risk of serious harm to the person, land or chattels of others which cannot be eliminated by the exercise of the utmost care, and (b) is not a matter of common usage. . . . An activity is a matter of common usage if it is customarily carried on by the great mass of mankind or by many people in the community. It does not cease to be so because it is carried on for a purpose peculiar to the individual who carries it on. Certain activities may be so generally carried on as to be regarded as customary. Thus, automobiles have come into such general use that their operation is a matter of common usage. This, together with the fact that the risk involved in the careful operation of a carefully maintained automobile is slight, is sufficient to prevent their operation from being an ultra-hazardous activity. However, the use of an automotive vehicle of such size and weight as to be incapable of safe control and to be likely to crush water and gas mains under the surface of the highway is not as yet a usual means of transportation and, therefore, the use of such an automobile is ultrahazardous.

"While blasting is recognized as a proper means of clearing woodland for cultivation and of excavating for building purposes, the conditions which require its use are usually of brief duration. It is generally required because of the peculiar character of the land and it is not a part of the customary processes of farming or of building operations. Likewise, the manufacture, storage, transportation and use of high explosives, although necessary to the construction of many public and private works, are carried on by a comparatively small number of persons and, therefore, are not matters of common usage. So, too, the very nature of oil lands and the essential interest of the public in the production of oil require that oil wells be drilled, but the dangers incident thereto are characteristic of oil lands and not of lands in general. . . . The rule stated . . . does not apply if the activity is carried on in pursuance of a public duty imposed upon the actor as a public officer or employee or as a common carrier. . . . The rule stated . . . does not apply where the person harmed by the unpreventable miscarriage of an ultrahazardous activity has reason to know of the risk which makes the activity ultrahazardous and (a) takes part in it, or (b) brings himself within the area which will be endangered by its miscarriage, (i) without a privilege, or (ii) in the exercise of a privilege derived from the consent of the person carrying on the activity, or (iii) as a member of the public entitled to the services of a public utility carrying on the activity. . . . (1) A plaintiff is not barred from recovery for harm done by the miscarriage of an ultrahazardous activity caused by his failure to exercise reasonable care to observe the fact that the activity is being carried on or by intentionally coming into the area which would be endangered by its miscarriage. (2) A plaintiff is barred from recovery for harm caused by the miscarriage of an ultrahazardous activity if, but only if, (a) he intentionally or negligently causes the activity to miscarry, or (b) after knowledge that it has miscarried or is about to miscarry, he fails to exercise reasonable care to avoid harm threatened thereby." Rest., Torts, secs. 519, 520, 521, 523. In the case of Green v. General Petroleum Corporation, supra, an oil well had "blown out" due to natural gas pressure while in the process of being drilled, and the plaintiff's property was damaged by debris being cast thereon. The court declared the driller of the well to be liable although he had used all care possible to avoid the accident, and announced the rule that: "Where one, in the conduct and maintenance of an enterprise lawful and proper in itself, deliberately does an act under known conditions, and, with knowledge that injury may result to another, proceeds, and injury is done to the other as the direct and proximate consequence of the act, however carefully done, the one who does the act and causes the injury should, in all fairness, be required to compensate the other for the damage done." Page 333 of 205 Cal., page 955 of 270.P.

There is considerable discussion in the briefs about the doctrine of the English case of Fletcher v. Rylands, L.R. 3 H.L. 330, and the latest expression there apparently limiting the doctrine (Read v. Lyons & Co., [1945] 1 All Eng. 106, see 35 Cal. L. Rev. 316.) and whether it is in effect in California. Whatever the situation may be in that regard, there can be no doubt that the case of Green v. General Petroleum Corporation, supra, enunciated a principle of absolute liability which is applicable to the instant case. It is not significant that a property damage, as distinguished from a personal injury, was there involved. The important factor is that certain activities under certain conditions may be so hazardous to the public generally, and of such relative infrequent occurrence, that it may well call for strict liability as the best public policy.

The above quoted evidence shows that the use of gas under the circumstances presented is a hazardous activity; that it is perilous and likely to cause injury even though the utmost care is used; that defendant Moore knew or should have known that injury might result; and that the use of it under these circumstances is not a matter of "common usage" within the meaning of the term. In regard to the last feature it may be used commonly by fumigators, but they are relatively few in number and are engaged in a specialized activity. It is not carried on generally by the public, especially under circumstances where many people are present, thus enhancing the hazard, nor is its use a common everyday practice. It is not a common usage within the definition: "An activity may be ultrahazardous because of the instrumentality which is used in carrying it on, the nature of the subject matter with which it deals or the condition which it creates." Rest., Torts, sec. 520(b), com. Cl. (b). And in this connection the instruction advising the jury that the usage was not common, was proper. . . .

The judgment against defendant Moore is affirmed. Plaintiff's appeal is dismissed.

Notes

1. Among the arguments for "strict liability" in the law are the following: (1) holding persons who engage in ultrahazardous activities strictly liable for the injuries they cause promotes the welfare of the victims by providing them with compensation which, under the fault system of liability, they might not be entitled to; (2) it benefits society as a whole by shifting the burden of loss from the individual to those who can better afford it, e.g., business organizations, or insurance companies. Consider the merits of these points in relation to the case of *Luthringer v. Moore.*

In connection with such cases, the question is often asked, "As between two innocent persons, who is the better 'risk-bearer'?" What are the philosophical implications of such a concept?

Are there in fact circumstances under which it is right (morally) to make an innocent person suffer a loss?

2. "Ignorance of the law is no excuse" is a legal maxim familiar to everybody. "Ignorance of the facts is an excuse" is less familiar, but perhaps better understood. Normally we do not hold persons responsible for their ignorance of the facts if such ignorance is not due to carelessness or lack of diligence. The latter is a moral as well as a legal principle. Whether the former has an analogue in morals is more questionable. Why?

There are, of course, exceptions to both rules in the law. Cf. *People v. Werner.* Is there a justification for the statutory exception in that case?

What special objections do you see to the application of the doctrine of strict liability in criminal law as contrasted with civil law? Do these same objections preclude its extension into the area of morals?

3. In the case of *People v. Koerber,* a distinction is introduced between voluntary drunkenness as an excuse and voluntary drunkenness as a ground for reducing the degree of the crime. Would it be altogether inaccurate to speak of the latter as a "partial excuse"? Would we then have to speak also of "partial responsibility" for acts? Does this make any sense?

4. Is it true that we never hold insane persons morally responsible for their acts? Aren't the inmates of mental institutions held accountable for many aspects of their behavior? Is there a parallel here with the legal

position regarding the torts of insane persons? Cf. *McGuire v. Almy.* If not, what extensions of or changes in the notion of moral responsibility would be required to hold an insane person (or the guardians of his estate) morally liable for the injuries he causes?

5. According to Judge Cardozo, "There is nothing to justify the belief that the words right and wrong, when they became limited by M'Naghten's case to the right and wrong of the particular act, cast off their meaning as terms of morals, and became terms of pure legality." The moral test of legal insanity is still the test applied by the vast majority of the courts today. Should it be? Would a more legal or more psychological test be better? What, if any, are the presuppositions of the M'Naghten test regarding morality, mental delusion, and the human personality?

6. A general rule in the law of negligence is that a person is responsible for all the proximate injuries resulting from his negligent act. This is not so, however, if some unforeseeable cause or act intervenes which either aggravates the injuries or causes quite different ones. To count as "unforeseeable" rather than as merely "unforeseen," the intervening agency must be, as the judge in the *Watson* case says, "something so unexpected or extraordinary as that he could not or ought not to have anticipated it." He specifically mentions that one is not bound to anticipate the criminal acts of others. Considering the high crime rate these days, why should this constitute an excuse?

3

WRONGS: JUSTIFICATIONS

In the previous chapter, all the cases involved attempts to escape responsibility by citing certain unusual states of mind or circumstances of the act which would excuse the wrongs committed. None of the defendants claimed a "right" to do what they were being charged with doing. In this chapter, a claim of right is a part of each defense offered. These rights—the right of the pedestrian to use the highways, the right of a seaman to make authoritative decisions during maritime emergencies, the right of self-preservation, the right of a property owner to protect his property against intruders, the right of an employee to protect his business interests—are all legally protected claims. A problem arises only when their assertion conflicts with the lawful interests of others and results in harm. When this occurs, it is necessary to re-evaluate the right so as to place responsibility for the harm or wrong. If the right outweighs the harm, the wrongdoer is "justified," and is relieved of legal responsibility; otherwise, he is not.

The problem of justification may, however, be expressed differently. Instead of posing it as a matter of "rights versus harms," it is perhaps more enlightening, for the purposes of ethical analysis at least, to look upon it as a "conflict of duties" problem. In each of these cases there is implicitly a "duty not to harm others" which is opposed by some other obligation. The task of assigning responsibility is then seen as a task of finding the means of assessing the greater duty.

One of the advantages of approaching the problem of justification in this way is that it encourages closer attention than has yet been given in this book to just what is meant by a "duty not to harm others." In fact, there seem to be as many such specific negative duties as there are positive ones, and our earlier suspicion that Ross's general classification of duties of this negative character overlaps with or at least parallels the others, is thus supported.

For example, in the first case, *Tedla v. Ellman,* the duty not to harm others turns out to be the duty not to disobey statutes designed for the protection of all users of the highways. The particular statute in question is one requiring pedestrians to walk on the left side of the highway so as to permit all the traffic in either direction to pass on their right. A problem arises when, as a justification of the violation of the statute, it is contended that under the circumstances strict conformity to the statutory requirement would have subjected the pedestrian to unreasonable risks. At the time of the accident there was extremely heavy traffic on the side on which the pedestrian was supposed to walk and almost none on the other side. It is argued that obedience to the statute would have meant the violation of another duty, namely, the duty of the pedestrian to use reasonable care. An interesting question is thereby raised: whether it is always reasonable to obey the law when the law itself, at least when strictly interpreted, is unreasonable.

A conflict between a duty not to disobey orders, which in the case of *United States v. Holmes* entails sacrificing the lives of shipwrecked passengers, and the duty to rescue lives is a particularly difficult one for the court, or anyone else for that matter, to resolve. Its difficulty is intensified when it is argued that the sacrifice of some of the passengers was required in order to rescue the remaining survivors. This argument from physical necessity clearly rests upon certain unexpressed assumptions about the value of human life in general, and, in particular, about the relative worth of one life as compared with another. Is life intrinsically valuable? Is one life worth more than another? Surely these are questions which can and ought to be asked.

Self-defense has, from time immemorial, been regarded as a basic human right and a justification for the most serious wrongs, up to and including homicide. It is odd to speak of it as a "duty," but to do so is not altogether without precedent. We sometimes speak of a person's duty to himself, for example. It is precisely in cases where this right or duty is admitted as a justification that an implied "duty to prevent another from causing harm" is also involved. In fact, the right of self-preservation has definite legal limitations. One of the most usual is referred to as a "duty to retreat." No one is justified, say the courts, if he uses force to repel an aggressor where ample opportunity is afforded him to avoid injuring the aggressor and save his own life as well. Whether he must "retreat to the wall" or act altogether reasonably "in the presence of an uplifted knife" is another matter.

Defense of one's property involves an essentially analogous problem. Here too the assertion of one's property right, where it constitutes a justification for injuring or killing another must also involve a duty not to harm another unnecessarily. The case of *State v. Childers* further amplifies the implied "duty not to harm" by understanding it as a "duty not to use one's property to the harm of others," e.g., by enticing another onto the property where spring guns are set, or by failing to warn would-be intruders of their presence.

The final case, *Watt v. Longsdon*, involves a conflict between the negative duty not to defame one's neighbor and the duty to speak the truth. Is a man justified in making statements about the marital infidelity of a fellow employee? Suppose he sincerely believes that the statements are true, even though they later turn out to be false. May he be justified (or "privileged") in some contexts and with reference to some persons (his employer, for example) and not to others (the man's wife)? Suppose that he owes a debt of gratitude to the latter. The complexity of this problem, involving as it does many separate considerations of an obviously moral kind, places severe strains upon the purely judicial methods of the judges. It is well calculated to make philosophers wonder what practical relevance ethical analysis might have in cases of this kind.

REASONABLENESS

Tedla v. Ellman

court of appeals of new york, 1939
280 n.y. 124, 19 n.e.2d 987

Action by Anna Tedla and her husband for damages resulting from injuries sustained by Anna Tedla, against Joseph Ellman and another, consolidated with action by Mary Bachek, as administratrix of the estate of John Bachek, deceased, to recover damages for death of deceased, against Joseph Ellman and another. From judgments of the Appellate Division of the Supreme Court, 253 App. Div. 764, 300 N.Y.S. 1051, affirming judgments in favor of plaintiffs entered upon a verdict in each case, the defendants appeal by permission.

LEHMAN, JUDGE. While walking along a highway, Anna Tedla and her brother, John Bachek, were struck by a passing automobile, operated by the defendant Ellman. She was injured and Bachek was killed. Bachek was a deaf-mute. His occupation was collecting and selling junk. His sister, Mrs. Tedla, was engaged in the same occupation. They often picked up junk at the incinerator of the village of Islip. At the time of the accident they were walking along "Sunrise Highway" and wheeling baby carriages containing junk and wood which they had picked up at the incinerator. It was about six o'clock, or a little earlier, on a Sunday evening in December. Darkness had already set in. Bachek was carrying a lighted lantern, or, at least, there is testimony to that effect. The jury found that the accident was due solely to the negligence of the operator of the automobile. The defendants do not, upon this appeal, challenge the finding of negligence on the part of the operator. They maintain, however, that Mrs. Tedla and her brother were guilty of contributory negligence as matter of law.

Sunrise Highway, at the place of the accident, consists of two roadways, separated by a grass plot. There are no footpaths along the highway and the center grass plot was soft. It is not unlawful for a pedestrian, wheeling a baby carriage, to use the roadway under such circumstances, but a pedestrian using the roadway is bound to exercise such care for his safety as a reasonably prudent person would use. The Vehicle and Traffic Law (Consol. Laws, c.71) provides that "Pedestrians walking or remaining on the paved portion, or traveled part of a roadway shall be subject to, and comply with, the rules governing vehicles, with respect to meeting and turning out, except that such pedestrians shall keep to the left of the center line thereof, and turn to their left instead of right side thereof, so as to permit all vehicles passing them in either direction to pass on their right. Such pedestrians shall not be subject to the rules governing vehicles as to giving signals." Section 85, subd. 6. Mrs. Tedla and her brother did not observe the statutory rule, and at the time of the accident were proceeding in easterly direction on the east bound or right-hand roadway. The defendants moved to dismiss the complaint on the ground, among others, that violation of the statutory rule constitutes contributory negligence as matter of law. They did not, in the courts below, urge that any negligence in other respect of Mrs. Tedla or her brother bars a recovery. The trial judge left to the jury the question whether failure to observe the statutory rule was a proximate cause of the accident; he left to the jury no question of other fault or negligence on the part of Mrs. Tedla or her brother, and the defendants did not request that any other question be submitted. Upon this appeal, the only question presented is whether, as matter of law, disregard of the statutory rule that pedestrians shall keep to the left of the center line of a highway constitutes contributory negligence which bars any recovery by the plaintiff. . . .

The plaintiffs showed by the testimony of a State policeman that "there were very few cars going east" at the time of the accident, but that going west there was "very heavy Sunday night traffic." Until the recent adoption of the new statutory rule for pedestrians, ordinary prudence would have dictated that pedestrians should not expose themselves to the danger of walking along the roadway upon which the "very heavy Sunday night traffic" was proceeding when they could walk in comparative safety along a roadway used by very few cars. It is said that now, by force of the statutory rule, pedestrians are guilty of contributory negligence as a matter of law when they use the safer roadway, unless that roadway is left of the center of the road. Disregard of the statutory rule of the road and observance of a rule based on immemorial custom, it is said, is negligence which as matter of law is a proximate cause of the accident, though observance of the statutory rule might, under the circumstances of the particular case, expose a pedestrian to serious danger from which he would be free if he followed the rule that had been established by custom. If that be true, then the Legislature has decreed that pedestrians must observe the general rule of conduct which it has prescribed for their safety even under circumstances where observance would subject them to unusual risk; that pedestrians are to be charged with negligence as matter of law for acting as prudence dictates. It is unreasonable to ascribe to the Legislature an intention that the statute should have so extraordinary a result, and the courts may not give to a statute an effect not intended by the Legislature.

The Legislature, when it enacted the statute, presumably knew that this court and the courts of other jurisdictions had established the general principle that omission by a plaintiff of a safeguard, prescribed by statute, against a recognized danger, constitutes negligence as matter of law which bars recovery for damage caused by incidence of the danger for which the safeguard was prescribed. The principle has been formulated in the Restatement of the Law of Torts: "A plaintiff who has violated a legislative enactment designed to prevent a certain type of dangerous situation is barred from recovery for a harm caused by a violation of the statute if, but only if, the harm was sustained by reason of a situation of that type." § 469. So where a plaintiff failed to place lights upon a vehicle, as required by statute, this court has said: "we think the unexcused omission of the statutory signals is more than some evidence of negligence. It is negligence in itself. Lights are intended for the guidance and protection of other travelers on the highway. Highway Law [Consol. Laws, c. 25] § 329-a. By the very terms of the hypothesis, to omit, willfully or heedlessly, the safeguards prescribed by law for the benefit of another that he may be preserved in life or limb, is to fall short of the standard of diligence to which those who live in organized society are under a duty to conform. That, we think is now the established rule in this State." Martin v. Herzog, 228 N.Y. 164, 168, 126 N.E. 814, 815, per Cardozo. J. The appellants lean heavily upon that and kindred cases and the principle established by them.

The analogy is, however, incomplete. The "established rule" should not be weakened either by subtle distinctions or by extension beyond its letter or spirit into a field where "by the very terms of the hypothesis" it can have no proper application. At times the indefinite and flexible standard of care of the traditional reasonably prudent man may be, in the opinion of the Legislature, an insufficient measure of the care which should be exercised to guard against a recognized danger; at times, the duty, imposed by custom, that no man shall use what is his to the harm of others provides insufficient safeguard for the preservation of the life or limb or property of others. Then the Legislature may by statute prescribe additional safeguards and may define duty and standard of care in rigid terms; and when the Legislature has spoken, the standard of care required is no longer what the reasonably prudent man would do under the circumstances but what the Legislature has commanded. That is the rule established by the courts and "by the very terms of the hypothesis" the rule applies where the Legislature has prescribed safeguards "for the benefit of another that he may be preserved in life or limb." In that field debate as to whether the safeguards so prescribed are reasonably necessary is ended by the legislative fiat. Obedience to that fiat cannot add to the danger, even assuming that the prescribed safeguards are not reasonably necessary and where the legislative anticipation of dangers is realized and harm results through heedless or willful omission of the prescribed safeguard, injury flows from wrong and the wrongdoer is properly held responsible for the consequent damages.

The statute upon which the defendants rely is of different character. It does not prescribe additional safeguards which pedestrians must provide for the preservation of the life or limb or property of others, or even of themselves, nor does it impose upon pedestrians a higher standard of care. What the statute does provide is rules of the road to be observed by pedestrians and by vehicles, so that all those who use the road may know how they and others should proceed, at least under usual circumstances. A general rule of conduct—and, specifically, a rule of the road—may accomplish its intended purpose under usual conditions, but, when the unusual occurs, strict observance may defeat the purpose of the rule and produce catastrophic results.

Negligence is failure to exercise the care required by law. Where a statute defines the standard of care and the safeguards required to meet a recognized danger, then, as we have said, no other measure may be applied in determining whether a person has carried out the duty of care imposed by law. Failure to observe the standard imposed by statute is negligence, as matter of law. On the other hand, where a statutory general rule of conduct fixes no definite standard of care which would under all circumstances tend to protect life, limb or property but merely codifies or supplements a common-law rule, which has always been subject to limitations and exceptions; or where the statutory rule of conduct regulates conflicting rights and obligations in manner calculated to promote public convenience and safety, then the statute, in the absence of clear language to the contrary, should not be construed as intended to wipe out the limitations and exceptions which judicial decisions have attached to the common-law duty; nor should it be construed as an inflexible command that the general rule of conduct intended to prevent accidents must be followed even under conditions when observance might cause accidents. We may assume reasonably that the Legislature directed pedestrians to keep to the left of the center of the road because that would cause them to face traffic approaching in that lane and would enable them to care for their own safety better than if the traffic approached them from the rear. We cannot assume reasonably that the Legislature intended that a statute enacted for the preservation of the life and limb of pedestrians must be observed when observance would subject them to more imminent danger. . . .

The generally accepted rule and the reasons for it are set

forth in the comment to section 286 of the Restatement of the Law of Torts: "Many statutes and ordinances are so worded as apparently to express a universally obligatory rule of conduct. Such enactments, however, may in view of their purpose and spirit be properly construed as intended to apply only to ordinary situations and to be subject to the qualification that the conduct prohibited thereby is not wrongful if, because of an emergency or the like, the circumstances justify an apparent disobedience to the letter of the enactment. . . . The provisions of statutes intended to codify and supplement the rules of conduct which are established by a course of judicial decision or by custom, are often construed as subject to the same limitations and exceptions as the rules which they supersede. Thus, a statute or ordinance requiring all persons to drive on the right side of the road may be construed as subject to an exception permitting travellers to drive upon the other side, if so doing is likely to prevent rather than cause the accidents which it is the purpose of the statute or ordinance to prevent."

Even under that construction of the statute, a pedestrian is, of course, at fault if he fails without good reason to observe the statutory rule of conduct. The general duty is established by the statute, and deviation from it without good cause is a wrong and the wrongdoer is responsible for the damages resulting from his wrong. . . .

In each action, the judgment should be affirmed, with costs.

O'BRIEN and FINCH, JJ., dissent on the authority of Martin v. Herzog, 228 N.Y. 164, 126 N.E. 814.

Judgments affirmed.

PHYSICAL NECESSITY

United States v. Holmes*

UNITED STATES CIRCUIT COURT, EASTERN DISTRICT OF
PENNSYLVANIA, 1842
1 WALL. JR. 1, 26 FED. CAS. 360, NO. 15, 383

The American ship William Brown, left Liverpool on
the 13th of March, 1841, bound for Philadelphia, in the United
States. She had on board (besides a heavy cargo) 17 of a crew, and
65 passengers, Scotch and Irish emigrants. About 10 o'clock on
the night of the 19th of April, when distant 250 miles southeast
of Cape Race, Newfoundland, the vessel struck an iceberg, and
began to fill so rapidly that it was evident she must soon go down.
The long-boat and jolly-boat were cleared away and lowered. The
captain, the second mate, 7 of the crew, and 1 passsenger got into
the jolly-boat. The first mate, 8 seamen, of whom the prisoner was
one (these 9 being the entire remainder of the crew), and 32 passengers, in all 41 persons got indiscriminately into the long-boat.
[The first mate and some of the crew of the long-boat were originally in the jolly-boat with the captain; but the mate understanding navigation, was transferred, with a chart, quadrant, and compass, to the long-boat; and some of the crew were exchanged.]
The remainder of the passengers, 31 persons were obliged to remain on board the ship. In an hour and a half from the time
when the ship struck, she went down, carrying with her every

* Reported by John William Wallace. See Appendix for an explanation of
the earlier and later reporting systems. Footnotes to this report are omitted,
except those deemed especially relevant or interesting, which are included
in the text in brackets in abbreviated form.

person who had not escaped to one or the other of the small boats. Thirty-one passengers thus perished. On the following morning (Tuesday) the captain, being about to part company with the long-boat, gave its crew several directions, and among other counsel, advised them to obey all the orders of the mate, as they would obey his, the captain's. This the crew promised that they would do. The long-boat was believed to be in general good condition, but she had not been in the water since leaving Liverpool, now thirty-five days; and as soon as she was launched, began to leak. She continued to leak the whole time; but the passengers had buckets, and tins, and by bailing, were able to reduce the water, so as to make her hold her own. The plug was about an inch and a half in diameter. It came out more than once, and finally, got lost; but its place was supplied by different expedients.

It appeared by the depositions of the captain, and of the second mate (the latter of whom had followed the sea twenty-one years; the former being, likewise, well experienced), that on Tuesday morning when the two boats parted company, the long-boat and all on board were in great jeopardy. [The captain and the others in the jolly-boat were picked up at sea after six days by a French ship. They afterwards came to Philadelphia where depositions of the captain and mate were taken.] . . . Without going into more detail, the evidence of both these officers went to show that, loaded as the long-boat was on Tuesday morning, the chances of living were much against her. But the captain thought, that even if lightened to the extent to which she afterwards was, "It would have been impossible to row her to land; and that the chances of her being picked up, were ninety-nine to one against her." It appeared, further, that on Monday night, when the passengers on the ship (then settling towards her head and clearly going down) were shrieking, and calling on the captain to take them off on his boat, the mate on the long-boat said to them: "Poor souls! you're only going down a short time before we do." And, further, that on the following morning, before the boats parted company, the mate, in the long-boat, told the captain, in the jolly-boat, that the long-boat was unmanageable, and, that unless the captain would take some of the long-boat's passengers, it would be necessary to cast lots and throw some overboard. "I know what you mean," or, as stated by one witness, "I know what you'll have to do," said the captain. "Don't speak of that now. Let it be the last resort." There was little or no wind at this time, but pieces of ice were floating about.

Notwithstanding all this, the long-boat, loaded as she is above described to have been, did survive throughout the night of Monday, the day of Tuesday, and until 10 o'clock of Tuesday night,—full twenty-four hours after the ship struck the iceberg. The crew rowed, turn about, at intervals, and the passengers bailed. On Tuesday morning, after the long-boat and jolly-boat parted, it began to rain, and continued to rain throughout the day and night of Tuesday. At night the wind began to freshen, the sea grew heavier, and once, or oftener, the waves splashed over the boat's bow so as to wet, all over, the passengers who were seated there. Pieces of ice were still floating around, and, during the day, icebergs had been seen. About 10 o'clock of Tuesday night, the prisoner and the rest of the crew began to throw over some of the passengers, and did not cease until they had thrown over 14 male passengers. These, with the exception of two married men and a small boy, constituted all the male passengers abroad. Not one of the crew was cast over. One of them, the cook, was a negro.

It was among the facts of this case that, during these solemn and distressful hours, scarce a remark appeared to have been made in regard to what was going to be done, nor, while it was being done, as to the necessity for doing it. None of the crew of the long-boat were present at the trial, to testify, and, with the exception of one small boy, all the witnesses from the long-boat were women,—mostly quite young. It is probable that, by Tuesday night . . . the witnesses had become considerably overpowered by exhaustion and cold, having been 24 hours in the boat. None of them spoke in a manner entirely explicit and satisfactory in regard to the most important point, viz., the degree and imminence of the jeopardy at 10 o'clock on Tuesday night, when the throwing over began. As has been stated, few words were spoken. It appeared, only, that, about 10 o'clock of Tuesday night, it being then dark, the rain falling rather heavily, the sea somewhat freshening, and the boat having considerable water in it, the mate, who had been bailing for some time, gave it up, exclaiming: "This work won't do. Help me, God. Men, go to work."

Some of the passengers cried out, about the same time: "The boat is sinking. The plug's out. God have mercy on our poor souls." Holmes and the crew did not proceed upon this order; and after a little while, the mate exclaimed again: "Men, you must go to work, or we shall all perish." They then went to work; and, as has been already stated, threw out, before they ended, 14 male passengers, and also 2 women. [It was a matter of doubt whether these women had been thrown over, or whether their sacrifice was an act of self-devotion and affection to their brother. When Holmes seized him, his sisters entreated for his life, and said that if he was thrown over they wished to be thrown over too; that "they wished to die the death of their brother." "Give me a dress to put around me," said one of the sisters, after her brother had been thrown out, "and I care not now to live longer."] The mate directed the crew "not to part man and wife, and not to throw over any women." There was no other principle of selection. There was no evidence of combination among the crew. No lots were cast, nor had the passengers, at any time, been either informed or consulted as to what was now done. Holmes was one of the persons who assisted in throwing the passengers over. The first man thrown over was one Riley, whom Holmes and the others told to stand up, which he did. They then threw him over, and afterwards Duffy, who, in vain, besought them to spare him, for the sake of his wife and children, who were on shore. They then seized a third man, but his wife being aboard, he was spared. Coming to Charles Conlin, the man exclaimed: "Holmes, dear, sure you won't put me out?" "Yes, Charley," said Holmes, "you must go, too." And so he was thrown over. Next was Francis Askin, for the manslaughter of whom the prisoner was indicted. When laid hold of, he offered Holmes five sovereigns to spare his life till morning, "when," said he, "if God don't send us some help, we'll draw lots, and if the lot falls on me, I'll go over like a man." Holmes said, "I don't want your money, Frank," and put him overboard. When one McAvoy was seized, he asked for five minutes to say his prayers, and, at the interposition of a negro, the cook, was allowed time to say them before he was cast overboard. It appeared, also, that when Askin was put out, he had struggled violently, yet the boat had not sunk. Two men, very stiff with cold, who had hidden themselves, were thrown over

after daylight on Wednesday morning, when, clearly, there was
no necessity for it. [The exact condition of these two men did not
appear. Some of the witnesses thought that they were too much
frozen to recover. Others swore differently.] On Wednesday morning, while yet in the boat, some of the witnesses had told the crew
that they (i.e., the crew) should be made to die the death they had
given to the others. The boat had provisions for six or seven days,
close allowance; that is to say, 75 pounds of bread, 6 gallons of
water, 8 or 10 pounds of meat, and a small bag of oatmeal. The
mate had a chart, quadrant, and compass. The weather was cold,
and the passengers, being half clothed, much benumbed. On
Wednesday morning the weather cleared, and early in the morning the long-boat was picked up by the ship "Crescent." All the
persons who had not been thrown overboard were thus saved.

On the other hand the character of the prisoner stood forth,
in many points, in manly and interesting relief. A Finn by birth,
he had followed the sea from youth, and his frame and counte-
nance would have made an artist's model for decision and
strength. He had been the last man of the crew to leave the sinking ship. His efforts to save the passengers, at the time the ship
struck, had been conspicuous, and, but that they were in discharge of duty, would have been called self-forgetful and most
generous. [On board the long-boat, a widowed mother, a Scots-
woman, and her three daughters had escaped; but, just as the
boat was about veering astern, and when there was great danger
of being drawn into the vortex of the sinking ship, it was discovered that one of the family, a sick sister, had been left behind
in the ship. Her mother was calling, "Isabel, Isabel, come, come!"
But the girl was too sick to hear or to mind. Holmes, hearing the
mother's cry, climbed up the ship's side (at great peril of his life,
as was testified), ran astern, and, hoisting the sick girl upon his
shoulders, swung himself and her over, by the tackle, by one arm,
into the long-boat below.] As a sailor, his captain and the second
mate testified that he had ever been obedient to orders, faithful to
his duty, and efficient in the performance of it,—"remarkably so,"
said the second mate. "He was kind and obliging in every respect," said the captain, "to the passengers, to his shipmates, and
to everybody. Never heard one speak against him. He was always
obedient to officers. I never had a better man on board ship. He

was a first rate man." (Captain's deposition.) While on the long-
boat, in order to protect the women, he had parted with all his
clothes, except his shirt and pantaloons; and his conduct and language to the women were kind. After Askin had been thrown out,
some one asked if any more were to be thrown over. "No," said
Holmes, "no more shall be thrown over. If any more are lost, we
will all be lost together." Of both passengers and crew, he finally
became the only one whose energies and whose hopes did not sink
into prostration. He was the first to descry the vessel which took
them up, and by his exertions the ship was made to see, and,
finally, to save them.

The prisoner was indicted under the act of April 30, 1790,
"for the punishment of certain crimes against the United States"
(1 Story's Laws 83 [1 Stat. 115]), an act which ordains (section 12)
that if any seaman, etc., shall commit manslaughter upon the
high seas, etc., on conviction, he shall be imprisoned not exceeding three years, and fined not exceeding one thousand dollars. . . .

The prosecution was conducted by Mr. Wm. M. Meredith,
U. S. Dist. Atty., Mr. Dallas, and O. Hopkinson; the defence by
David Paul Brown, Mr. Hazlehurst, and Mr. Armstrong.

Mr. Dallas. The prisoner is charged with "unlawful homicide," as distinguished from that sort which is malicious. His defence is that the homicide was necessary to self-preservation. First,
then, we ask: Was the homicide thus necessary? That is to say,
was the danger instant, overwhelming, leaving no choice of
means, no moment for deliberation? For, unless the danger were
of this sort, the prisoner, under any admission, had no right, without notice or consultation, or lot, to sacrifice the lives of 16 fellow
beings. Peril, even extreme peril, is not enough to justify a sacrifice such as this was. Nor would even the certainty of death be
enough, if death were yet prospective. It must be instant. The law
regards every man's life as of equal value. It regards it, likewise,
as of sacred value. Nor may any man take away his brother's life,
but where the sacrifice is indispensable to save his own. (Mr. Dallas then examined the evidence, and contended that the danger
was not so extreme as is requisite to justify homicide.) But it will
be answered, that death being certain, there was no obligation to
wait until the moment of death had arrived. Admitting, then, the

fact that death was certain, and that the safety of some persons
was to be promoted by an early sacrifice of the others, what law,
we ask, gives a crew, in such a case, to be the arbiters of life and
death, settling, for themselves, both the time and the extent of the
necessity? No. We protest against giving to seamen the power thus
to make jettison of human beings, as of so much cargo; of allowing sailors, for their own safety, to throw overboard, whenever
they may like, whomsoever they may choose. If the mate and seamen believed that the ultimate safety of a portion was to be advanced by the sacrifice of another portion, it was the clear duty of
that officer, and of the seamen, to give full notice to all on board.
Common settlement would, then, have fixed the principle of sacrifice, and, the mode of selection involving all, a sacrifice of any
would have been resorted to only in dire extremity. Thus far, the
argument admits that, at sea, sailor and passenger stand upon the
same base, and in equal relations. But we take, third, stronger
ground. The seaman, we hold, is bound, beyond the passenger, to
encounter the perils of the sea. To the last extremity, to death itself, must he protect the passenger. It is his duty. It is on account
of these risks that he is paid. It is because the sailor is expected to
expose himself to every danger, that, beyond all mankind, by
every law, his wages are secured to him. It is for this exposure
that the seamen's claims are a "sacred lien," and "that if only a
single nail of the ship is left, they are entitled to it." 3 Kent.
Comm. 197, and in note. Exposure, risk, hardship, death, are the
sailor's vocation,—the seaman's daily bread. He must perform
whatever belongs to his duty. To this effect speaks Lord Bacon,
when he says "that the law imposeth it upon every subject that
he prefer the urgent service of his prince and country before the
safety of his life." His lordship goes on to say that, "if a man be
commanded to bring ordnance or munition to relieve any of the
king's towns that are distressed, then he cannot, for any danger
of tempest, justify the throwing of them overboard; for there it
holdeth which was spoken by the Roman when he alleged the
same necessity of weather to hold him from embarking: 'Necesse
est et ut eam; non ut vivam.' " ["It is necessary that I go, not that
I live."] 13 Bacon's Works, by Montagu (Lond. 1831) p. 161. No
other doctrine than this one can be adopted. Promulgate as law
that the prisoner is guiltless, and our marine will be disgraced in

the eyes of civilized nations. The thousand ships which now traverse the ocean in safety will be consigned to the absolute power of their crews, and, worse than the dangers of the sea, will be added such as come from the violence of men more reckless than any upon earth.

Mr. Armstrong opened the defence, and was followed by Mr. Brown.

We protest against the prisoner being made a victim to the reputation of the marine law of the country. It cannot be, God forbid that it should ever be, that the sacrifice of innocence shall be the price at which the name and honour of American jurisprudence is to be preserved in this country, or in foreign lands. The malediction of an unrighteous sentence will rest more heavily on the law, than on the prisoner. This court (it would be indecent to think otherwise) will administer the law, "uncaring consequences." But this case should be tried in a long-boat sunk down to its very gunwale with 41 half naked, starved, and shivering wretches, the boat leaking from below, filling from above, a hundred leagues from land, at midnight, surrounded by ice, unmanageable from its load, and subject to certain destruction from the change of the most changeful of the elements, the winds and the waves. To these superadd the horrours of famine and the recklessness of despair, madness, and all the prospects, past utterance, of this unutterable condition. Fairly to sit in judgment on the prisoner, we should, then, be actually translated to his situation. It was a conjuncture which no fancy can imagine. Terrour had assumed the throne of reason, and passion had become judgment. Are the United States to come here, now, a year after the events, when it is impossible to estimate the elements which combined to make the risk, or to say to what extent the jeopardy was imminent? Are they, with square, rule, and compass, deliberately to measure this boat in this room, to weigh these passengers, call in philosophers, discuss specific gravities, calculate by the tables of a life insurance company the chances of life, and because they, these judges find that, by their calculation, this unfortunate boat's crew might have had the thousandth part of one poor chance of escape, to condemn this prisoner to chains and a dungeon for what he did in the terrour and darkness of that dark and terrible night. Such a mode of testing men's acts and motives is monstrous.

We contend, therefore, that what is honestly and reasonably believed to be certain death will justify self-defence to the degree
requisite for excuse. According to Dr. Rutherford (Inst. Nat. Law,
bk. 1, c. 16, § 5): "This law,"—i.e. the law of nature,—"cannot be
supposed to oblige a man to expose his life to such dangers as may
be guarded against, and to wait till the danger is just coming
upon him, before it allows him to secure himself." In other words,
he need not wait till the certainty of the danger has been proved,
past doubt, by its result. Yet this is the doctrine of the prosecution. They ask us to wait until the boat has sunk. We may, then,
make an effort to prevent her from sinking. They tell us to wait
till all are drowned. We may, then, make endeavours to save a
part. They command us to stand still till we are all lost, past possibility of redemption, and then we may rescue as many as can
be saved. Where the danger is instantaneous, the mind is too
much disturbed, says Rutherford, in a passage hereafter cited, to
deliberate upon the method of providing for one's own safety
with the least hurt to an aggressor. The same author then proceeds: "I see not, therefore, any want of benevolence which can
be reasonably charged upon a man in these circumstances, if he
takes the most obvious way of preserving himself, though perhaps
some other method might have been found out, which would have
preserved him as effectually, and have produced less hurt to the
aggressor, if he had been calm enough, and had been allowed time
enough to deliberate about it." Rutherf. Inst. Nat. Law, bk. 1,
c. 16, § 5. Nor is this the language of approved text writers alone.
The doctrine has the solemnity of judicial establishment. In
Grainger v. State, 5 Yerg. 459, the supreme court of Tennessee
deliberately adjudge, that "if a man, though in no great danger of
serious bodily harm, through fear, alarm, or cowardice, kill another under the impression that great bodily injury is about to be
inflicted on him, it is neither manslaughter nor murder, but self-
defence. . . ."

Counsel say that lots are the law of the ocean. Lots, in cases
of famine, where means of subsistence are wanting for all the
crew, is what the history of maritime disaster records; but who has
ever told of casting lots at midnight, in a sinking boat, in the
midst of darkness, of rain, of terrour, and of confusion? To cast
lots when all are going down, but to decide who shall be spared,

to cast lots when the question is, whether any can be saved, is a plan easy to suggest, rather difficult to put in practice. The danger was instantaneous, a case, says Rutherford . . . when "the mind is too much disturbed to deliberate," and where, if it were "more calm," there is no time for deliberation. The sailors adopted the only principle of selection which was possible in an emergency like theirs,—a principle more humane than lots. Man and wife were not torn asunder, and the women were all preserved. Lots would have rendered impossible this clear dictate of humanity. But again: The crew either were in their ordinary and original state of subordination to their officers, or they were in a state of nature. If in the former state, they are excusable in law, for having obeyed the order of the mate,—an order twice imperatively given. Independent of the mate's general authority in the captain's absence, the captain had pointedly directed the crew to obey all the mate's orders as they would his, the captain's; and the crew had promised to do so. It imports not to declare that a crew is not bound to obey an unlawful order, for to say that this order was unlawful is to postulate what remains to be proved. Who is to judge of the unlawfulness? The circumstances were peculiar. The occasion was emergent, without precedent, or parallel. The lawfulness of the order is the very question which we are disputing; a question about which this whole community has been agitated, and is still divided; the discussion of which crowds this room with auditors past former example; a question which this court, with all its resources, is now engaged in considering, as such a question demands to be considered, most deliberately, most anxiously, most cautiously. It is no part of a sailor's duty to moralize and to speculate, in such a moment as this was, upon the orders of his superiour officers. The commander of a ship, like the commander of an army, "gives desperate commands. He requires instantaneous obedience." The sailor, like the soldier, obeys by instinct. . . .

Whether the mate, if on trial here, would be found innocent, is a question which we need not decide. That question is a different one from the guilt or innocence of the prisoner, and one more difficult. But if the whole company were reduced to a state of nature, then the sailors were bound to no duty, not mutual, to the passengers. The contract of the shipping articles had become dissolved by an unforeseen and overwhelming necessity. The sailor was no longer a sailor, but a drowning man. Having fairly done his duty to the last extremity, he was not to lose the rights of a human being, because he wore a roundabout instead of a frock coat. We do not seek authorities for such doctrine. The instinct of these men's hearts is our authority,—the best authority. Whoever opposes it must be wrong, for he opposes human nature. All the contemplated conditions, all the contemplated possibilities of the voyage, were ended. The parties, sailor and passenger, were in a new state. All persons on board the vessel became equal. All became their own lawgivers; for artificial distinctions cease to prevail when men are reduced to the equality of nature. Every man on board had a right to make law with his own right hand, and the law which did prevail on that awful night having been the law of necessity, and the law of nature too, it is the law which will be upheld by this court, to the liberation of this prisoner. . . .

BALDWIN, CIRCUIT JUSTICE, charging jury, alluded to the touching character of the case; and, after stating to the jury what was the offence laid in the indictment, his honour explained, with particularity, the distinction between murder and manslaughter. He said that malice was of the essence of murder, while want of criminal intention was consistent with the nature of manslaughter. He impressed strongly upon the jury, that the mere absence of malice did not render homicide excusable. . . .

In such cases the law neither excuses the act nor permits it to be justified as innocent; but, although inflicting some punishment, she yet looks with a benignant eye, through the thing done, to the mind and to the heart; and when, on a view of all the circumstances connected with the act, no evil spirit is discerned, her humanity forbids the exaction of life for life. But though, said the court, cases of this kind are viewed with tenderness, and punished with mercy, we must yet bear in mind that man, in taking away the life of a fellow being, assumes an awful responsibility to God, and to society; and that the administrators of public justice do themselves assume that responsibility if, when called on to pass judicially upon the act, they yield to the indulgence of misapplied humanity. It is one thing to give a favourable interpretation to evidence in order to mitigate an offence. It is a different thing when we are asked, not to extenuate, but to justify, the act. In the former case, as I have said, our decision may in some degree be swayed by feelings of humanity; while in the latter, it is the law of necessity alone which can disarm the vindicatory justice of the country. Where, indeed, a case does arise, embraced by this "law of necessity," the penal laws pass over such case in silence; for law is made to meet but the ordinary exigencies of life. But the case does not become "a case of necessity," unless all ordinary means of self preservation have been exhausted. The peril must be instant, overwhelming, leaving no alternative but to lose our own life, or to take the life of another person. An illustration of this principle occurs in the ordinary case of self-defense against lawless violence. . . . For example, suppose that two persons who owe no duty to one another that is not mutual should, by accident, not attributable to either, be placed in a situation where both cannot survive. Neither is bound to save the other's life by sacrificing his own, nor would either commit a crime in saving his own life in a struggle for the only means of safety. Of this description of cases are those which have been cited to you by counsel, from writers on natural law,—cases which we rather leave to your imagination than attempt minutely to describe. And I again state that when this great "law of necessity" does apply, and is not improperly exercised, the taking of life is devested of unlawfulness.

But in applying this law, we must look not only to the jeopardy in which the parties are, but also to the relations in which they stand. . . . The passenger stands in a position different from that of the officers and seamen. It is the sailor who must encounter the hardships and perils of the voyage. Nor can this relation be changed when the ship is lost by tempest or other danger of the sea, and all on board have betaken themselves, for safety, to the small boats; for imminence of danger can not absolve from duty. The sailor is bound, as before, to undergo whatever hazard is necessary to preserve the boat and the passengers. Should the emergency become so extreme as to call for the sacrifice of life, there can be no reason why the law does not still remain the same. The passenger, not being bound either to labour or to incur the risk of life, cannot be bound to sacrifice his existence to preserve the sailor's. The captain, indeed, and a sufficient number of seamen to navigate the boat, must be preserved; for, except these abide in the ship, all will perish. But if there be more seamen than are necessary to manage the boat, the supernumerary sailors have no right, for their safety, to sacrifice the passengers. The sailors and passengers, in fact, cannot be regarded as in equal positions. The sailor (to use the language of a distinguished writer) owes more benevolence to another than to himself. He is bound to set a greater value on the life of others than on his own. And while we admit that sailor and sailor may lawfully struggle with each other for the plank which can save but one, we think that, if the passenger is on the plank, even "the law of necessity" justifies not the sailor who takes it from him. . . .

But, in addition, if the source of the danger have been obvious, and destruction ascertained to be certainly about to arrive, though at a future time, there should be consultation, and some mode of selection fixed, by which those in equal relations may have equal chance for their life. By what mode, then, should selection be made? The question is not without difficulty; nor do we know of any rule prescribed, either by statute or by common law, or even by speculative writers on the law of nature. In fact, no rule of general application can be prescribed for contingencies which are wholly unforeseen. There is, however, one condition of extremity for which all writers have prescribed the same rule. When the ship is in no danger of sinking, but all sustenance is exhausted, and a sacrifice of one person is necessary to appease the hunger of others, the selection is by lot. This mode is resorted to as the fairest mode, and, in some sort, as an appeal to God, for selection of the victim. This manner, obviously, was regarded by the mate, in parting with the captain, as the one which it was proper to adopt, in case the long-boat could not live with all who were on board on Tuesday morning. The same manner, as would appear from the response given to the mate, had already suggested itself to the captain. For ourselves, we can conceive of no mode so consonant both to humanity and to justice; and the occasion, we think, must be peculiar which will dispense with its exercise. If, indeed, the peril be instant and overwhelming, leaving no chance of means, and no moment for deliberation, then, of course, there is no power to consult, to cast lots, or in any such way to decide; but even where the final disaster is thus sudden, if it have been foreseen as certainly about to arrive, if no new cause of danger have arisen to bring on the closing catastrophe, if time have existed to cast lots, and to select the victims, then, as we have said, sortition should be adopted. In no other than this or some like way are those having equal rights put upon an equal footing, and in no other way is it possible to guard against partiality and oppression, violence, and conflict. What scene, indeed, more horrible, can imagination draw than a struggle between sailor and sailor, passenger and passenger, or, it may be, a mixed affray, in which, promiscuously, all destroy one another? This, too, in circumstances which have allowed time to decide, with justice, whose life should be calmly surrendered.

When the selection has been made by lots, the victim yields of course to his fate, or, if he resist, force may be employed to coerce submission. Whether or not "a case of necessity" has arisen, or whether the law under which death has been inflicted have been so exercised as to hold the executioner harmless, cannot depend on his own opinion; for no man may pass upon his own conduct when it concerns the rights, and especially, when it affects the lives, of others. We have already stated to you that, by the law of the land, homicide is sometimes justifiable; and the law defines the occasions in which it is so. The transaction must, therefore, be justified to the law; and the person accused rests under obligation to satisfy those who judicially scrutinize his case that it really transcended ordinary rules. In fact, any other principle would be followed by pernicious results, and, moreover, would not be practicable in application. Opinion or belief may be assumed, whether it exist or not; and if this mere opinion of the sailors will justify them in making a sacrifice of the passengers, of course the mere opinion of the passengers would, in turn, justify these in making a sacrifice of the sailors. The passengers may have confidence in their own capacity to manage and preserve the boat, or the effort of either sailors or passengers to save the boat, may be clearly unavailing; and what, then, in a struggle against force and numbers, becomes of the safety of the seamen? Hard as is a seaman's life, would it not become yet more perilous if the passengers, who may outnumber them tenfold, should be allowed to judge when the dangers of the sea will justify a sacrifice of life? We are, therefore, satisfied, that, in requiring proof, which shall be satisfactory to you, of the existence of the necessity, we are fixing the rule which is, not merely the only one which is practicable, but, moreover, the only one which will secure the safety of the sailors themselves.

The court said, briefly, that the principles which had been laid down by them, as applicable to the crew, applied to the mate likewise, and that his order (on which much stress had been laid), if an unlawful order, would be no justification to the seamen, for that even seamen are not justified, in law, by obedience to commands which are unlawful. The court added that the case was one which involved questions of gravest consideration, and, as the facts, in some sort, were without precedent, that the court preferred to state the law, in the shape of such general principles as would comprehend the case, under any view which the jury might take of the evidence.

After a few remarks upon the evidence, the case was given to the jury, who, about 16 hours afterwards, and after having once returned to the bar, unable to agree, with some difficulty, found a verdict of guilty. The prisoner was, however, recommended to the mercy of the court. On the same day a rule was obtained to show cause why judgment should not be arrested and a new trial granted. The following ground was relied on for a new trial: Because the court, instead of telling the jury that, in a state of imminent and deadly peril, all men are reduced to a state of nature, and that there is, then, no distinction between the rights of sailor and passenger, adopted a contrary doctrine, and charged the jury accordingly.

Mr. Brown subsequently showed cause. He insisted largely upon the existence of the state of nature, as distinguished from the social state, and contended that to this state of nature the persons in the long-boat had become reduced on Tuesday night, at 10 o'clock, when Askin was thrown overboard. He iterated, illustrated, and enforced the argument contained in the closing part of the defence. For the arrest of judgment he argued that the indictment was defective in not stating the name of the boat on which the homicide was alleged to have been committed; that the courts in this respect wanted certainty. The United States did not reply.

THE COURT held the application for some days under advisement, and, at a subsequent day, discharged the rule. They said that . . . no error had been perceived by the court in its instructions to the jury. It is true, said the court, as is known by every one, that we do find in the text writers, and sometimes in judicial opinions, the phrases, "the law of nature," "the principles of natural right," and other expressions of a like signification; but, as applied to civilized men, nothing more can be meant by those expressions than that there are certain great and fundamental principles of justice which, in the constitution of nature, lie at the foundation and make part of all civil law, independently of express adoption or enactment. And to give to the expressions any other signification, to claim them as shewing an independent code, and one contrariant to those settled principles which, however modified, make a part of civil law in all Christian nations, would be to make the writers who use the expressions lay down as rules of action, principles which in their nature, admit of no practical ascertainment or application. The law of nature forms part of the municipal law; and, in a proper case (as of self-defence), homicide is justifiable, not because the municipal law is subverted by the law of nature, but because no rule of the municipal law makes homicide in such cases, criminal. It is, said the court, the municipal or civil law, as thus comprehensive, as founded in moral and social justice,—the law of the land, in short, as existing and administered amongst us and all enlightened nations,—that regulates the social duties of men, the duties of man towards his neighbour, everywhere. Everywhere are civilized men under its protection; everywhere, subject to its authority. It is part of the universal law. We cannot escape it in a case where it is applicable; and if, for the decision of any question, the proper rule is to be found in the municipal law, no code can be referred to as annulling its authority. Varying however, or however modified, the laws of all civilized nations, and, indeed, the very nature of the social constitution, place sailors and passengers in different relations. And, without stopping to speculate upon over nice questions not before us, or to involve ourselves in the labyrinth of ethical subtleties, we may safely say that the sailor's duty is the protection of the persons intrusted to his care, not their sacrifice,—a duty we must again declare our opinion, that rests on him in every emergency of his calling, and from which it would be senseless, indeed, to absolve him exactly at those times when the obligation is most needed.

Respecting the form of the counts, the court said that the locality of the offence was sufficiently expressed, and that, in a case so peculiar, it was impossible to express the place with more precision.

When the prisoner was brought up for sentence, the learned judge said to him, that many circumstances in the affair were of a character to commend him to regard, yet, that the case was one in which some punishment was demanded; that it was in the power of the court to inflict the penalty of an imprisonment for a term of three years, and a fine of $1,000, but, in view of all the circumstances, and especially as the prisoner had been already confined in gaol several months, that the court would make the punishment more lenient. The convict was then sentenced to undergo an imprisonment in the Eastern Penitentiary of Pennsylvania, (solitary confinement) at hard labour, for the term of six months, and to pay a fine of $20.

SELF-DEFENSE

Brown v. United States

supreme court of the united states, 1921
256 u.s. 335, 41 sup. ct. 501

Mr. Justice Holmes delivered the opinion of the Court.

The petitioner was convicted of murder in the second degree committed upon one Hermis at a place in Texas within the exclusive jurisdiction of the United States, and the judgment was affirmed by the Circuit Court of Appeals. 257 Fed. 46, 168 C.C.A. 258. A writ of certiorari was granted by this Court. . . .

The other question concerns the instructions at the trial. There had been trouble between Hermis and the defendant for a long time. There was evidence that Hermis had twice assaulted the defendant with a knife and had made threats communicated to the defendant that the next time, one of them would go off in a black box. On the day in question the defendant was at the place above mentioned superintending excavation work for a postoffice. In view of Hermis's threats he had taken a pistol with him and had laid it in his coat upon a dump. Hermis was driven up by a witness, in a cart to be loaded, and the defendant said that certain earth was not to be removed, whereupon Hermis came toward him, the defendant says, with a knife. The defendant retreated some twenty or twenty-five feet to where his coat was and got his pistol. Hermis was striking at him and the defendant fired four shots and killed him. The judge instructed the jury among other things that "it is necessary to remember, in considering the question of self defence, that the party assaulted is always under the obligation to retreat so long as retreat is open to him, provided that he can do so without subjecting himself to the danger of death or great bodily harm." The instruction was reinforced by the further intimation that unless "retreat would have appeared to a man of reasonable prudence, in the position of the defendant, as involving danger of death or serious bodily harm" the defendant was not entitled to stand his ground. An instruction to the effect that if the defendant had reasonable grounds of apprehension that he was in danger of losing his life or of suffering serious bodily harm from Hermis he was not bound to retreat was refused. So the question is brought out with sufficient clearness whether the formula laid down by the Court and often repeated by the ancient law is adequate to the protection of the defendant's rights.

It is useless to go into the developments of the law from the time when a man who had killed another no matter how innocently had to get his pardon, whether of grace or of course. Concrete cases or illustrations stated in the early law in conditions very different from the present, like the reference to retreat in Coke, Third Inst. 55, and elsewhere, have had a tendency to ossify into specific rules without much regard for reason. Other examples may be found in the law as to trespass ab initio, Commonwealth v. Rubin, 165 Mass. 453, 43 N.E. 200, and as to fresh complaint after rape. Commonwealth v. Cleary, 172 Mass. 175, 51 N.E. 746. Rationally the failure to retreat is a circumstance to be considered with all the others in order to determine whether the defendant went farther than he was justified in doing; not a categorical proof of guilt. The law has grown, and even if historical mistakes have contributed to its growth it has tended in the direction of rules consistent with human nature. Many respectable writers agree that if a man reasonably believes that he is in immediate danger of death or grievous bodily harm from his assailant he may stand his ground and that if he kills him he has not exceeded the bounds of lawful self defence. That has been the decision of this Court. Beard v. United States, 158 U.S. 550, 559, 15 Sup. Ct. 962, 39 L. Ed. 1086. Detached reflection cannot be demanded in the presence of an uplifted knife. Therefore in this Court, at least, it is not a condition of immunity that one in that situation should pause to consider whether a reasonable man might not think it possible to fly with safety or to disable his assailant rather than to kill him. Rowe v. United States, 164 U.S. 546, 558, 17 Sup. Ct. 172, 41 L. Ed. 547. The law of Texas very strongly adopts these views as is shown by many cases, of which it is enough to cite two. Cooper v. State, 49 Tex. Cr. R. 28, 38, 89 S.W. 1068. Baltrip v. State, 30 Tex. App. 545, 549, 17 S.W. 1106.

Judgment reversed.

MR. JUSTICE PITNEY and MR. JUSTICE CLARKE dissent.

DEFENSE OF PROPERTY

State v. Childers

supreme court of ohio, 1938
133 ohio st. 508, 14 n.e.2d 767

Arn Childers was convicted of unlawfully shooting with intent to wound, and he appeals. . . .

Evidence was introduced which showed that the defendant, Childers, owned a farm which was some distance from the house in which he resided. On the farm was a field of watermelons planted by a tenant, but which were at the time in question under the control of Childers.

A few days before September 1, 1935, considerable damage was done to the watermelon crop, apparently by some boys in the neighborhood. The evidence shows that one of these boys was Daniel Earl Wagoner of Huntington, W. Va., who was then about 14 years of age. He was visiting his grandfather who lived on a farm adjoining that of Childers in Gallia county.

After the damage was done to his melons, Childers set six spring guns, one concealed at each end of the melon patch. Attached to the triggers were small wires which went all around the patch. The guns so placed and set were single-barreled shotguns loaded with ordinary type of shells. The wires were so arranged that if anyone came in contact with them, the guns would be discharged. The defendant claimed that there were two notices, written on pieces of paper, saying "Dangerous, don't go in this patch. Go back out," which were placed at one end of the patch.

On or about September 1, 1935, when young Wagoner entered the patch, one of the guns was discharged and he received about 150 shot, principally in his right side, arm and leg. He was seriously wounded, and remained in the hospital 18 days. Upon these facts in brief, an indictment was returned against Childers. At the trial, Childers admitted setting the guns, after his melon patch had been destroyed, for the purpose of preventing anyone from again coming on that part of his premises. Young Wagoner testified that, while he had been in the patch on the Sunday before the shooting, he did not see any notices on September 1st, and that he thought the watermelons belonged to members of his family.

Upon this evidence, the jury found the defendant, Childers, guilty as he stood charged in the indictment. After an affirmance by the Court of Appeals, the defendant filed an appeal as of right, and a motion for leave to appeal. The motion was allowed by this court.

GORMAN, J. . . . The principal question involved is whether the facts proved warrant a conviction of Childers of the offense of shooting with intent to wound. This is the first time in its history that this court has been called upon to pass upon the legality of spring guns, although there is no dearth of such cases in other jurisdictions. . . .

At early common law, the setting of a spring gun was not in itself unlawful, and if a person was killed by it while attempting to commit a felony no criminal liability ensued. Deane v. Clayton, 1817, 7 Taunt. 489; Ilott v. Wilkes, 1820, 3 Barn. & Ald. 304. This rule in England has now been changed by statute to cover acts such as this. See 14 & 15 Vict. c. 19, s. 4 and 54 & 55 Vict. c. 69, s. 1. In this country, at least one State has adopted a statute making spring guns unlawful. Schmidt v. State, 159 Wis. 15, 149 N.W. 388, Ann. Cas. 1916E, 107.

However, the early common law of England has never been followed in this country. . . . By the overwhelming weight of authority, a person is not justified in taking human life or inflicting bodily harm upon the person of another by means of traps, spring guns, or other instruments of destruction, unless as a matter of law, he would have been justified had he been personally present and had taken the life or inflicted the bodily harm with his own hands. . . .

Tested by these principles, one might set a spring gun in his own home, and if its discharge prevented the ingress of a burglar, he might be justified because if he had been present he could have fired the shot. Has he the right, however, to set such a gun in an open field to prevent trespassers from entering his melon patch? . . .

No one should be permitted to do indirectly what he may not do directly. Defendant's absence from the scene of the shooting should not enlarge his rights. In this case the facts are to be considered just as if Childers, himself, was in the melon patch and fired the shot, or as if he had stationed another there to fire a shot in case trespassers entered the melon patch. Childers knew that if anyone came in contact with the wires the gun would be discharged. It was not only the natural and probable consequence that bodily injuries would be received in that event, but it was also his intention that they should be inflicted.

Daniel Earl Wagoner was a boy 14 years of age. He was a mere trespasser entering upon Childers' land to commit at most a petit larceny by eating his melons. While a person has a right to protect his property from a trespass, and, after warning or notice to the trespasser, use such force as is reasonably necessary so to do, he cannot unlawfully use firearms to expel the intruder where he has no reasonable ground to fear the trespasser will do him great bodily harm. . . .

In accordance with the great weight of authority, one who sets a spring gun or trap does so at his peril. If it is set in a dwelling house and prevents the entrance of a felon, the justification may be sufficient to acquit the owner. If one the other hand it inflicts death or great bodily harm on an innocent person, or one who is a mere trespasser, the one who sets the trap must suffer the consequences. He is presumed to intend the natural and probable consequences of his voluntary act. It becomes as much of an assault on another as if he was personally present and pulled the trigger.

If Childers was vexed by secret trespassers or marauders, he could have found protection by his own vigilance within lawful limits. He could have provided a stronger inclosure or kept a more constant watch. If these had failed, an appeal to the agencies of the law would no doubt have given him adequate protection. His reckless disregard for the value of human life can find neither sanction within the law, nor sympathy without, from this court.

By setting the trap, Childers must be held responsible for that which happened just as if he had been personally present. The boy, Wagoner, was a mere trespasser and unarmed. Childers could not maintain a claim of self-defense or that the shooting was accidental. Under such circumstances, the jury was fully warranted in finding him guilty of a violation of the provisions of Section 12420, General Code.

Upon a review of the entire record, this court is of the opinion that the judgment of the Court of Appeals should be, and the same hereby is, affirmed.

Judgment affirmed.

PRIVILEGE

WATT v. LONGSDON

COURT OF APPEAL (ENGLAND), 1929
[1930] 1 K.B. 130 (C.A.)

SCRUTTON, L. J. This case raises, amongst other matters, the extremely difficult question, equally important in its legal and social aspect, as to the circumstances, if any, in which a person will be justified in giving to one partner to a marriage information which that person honestly believes to be correct, but which is in fact untrue, about the matrimonial delinquencies of the other party to the marriage. The question becomes more difficult if the answer in law turns on the existence or non-existence of a social or moral duty, a question which the judge is to determine, without any evidence, by the light of his own knowledge of the world, and his own views on social morality, a subject matter on which views vary in different ages, in different countries, and even as between man and man.

The Scottish Petroleum Company, which carried on business, amongst other places, in Morocco, had in Casa Blanca, a port in Morocco, a manager named Browne, and a managing director named Watt. The company had in England a chairman named Singer, who held a very large proportion of shares in the company, and also another director, Longsdon, a young man under thirty years of age. The latter had been in Morocco in business and friendly relations with Watt and Browne, and was a friend of Mrs. Watt, who had nursed him in an illness. The company went into voluntary liquidation in November, 1927, and Longsdon was appointed liquidator. In April, 1928, Mrs. Watt was in

England, and her husband in Casa Blanca. It is not clear, and
there is no evidence, what the effect of the liquidation had been
on the actual employment of Watt and Browne, that is, whether
they, or either of them, still received a salary. Watt's directorship
was, under the Companies Act, in a state of suspended animation.
Under these circumstances Longsdon in England received at the
beginning of May from Browne in Casa Blanca a letter stating
that Watt had left for Lisbon to look for a job, that he had left a
bill for 88 *l.* for whisky unpaid, and that he had been for two
months in immoral relations with his housemaid, who was now
publicly raising claims against him for money matters. The
woman was described as an old woman, stone deaf, almost blind,
and with dyed hair. A number of details were given which
Browne said Watt's cook had corroborated. The information was
mixed up with an allegation that Watt had been scheming to
compromise or seduce Mrs. Browne. The letter concluded: "From
a letter shown to me by Mr. Watt I know how bitterly disap-
pointed Mrs. Watt is, and how very much troubled she is. It
would therefore perhaps be better not to show her this letter as it
could only increase most terribly her own feelings in regard to her
husband. These awful facts might be the cause of a breakdown to
her, and I think she has enough to cope with at present. Mr.
Singer, however, should perhaps know." On May 5, Longsdon,
without making inquiries, sent Browne's letter on to Singer, the
chairman of the board of directors. At the trial Watt's counsel
put in Longsdon's answer to interrogatory 5 that he believed the
statements in the letter to be true. On May 5 Longsdon wrote a
long letter to Browne, in which he said that he had long suspected
Watt's immorality, but had no proof; that he thought it wicked
and cruel that Mrs. Watt, a very old friend of the writer's, should
be in the dark when Watt might return to her—did not Browne
agree?—that he (Longsdon) would not speak until he had a sworn
statement in his possession, "and only with such proof would I
speak, for an interferer between husband and wife nearly always
comes off the worst." Could Browne get a sworn statement? "It
may even be necessary for you to bribe the women to do such, and
if only a matter of a few hundred francs I will pay it and of course
the legal expenses." Longsdon's letter describes one of the women
who was to make this sworn statement as "a prostitute all her

life," a description not contained in Browne's letter. Watt returned to England in May. Without waiting for the sworn statement, on May 12, Longsdon sent the letter to Mrs. Watt. Mr. and Mrs. Watt separated, and Mrs. Watt instituted proceedings for divorce, which apparently are still pending.

Mr. Watt then instituted proceedings against Longsdon for libel—namely (1.) the publication of Browne's letter to Singer; (2.) the publication of the same letter to Mrs. Watt; (3.) Longsdon's letter of May 5 to Browne. The claim alleged: "The plaintiff, the defendant, and one E. A. Browne were at all material times in the employment in Morocco of the Scottish Petroleum Company, Ld., a company now in liquidation, of which one W. M. G. Singer was chairman and had a controlling interest therein," and the defence admitted it: "The facts alleged in paragraph 1 of the statement of claim are admitted." The plaintiff also put in at the trial the defendant's answers to interrogatories that his only information on the subject was derived from Browne's letter, that he made no further inquiries, and that he believed that all the statements in Browne's letter, and in the defendant's letter of May 12 were true. The defendant did not justify, but pleaded privilege. The case was tried before Horridge J. and a jury. The learned judge held that all three publications were privileged, and that there was no evidence of malice fit to be left to the jury. He therefore entered judgment for the defendant. The plaintiff appeals.

The learned judge appears to have taken the view that the authorities justify him in holding that if "there is an obvious interest in the person to whom a communication is made which causes him to be a proper recipient of a statement," even if the party making the communication had no moral or social duty to the party to whom the communication is made, the occasion is privileged. . . .

By the law of England there are occasions on which a person may make defamatory statements about another which are untrue without incurring any legal liability for his statements. These occasions are called privileged occasions. A reason frequently given for this privilege is that the allegation that the speaker has "unlawfully and maliciously published," is displaced by proof that the speaker had either a duty or an interest to publish, and that this duty or interest confers the privilege. But communications made on these occasions may lose their privilege: (1.) they may exceed the privilege of the occasion by going beyond the limits of the duty or interest, or (2.) they may be published with express malice, so that the occasion is not being legitimately used, but abused. . . . The classical definition of "privileged occasions" is that of Parke B. in Toogood v. Spyring, a case where the tenant of a farm complained to the agent of the landlord, who had sent a workman to do repairs, that the workman had broken into the tenant's cellar, got drunk on the tenant's cider, and spoilt the work he was sent to do. The workman sued the tenant. Parke B. gave the explanation of privileged occasions in these words: "In general, an action lies for the malicious publication of statements which are false in fact, and injurious to the character of another (within the well-known limits as to verbal slander), and the law considers such publication as malicious, unless it is fairly made by a person in the discharge of some public or private duty, whether legal or moral, or in the conduct of his own affairs, in matters where his interest is concerned. In such cases, the occasion prevents the inference of malice, which the law draws from unauthorized communications, and affords a qualified defence depending upon the absence of actual malice. If fairly warranted by any reasonable occasion or exigency, and honestly made, such communications are protected for the common convenience and welfare of society; and the law has not restricted the right to make them within any narrow limits." It will be seen that the learned judge requires: (1.) a public or private duty to communicate, whether legal or moral; (2.) that the communication should be "fairly warranted by any reasonable occasion or exigency"; (3.) or a statement in the conduct of his own affairs where his interest is concerned. Parke B. had given several other definitions in slightly varying terms. For instance, in Cockayne v. Hodgkisson he had directed the jury "Where the writer is acting on any duty, legal or moral, towards the person to whom he writes, or where he has, by his situation, to protect the interests of another, that which he writes under such circumstances is a privileged communication." This adds to the protection of his own interest spoken of in Toogood v. Spyring the protection of the interests of another where the situation of the writer requires him to protect those interests.

This, I think, involves that his "situation" imposes on him a legal or moral duty.

The question whether the occasion was privileged is for the judge, and so far as "duty" is concerned, the question is: Was there a duty, legal, moral, or social, to communicate? As to legal duty, the judge should have no difficulty; the judge should know the law; but as to moral or social duties of imperfect obligation, the task is far more troublesome. The judge has no evidence as to the view the community takes of moral or social duties. . . . Is the judge merely to give his own view of moral and social duty, though he thinks a considerable portion of the community hold a different opinion? Or is he to endeavour to ascertain what view "the great mass of right-minded men" would take? It is not surprising that with such a standard both judges and text-writers treat the matter as one of great difficulty in which no definite line can be drawn. . . .

A conspicuous instance of the difficulties which arise when judges have to determine the existence of duties, not legal, but moral or social, by the inner light of their own conscience and judgment and knowledge of the world, is to be found in the case of Coxhead v. Richards. A correct appreciation of what was the difference of opinion in that case is, in my opinion, of great importance in the decision of the present case. The short facts were that Cass, the mate of a ship, wrote to Richards, an intimate friend of his, a letter stating that on a voyage from the Channel to Wales, which was going to continue to Eastern ports, the captain, Coxhead, had by his drunkenness endangered the safety of the ship, and the lives of the crew; and Cass asked Richards' advice what he should do in view of the risk of repetition of this danger on the voyage to the East. Richards, after consulting "an Elder Brother of the Trinity House, and an eminent shipowner," sent this letter to Ward, the owner of the ship. Richards did not know Ward, and had no interest in the ship. The owner dismissed the captain, who thereupon brought an action against Richards. The judge at the trial directed the jury, if they should think that the communication was strictly honest, and made solely in the execution of what he believed to be a duty, to find for the defendant. They did so, while finding that the plea of justification failed. The plaintiff then moved for a new trial, on which motion the

Court after two hearings was equally divided. It is not very clear whether the judges differed on a general principle, or on its application to the facts of the case. I understand Tindal C.J. to have taken the view that if a man has information materially affecting the interests of another, and honestly communicates it to that other, he is protected, though he has no personal interest in the subject matter, and that his protection arises from "the various social duties by which men are bound to each other," and that it was the duty of the defendant to comunicate this information to the owner. Erle J. appears to put the matter on "information given to protect damage from misconduct," "the importance of the information to the interest of the receiver," and says that a person having such information is justified in communicating it to the person interested, though the speaker did not stand in any relation to the recipient, and was a volunteer. He does not expressly refer to any social duty. On the other hand, Coltman and Cresswell JJ. both appear to me to hold that in such circumstances there was no moral duty, for that any tendency that way was counterbalanced by the moral duty not to slander your neighbour. . . .

Lastly, in Stuart v. Bell there was again a difference of opinion, though not an equal division of the judges, as in Coxhead v. Richards. Stanley, the explorer, and his valet, Stuart, were staying with the mayor of Newcastle, Bell. The Edinburgh police made a very carefully worded communication to the Newcastle police that there had been a robbery in Edinburgh at an hotel where Stuart was staying, and it might be well to make very careful and cautious inquiry into the matter. The Newcastle police showed the letter to the mayor, who after consideration showed it to Stanley, who dismissed Stuart. Stuart sued the mayor. Lindley and Kay L.JJ. held that the mayor had a moral duty to communicate, and Stanley a material interest to receive the communication; Lopes L.J. held that in the circumstances there was no moral duty to communicate, though in some circumstances there might be such a duty in a host towards a guest. I myself should have agreed with the majority, but the difference of opinion between such experienced judges shows the difficulty of the question.

In my opinion Horridge J. went too far in holding that there could be a privileged occasion on the ground of interest in the recipient without any duty to communicate on the part of the person making the communication. But that does not settle the question, for it is necessary to consider, in the present case, whether there was, as to each communication, a duty to communicate, and an interest in the recipient.

First as to the communication between Longsdon and Singer, I think the case must proceed on the admission that at all material times Watt, Longsdon and Browne were in the employment of the same company, and the evidence afforded by the answer to the interrogatory put in by the plaintiff that Longsdon believed the statements in Browne's letter. In my view on these facts there was a duty, both from a moral and a material point of view, on Longsdon to communicate the letter to Singer, the chairman of his company, who, apart from questions of present employment, might be asked by Watt for a testimonial to a future employer. Equally, I think Longsdon receiving the letter from Browne, might discuss the matter with him, and ask for further information, on the ground of a common interest in the affairs of the company, and to obtain further information for the chairman. I should therefore agree with the view of Horridge J. that these two occasions were privileged, though for different reasons. Horridge J. further held that there was no evidence of malice fit to be left to the jury, and, while I think some of Longsdon's action and language in this respect was unfortunate, as the plaintiff has put in the answer that Longsdon believed the truth of the statements in Browne's and his own letter, like Lord Dunedin in Adam v. Ward, I should not try excess with too nice scales, and I do not dissent from his view as to malice. As to the communications to Singer and Browne, in my opinion the appeal should fail, but as both my brethren take the view that there was evidence of malice which should be left to the jury, there must, of course, be a new trial as to the claim based on these two publications.

The communication to Mrs. Watt stands on a different footing. I have no intention of writing an exhaustive treatise on the circumstances when a stranger or a friend should communicate to husband or wife information he receives as to the conduct of the other party to the marriage. I am clear that it is impossible to say he is always under a moral or social duty to do so; it is equally impossible to say he is never under such a duty. It must depend on the circumstances of each case, the nature of the information, and the relation of speaker and recipient. It cannot, on the one hand, be the duty even of a friend to communicate all the gossip the friend hears at men's clubs or women's bridge parties to one of the spouses affected. On the other hand, most men would hold that it was the moral duty of a doctor who attended his sister in law, and believed her to be suffering from a miscarriage, for which an absent husband could not be responsible, to communicate that fact to his wife and the husband. . . . If this is so, the decision must turn on the circumstances of each case, the judge being much influenced by the consideration that as a general rule it is not desirable for any one, even a mother in law, to interfere in the affairs of man and wife. Using the best judgment I can in this difficult matter, I have come to the conclusion that there was not a moral or social duty in Longsdon to make this communication to Mrs. Watt such as to make the occasion privileged, and that there must be a new trial so far as it relates to the claim for publication of a libel to Mrs. Watt. The communications to Singer and Browne being made on a privileged occasion, there must be a new trial of the issue as to malice defeating the privilege. There must also be a new trial on the complaint as to publication to Mrs. Watt, the occasion being held not to be privileged. The plaintiff must have the costs of this appeal; the costs of the first trial must abide the result of the second trial, the issues being separated.

GREER L.J. The question involved in this appeal is one that, in my judgment, would be easy to answer if it were not for the difficulties occasioned by some of the earlier decisions on the subject of privileged occasions in the law of libel. Notwithstanding the serious difference of judicial opinion in the cases of Coxhead v. Richards; Blackham v. Pugh; and Bennett v. Deacon, the rule of law we have to apply in the present case has been finally accepted in the form stated by Lord Atkinson in Adams v. Ward: "A privileged occasion is . . . an occasion where the person who makes a communication has an interest or a duty, legal, social, or moral, to make it to the person to whom it is made, and the person to whom it is so made has a corresponding interest or duty to receive it. This reciprocity is essential. . . ." It is suggested,

however, on the authority of Willes J.'s approval of the decision
of Tindal C.J. and Erle J. in Coxhead v. Richards, in Amann v.
Damm, and the similar approval of Blackburn J. in Davies v.
Snead, and of the judgment of Lindley L.J. in Stuart v. Bell, that
it is unnecessary that there should be any duty in the person
making the communication, and that it is sufficient if there is
either a duty on his part or an interest in the person receiving the
communication. It is clear, however, that what was said by Willes
J. in Amann v. Damm was merely obiter, and that he was not
considering the question whether interest in the recipient was
sufficient to establish a privileged occasion; and the observations
relied on in the present case by Horridge J. in the judgment of
Blackburn J. in Davies v. Snead do not support the proposition
for which they were cited. Blackburn J. is in effect treating the
judgments of Tindal C.J. and Erle J. as based on the duty of the
defendant to make the communication in question. He points out
that the result of those two judgments, afterwards followed in
Blackham v. Pugh, "is that where a person is so situated that it
becomes right in the interests of society that he should tell a third
person certain facts, then if he bona fide and without malice does
tell them it is a privileged communication." These words clearly
indicate that the privileged occasion is based on a duty in the
person making the communication to do what is right in the interests of society. It may be, of course, that the interest of the
person receiving the communication is of such a character as by
its very nature to create a social duty in another under the circumstances to make the communication that he does in fact make.
In such a case the cause of the privileged occasion is not merely
the interest of the recipient; it is that interest plus the corresponding social duty which arises in the circumstances of the case
by reason of the nature of the interest. It is however unfortunate
that Lindley L.J. in Stuart v. Bell uses the words quoted by
Horridge J., which appear to indicate that the occasion of privilege may arise either out of the moral or social duty of the person
making the communication, or out of the interest of the person
receiving it. It is quite clear, however, that the Lord Justice and
the other members of the Court of Appeal did not decide the
case on the ground that the existence of the recipient's interest
was sufficient in itself to give rise to privilege. In his judgment

Lindley L.J. cites with approval the following words from the judgment of Parke B. in Toogood v. Spyring: "If fairly warranted by any reasonable occasion or exigency, and honestly made, such communications are protected for the common convenience and welfare of society." These words seem to me to indicate that there must be the warrant of some social duty created by the "reasonable occasion or exigency." Assuming that the defendant has no common interest with the person to whom the libel is published, and it is necessary that there should be some moral or social duty to make the communication, what is the test by which duty is to be determined? This may be a question which it is very difficult to answer. Opinions may easily differ as to whether the circumstances are such as to make the communication a moral or social duty. Similar questions of degree arise in many cases, and are left to the determination of a jury. In negligence cases, what the reasonably careful man would do is left to be determined by a jury whenever it is a question in which opinions may differ. But it is well settled that whether an occasion be privileged or not is a question for the judge, though he may ask the jury to determine any particular facts that are in dispute. The only guide one can get from previous decisions is to be obtained from the judgments of the Court of Appeal in Stuart v. Bell. There Lindley L.J. says: "I take moral or social duty to mean a duty recognized by English people of ordinary intelligence and moral principle, but at the same time not a duty enforceable by legal proceedings, whether civil or criminal." Would the great mass of right-minded men in the position of the defendant have considered it their duty, under the circumstances, to make the communication? Kay L.J. says: "The true mode of judging upon the question is to put oneself as much as possible in the position of the defendant." I think applied in forming an opinion on the question whether a privileged tests are as near as one can reasonably get to the tests to be leged occasion arising out of a moral or social duty has or has not arisen.

In my judgment no right-minded man in the position of the defendant, a friend of the plaintiff and of his wife, would have thought it right to communicate the horrible accusations contained in Mr. Browne's letter to the plaintiff's wife. The information came to Mr. Browne from a very doubtful source, and in my judgment no reasonably right-minded person could think it his duty, without obtaining some corroboration of the story, and without first communicating with the plaintiff, to pass on these outrageous charges of marital infidelity of a gross kind, and drunkenness and dishonesty, to the plaintiff's wife. As regards the publication to the plaintiff's wife, the occasion was not privileged, and it is unnecessary to consider whether there was evidence of express malice. As regards the publication to the chairman of the company, who owned nearly all the shares, and to Mr. Browne, I think on the facts as pleaded there was between the defendant and the recipients of the letters a common interest which would make the occasion privileged, but I also think there is intrinsic evidence in the letter to Browne, and evidence in the hasty and unjustifiable communication to the plaintiff's wife, which would be sufficient to entitle the plaintiff to ask for a verdict on these publications on the ground of express malice.

The plaintiff's counsel put in as part of his case the defendant's answers to interrogatories 5 and 8, which were to the effect that the defendant believed all the matters alleged in Browne's letter, which he published to the plaintiff's wife and to Mr. Singer, to be true. It was suggested that this belief made it impossible to say that the publication was malicious. I do not agree with this view. Malice is a state of mind. . . . A man may believe in the truth of a defamatory statement, and yet when he publishes it be reckness whether his belief be well founded or not. His motive for publishing a libel on a privileged occasion may be an improper one, even though he believes the statement to be true. He may be moved by hatred or dislike, or a desire to injure the subject of the libel, and may be using the occasion for that purpose, and if he is doing so the publication will be maliciously made, even though he may believe the defamatory statements to be true. . . .

I think the defendant's conduct in disseminating the gross charges that he did to the plaintiff's wife, and to Mr. Singer, and repeating and to some extent adding to them in his letter to Mr. Browne, and his offer to provide funds for procuring the evidence of the two women in Casa Blanca, affords some evidence of malice which ought to have been left to the jury. It is not for us to weigh the evidence. It will be for the jury to decide whether they are satisfied that in publishing the libels the defendant was in fact giving effect to his malicious or otherwise improper feelings towards the plaintiff, and was not merely using the occasion for the protection of the interests of himself and his two correspondents.

[The separate opinion of RUSSELL L.J. is omitted.]
Appeal allowed. New trial ordered.

Notes

1. The legal justification of the defendant's act in *Watt v. Longsdon* depends squarely on the question whether he had the moral duty he claims he had. If he had such a moral duty, the occasion was privileged; otherwise, not. The problem is particularly well focused because of the settled legal rule that although the jury may be asked to determine any facts that are in dispute, the question whether an occasion is privileged is a matter solely for the judge to decide. Judge Scrutton complains that the court must decide "without any evidence." The judges must exercise their "best judgment." Would it have been better to scrap the legal rule and allow the jury to decide? Should he have called in "moral experts"? Who would they be? Should he have taken time out and conducted some kind of poll of public opinion?

2. All, or nearly all, of the types of justification mentioned in this chapter can be viewed as forms of one type, namely, the protection of one's own welfare. Even privilege is discussed in terms of the defendant's own "material interest." In each case there is a claim of "right," but is it not "his right" rather than what is generally right that is claimed? Perhaps this reflects a narrowness in the law. If this is so, and that as far as morals are concerned there are other distinctive types of justification, what would they be?

3. Is the "duty to retreat" spoken of by Justice Holmes in *Brown v. United States* a moral obligation? If so, on what ethical theory could it best be explained? Wouldn't it be more manly, more courageous, to stand one's ground rather than to retreat? If he must retreat, how far must he retreat, and for how long? Should it make a difference whether he is being attacked in his home?

4. In connection with the shipwreck case of *United States v. Holmes*, critically examine the following statements:

   (a) "The seaman, we hold, is bound, beyond the passenger, to encounter the perils of the sea. To the last extremity, to death itself, must he protect the passenger. It is his duty. It is on account of these risks that he is paid." (Attorney for the Prosecution)

   (b) "It is no part of a sailor's duty to moralize and to speculate, in such a moment as this was, upon the orders of his superiour officers." (Counsel for the Defense)

   (c) "And while we admit that sailor and sailor may lawfully struggle with each other for the plank which can save but one, we think that, if the passenger is on the plank, even 'the law of necessity' justifies not the sailor who takes it from him." (The Judge)

(d) "For ourselves, we can conceive of no mode so consonant both to humanity and to justice [than that of casting lots]; and the occasion, we think, must be peculiar which will dispense with its exercise." (The Judge)

5. Compare the "reasonable" behavior of the pedestrians in *Tedla v. Ellman* with the equally "reasonable" behavior of the pest eradicator in *Luthringer v. Moore* (Chapter 2). All were engaged in hazardous activities. Why was the reasonableness of the former a "justification" of their violation of a statute, and the reasonableness of the other not even an "excuse" for injuries which could not practically have been avoided?

II

PROBLEMS OF
JUSTIFYING A JUDGMENT

4

ACTS AND CAUSES OF ACTION

For the human misery caused exclusively by natural events such as floods, cyclones, and earthquakes, no man is held responsible. These so-called "acts of God" do not fall within the range of acts which can be legally or morally judged. Yet, as the case of *Kimble v. MacKintosh Hemphill Co.* shows, the distinction between an act of God and a human act is not always an easy one to make. Someone is injured as a result of a wind storm. So far there is no difficulty. There is also no basis for an assignment of responsibility. But as soon as it is discovered that the storm and its consequences could have been anticipated, it becomes a problem whether the injury was caused by an act of God, or by a human act or failure to act.

The distinction between an act and an omission is not as obvious, or as free from difficulty, as one might initially take it to be either. If a person has done nothing, how has he done something for which he can be held responsible? Yet, as the *Kimble* case also points out, a failure to inspect and repair a defective roof may, under certain circumstances, be as much an act as any other.

On the other hand, there are "acts" of insane, drunken, and ignorant persons which, under some circumstances, many would prefer not to call acts, because, it is said, they are "involuntary." Such cases were considered in Chapter 2. Yet, as the cases indicate, neither insanity, drunkenness, nor ignorance will always excuse one from responsibility for what he has done.

Surely there is a need, both from the standpoint of practical decision making and from a theoretical viewpoint, for a distinction between acts, or the kind of conduct for which we hold persons responsible, and other physical events or physical behavior for which we hold no one responsible. Practically, it is necessary so that judges may determine whether the alleged wrong constitutes a *cause of action,* i.e., grounds for holding a person legally responsible. Thus, for example, in *State v. Rider* it is made clear that a mere intent to commit a crime is not a crime. There must be an "overt act." In *Vosburg v. Putney,* there is overt behavior (a "kicking"), but whether this constitutes a tortious *act* of battery is very much in doubt, since the defendant "didn't intend to harm." In *Palsgraf v. Long Island R. R. Co.,* what counts as an act is a non-intentional infliction of bodily injury, which, as it turns out, fails as basis for a suit, not because the act is unintentional, but because the act was not a wrong in relation to the plaintiff. Difficult as it is to define, liability in these and all other cases, whether criminal or civil, requires the occurrence of an "act."

Theoretically, the individual act is the subject of the legal judgment, that is, what is being judged, and so is logically prior to any other consideration in the assignment of responsibility. Substantive questions regarding underlying duties, and the excuses and justifications for their violations, such as those discussed in Part I, become issues only after a cause of action has been established. And this requires, minimally, the showing that an act has occurred.

It is apparent, however, that the question, "what is an act?" is not an easy one to answer. Philosophers have had much to say about the topic. The traditional philosophical theory, and the one commonly espoused by judges, is the view that an act is a bodily movement accompanied or preceded by a volition as its cause. Another philosophical account treats an act as a type of behavior which would have been different from what it was had a different choice been made by the agent. Still another is the view that acts are those instances of human behavior for which either (1) the agent is in fact held responsible, or (2) would be held responsible except for certain excusing conditions. A fourth view treats acts as instances of behavior which follow, and can be described in terms of, some rule, practice, or social convention. On this view, for example, a chess move is an act but knocking over a chessman is not.*

All these theories are illustrated by the following cases. Some, however, are more strongly suggested by certain cases than they are by others. The reasoning in *Vosbury v. Putney,* for example, lends itself to the "rule" theory, if it may be called that, whereas the case of *State v. Rider* appears to adopt the "volition" theory.

* For a fuller treatment of these and other theories, consult the following excellent articles: H. L. A. Hart, "The Ascription of Responsibility and Rights," reprinted in *Logic and Language,* 1st series, ed. Antony Flew (Oxford, Basil Blackwell, 1951), pp. 145-166; and A. I. Melden, "Action," reprinted in *Freedom and Responsibility,* ed. Herbert Morris (Stanford, Stanford Univ. Press, 1961), pp. 149-157.

Since, however, our approach has been to "let the lawyers speak for themselves," it is well not to overlook the distinctive ways in which lawyers and jurists apply themselves to the question, "what is an act?" There are, no doubt, philosophical assumptions underlying their thoughts and words, but their methods are sometimes dictated by considerations which philosophers rarely consider, and these especially need to be noted.

It is a mistake to suppose that in determining what is the act in a given case judges consider only mental states or physical movements, or that they mechanically apply the common definition of an act as a voluntary bodily movement. In cases like *Vosburg v. Putney* the definition by no means obviously applies, and yet an act is found nevertheless. On the other hand, in many cases the definition easily applies. In the case of *People v. Lewis,* there is no issue about the existence of voluntary bodily movements. The defendant shoots a man who then cuts his own throat. The issue is whether the defendant killed anybody. Unless he did, he can't be held responsible for murder, and it won't do to say that the victim both committed suicide and was murdered. He cannot die twice. In deciding that the defendant did commit an act of murder, others factors beside the defendant's movements and volitions have to be taken into account.

Among the other factors which guide judges in making these assessments of acts are various causal considerations. For example, in troublesome cases like *People v. Lewis,* they often ask whether what the defendant did *might have caused* death even if there had been no intervening causes. Or again, in *Palsgraf v. Long Island R. R. Co.,* Judge Andrews, in his dissenting opinion, asks whether given the physical event (an explosion) the injury which occurred was predictable. Similarly, in *Kimble v. MacKintosh Hemphill Co.,* the ability to anticipate the effects of a storm is a crucial factor in distinguishing a human act from an "act of God."

Sometimes judges look to particular social relationships for aids in assessing and describing an act. For example, in *Palsgraf,* Judge Cardozo is very much concerned about the relationships between the principal parties. A's act relative to B, to whom A owes a duty, may not be an act relative to C, if A owes no similar duty to C. This seems to be an essential part of his reasoning. In a somewhat different way, the judge in *People v. Lewis* finds it relevant, although not determinative, to consider the fact that the defendant and the deceased were brothers-in-law.

In "cases of first impression," judges often resort to analogies. If the case is a "first case" in the sense of presenting a novel fact situation, it is very useful and sometimes essential in describing an act to compare it to other well recognized acts. How else can it be subsumed under or shown relevant to an existing rule of law? If, on the other hand, it is novel in the sense of raising a question about the existence of an actionable right (a right which the law recognizes as enforceable), then the problem of locating the act is even more difficult, but here too analogy is useful. *Hinish v. Meier & Frank Co.* illustrates the latter type of case. The claim is made that "there is no such thing" as an invasion of one's right of privacy, since there is no "right of privacy." Although preserving his judicial prerogative to assert the existence of the right, the judge nevertheless does liken this right to a property right, and an invasion of one's privacy to an invasion of one's property.

Many other types of factors are taken into account in identifying acts in given cases. No single set of criteria emerges as a definitive way of characterizing all acts. And certainly in none of the cases do we find anything like a "pure act." The question, therefore, whether a general criterion of "act" can be found remains an open one.

AN ACT OF GOD

KIMBLE V. MACKINTOSH HEMPHILL CO.

SUPREME COURT OF PENNSYLVANIA, 1948
359 PA. 461, 59 A.2D 68

MAXEY, CHIEF JUSTICE. Virginia M. Kimble, wife of decedent Harry P. Kimble, instituted two actions in trespass to recover damages sustained as a result of her husband's death allegedly caused by the roof of defendant's foundry falling upon him. The first suit was a "death action" brought by plaintiff to recover expenses and for financial loss suffered by her and her children. The second suit was a "survival action" whereby plaintiff as administratrix of decedent's estate sought to recover the present worth of Harry P. Kimble's future earnings. These were cumulative suits. The jury returned a verdict in favor of plaintiff as personal representative of decedent in the sum of $5,823.20 and in favor of plaintiff as administratrix of the estate of Harry P. Kimble in the sum of $10,000. Defendant's motion for judgment n. o. v. was denied. The appeal followed.

Defendant is the owner and operator of a plant in Midland, Pennsylvania, where it manufactures castings and other products. The main part of the plant consists of a foundry building 740 feet long, 150 feet wide, and 64 feet high, with a monitor roof. The framework of the roof consists of steel trusses to which are attached steel purlins extending from the comb of the roof to the eaves. Wooden nailers are bolted to the purlins by carriage bolts. Spiked to the purlins and extending lengthwise of the building is 2x6 wooden sheathing. Over this sheathing is 1x8 sheathing, laid crosswise of the underlying sheathing. The lower deck was spiked to the nailers in the purlins, and the top deck was nailed to the under deck.

Plaintiff's decedent was employed by the Treadwell Construction Company as a brakeman on a "dinkey" engine used to shift railroad freight cars. On November 14, 1944, the defendant company leased to the Construction Company trackage and operating rights over a railroad siding serving the defendant's plant and connecting with the Pennsylvania Railroad Company. The Construction Company agreed to move defendant's freight cars to and from its plant. These cars were moved by the engine owned by the Construction Company and operated by its employees.

Mike Rubino, who operated the engine on which decedent was brakeman, testified that about 12:30 P.M. on March 31, 1945, he heard a "tearing or ripping of boards" as he sat in the cab watching Kimble, who had left the cab, walk the length of the engine in the direction of one Boice, defendant's employee, to receive instructions regarding the movement of defendant's cars. Kimble was struck by boards and timbers falling from the roof of defendant's foundry building. Decedent died an hour later from injuries thus sustained. When the crash came, Rubino was almost struck by a piece of board. He immediately got out of the cab to look for Kimble. He testified: "I didn't spend more than ten or fifteen seconds [looking for Kimble]. I had to run, because that other roof was coming down." The first section hit the engine and the second section "hit about ten or fifteen feet away, towards the east." About three seconds elapsed between the falling of the two sections, which measured 100 feet long, 22 feet wide and weighed 12 tons.

Defendant's liability is predicated upon its failure to maintain the roof in a safe condition and in failing to inspect, discover and correct its faulty condition. Witnesses testified that the lumber in the roof was rotted. James H. Cregar, a shipping helper at Treadwell, when asked "what was the condition of this part of roof lumber, and what not, that you found there on Harry Kimble?" replied: "Well, the roofing, why, it was good, but the other stuff was all rotten." He described "the other stuff" as "heavy boards; it was rotten; there wasn't anything to it. That was one reason we didn't have any trouble getting it off of him." Charles

O. Baker, another employee in the shipping department at Treadwell testified that "the lumber was in very poor condition. These two by fours that was bolted on to the purlins was very rotten, and the bolts had pulled right through the bolt holes, and the two by fours were rotted, and that is why they ripped loose in the roof. Otherwise, it wouldn't have come off like that; it probably would have busted up in different pieces, and part of it would have stuck to the roof. . . ." When asked: "What was the condition of the two by fours, that you saw on the ground?" he answered: "Why, the bolt holes were rotted out of it."

Arthur Williams, construction superintendent for the Nellis Company, which had the job of repairing the foundry building for defendant company on April 1, 1945, made an examination of that part of the monitor from which the roof was gone and found it "in very bad shape." When questioned as to the condition of the nailers on that date, he said: "They were rotten." The bolts "were rusted away." As for the nailers and the tongue and groove in the part of the blown off roof, he stated "The nailers were not much account, at all." Mr. Williams was asked: "Could the condition of these nailers, and this tongue and groove, nailed to the nailers . . . have been disclosed by an inspection from the interior of that building, on March 31st, 1945, or a reasonable length of time ahead of that date?" He replied: "Yes, it could." There was other testimony of the same purport.

Defendant disclaims liability alleging (1) that the proximate cause of the fatality was a cyclonic wind of an extraordinary intensity and that this relieved defendant from liability irrespective of whether or not its claimed antecedent negligence was a substantial factor in bringing about the harm. . . .

Defendant called a number of witnesses to prove that the winds at the time of decedent's injuries were of an unusually severe velocity such as had never occurred in that vicinity before and could not have been reasonably anticipated by it, and which ordinary skill and foresight could not guard against. . . .

W. S. Brontzman, employee of the U. S. Weather Bureau in charge of the Pittsburgh office, testified that at 12:28 P.M. the wind in Pittsburgh at the Allegheny County Airport (which is 30 to 35 miles from Midland) was south-southwest a velocity of 38 miles per hour with 50 mile per hour gusts. . . .

Plaintiff's witnesses contradicted the evidence with regard to the severity of the wind on the date of the accident. Mr. Cregar was asked: "What was the condition of the weather, in Midland, about a quarter to one, or thereabouts, on the 31st day of March, 1945, in the vicinity of those two plants, Treadwell and Mackintosh Hemphill?" He answered: "Well, in my judgment—you are referring to the wind, is that what you are referring to? Q. All right; let's go to the wind. A. To my judgment, the wind wasn't any stronger, at the time I was out there, than it was several times that I have seen it around that vicinity, before." He added: "There was a high wind . . . I have seen winds just as heavy as that."

Defendant contends that the court erred in submitting the question of negligence to the jury and should have declared as a matter of law that an act of God was responsible for Kimble's death. Whether or not the fatal injury to plaintiff's decedent was due to an act of God or to defendant's negligence was a question of fact for the jury. The condition of the roof, the intensity of the wind on the date of the accident and on previous occasions at the same place were factual questions. The charge of the court was comprehensive and accurate. The trial judge charged: "It is the law that no person is answerable for what is termed an act of Providence, that is, if some visitation of Providence comes along that in our ordinary experience we are not . . . anticipating, then no one can be held to answer for that act, so that if the wind on this day was of such severity that it could not be reasonably anticipated by the Defendant, and that by reason of that wind, a part of the roof was blown off, then the Defendant would not be liable. However, if the storm were not of that severity, if it were only such a storm as occasionally happens, but is reasonably to be anticipated on occasions of every year or two, then that would not be an act of Providence . . . if they were such as were reasonably to be expected to occur occasionally, then such storms should be guarded against. An act of Providence as related to cases of injurious negligence is one against which ordinary skill and foresight is not expected to provide. Whether the injury in this case is attributable to such a cause or is the consequence of negligence is a question of fact for you to determine. . . . Even if, with an extraordinary wind or storm there is concurring negligence, the party chargeable with it will be relieved from liability if the wind or storm is so overwhelming in character that it would of itself have produced the injury complained of, independently of negligence if there were negligence. . . ."

In the instant case, defendant by using ordinary diligence and attention could have prevented the serious consequences which resulted from its failure to inspect and correct the faulty condition of the foundry roof. We said in Fitzpatrick v. Penfield, 267 Pa. 564, 109 A. 653, 655: "High winds are not of infrequent occurrence, and this particular wind was termed an ordinary wind occurring three or four times in a year. It was not an unusual one, and it was for the jury to find under all the evidence whether it was likely to have occurred, and should have been provided against. We cannot say that the intervening cause was vis major. One who fails in his duty to remedy a defective or dangerous condition is liable for injuries resulting therefrom, although the immediate cause of the injury is the wind. . . . The causal connection is not broken, and the original wrongdoer is liable for the injury sustained. . . ."

The judgment is affirmed.

PATTERSON, JUSTICE (dissenting). The majority holds that appellant company was under a duty to anticipate, as within the realm of reasonable probability, a wind of such intensity and velocity as would tear loose a 12-ton section of roof, break it in half, and carry it over 100 feet. There is no proof of any similar occurrence and the judgment of the court below should be reversed for the reason that appellee has failed to prove a violation of duty owed to the decedent.

A section of a roof weighing 12 tons being ripped loose and carried through the air more than 100 feet is a possibility but certainly not a reasonable probability where there is no proof of a similar occurrence in or about the immediate vicinity. The event was not within the foreseeable risk of harm. The orbit of duty is determined by the reasonable foreseeable risk of harm. In Irwin Savings & Trust Company v. Pennsylvania R. Company, 349 Pa. 278, 284, 37 A.2d 432, 435, Mr. Justice Drew, quoting from South-Side Passenger Ry. Co. v. Trich, 117 Pa. 390, 399, 11 A. 627, 2 Am. St. Rep. 672, said: " 'To impose such a standard of care as requires, in the ordinary affairs of life, precaution on the part of individuals against all the possibilities which may occur, is establishing a degree of responsibility quite beyond any legal limitations which have yet been declared.' "

Negligence does not of itself create liability. Back of the negligent act or failure to act must be sought and found a duty to the person injured, the observance of which would have averted or avoided the injury. Even though it be assumed that the roof was negligently maintained, the unusually high wind was an independent intervening force effecting an unforeseeable event for which appellant should not be held responsible. The duty extended only to reasonably foreseeable circumstances and injury which appellant could reasonably anticipate as a result of such negligence. The event which is the basis for the instant suit was clearly beyond the periphery of the duty.

The judgment of the court below should be reversed and here entered for appellant.

AN OVERT ACT

State v. Rider

SUPREME COURT OF MISSOURI, 1886
90 MO. 54, 1 S.W. 825

HENRY, C. J. At the September term, 1885, of the Saline criminal court, the defendant was indicted for murder for killing one R. P. Tallent, and was tried at the November term of said court, 1885, and convicted of murder in the first degree. From that judgment he has appealed to this court.

The evidence for the state proved that he killed the deceased, and of that fact there is no question. It also tended to prove that he armed himself with a gun, and sought the deceased with the intent to kill him. The evidence tended to prove that the relations between the defendant and his wife were not of the most agreeable character, and that the deceased was criminally intimate with her, and on the day of the homicide had taken her off in a skiff to Brunswick. That the defendant went in search of his wife to the residence of the deceased, armed with a shot gun, and met the latter near his residence. What then occurred no one witnessed, except the parties engaged, but the defendant testified as follows: "Well, me and Mr. Merrill went to this path that was leading toward the river. When we come to that path Mr. Merrill stopped, and I went on in the direction of Mr. Tallent's house, to see if I could learn anything about where my wife was, and I discovered no sign of her there, and I started back north on this path, going down on the slough bank; after going down some distance from the bank I meets Mr. Tallent; I spoke to Mr. Tallent and asked him if he knew where my wife was, and he made this remark: 'I have taken her where you won't find her;' and he says, 'God damn you, we will settle this right here.' He started at me with his axe in a striking position, and I bid Mr. Tallent to stop; then he advanced a few feet, and I fired. I fired one time." The axe of deceased, found on the ground, had a shot in the handle near the end farthest from the blade, and on the same side as the blade, and this evidence had a tendency to corroborate the testimony of the accused, showing that the axe was pointing in the direction from which the shot came, and was held in an upright position.

The court, for the state, instructed the jury as follows:

"The court instructs the jury, that if they believe from the evidence that prior to the killing of the deceased, the defendant prepared and armed himself with a gun, and went in search of, and sought out, deceased, with the intention of killing him, or shooting him, or doing him some great bodily harm, and that he did find, overtake, or intercept, deceased, and did shoot and kill deceased while he was returning from the river to his home, then it makes no difference who commenced the assault, and the jury shall not acquit the defendant; and the jury are further instructed that in such case they shall disregard any and all testimony tending to show that the character or reputation of deceased for turbulency, violence, peace and quiet was bad, and they shall further disregard any and all evidence of threats made by deceased against the defendant."

The mere intent to commit a crime is not a crime. An attempt to perpetrate it is necessary to constitute guilt in law. One may arm himself with the purpose of seeking and killing an adversary, and may seek and find him, yet, if guilty of no overt act, commits no crime. It has been repeatedly held in this and nearly every state in the Union, that one against whom threats have been made by another is not justifiable in assaulting him unless the threatener makes some attempt to execute his threats. A threat to kill but indicates an intent or purpose to kill; and the unexpressed purpose or intent certainly affords no better excuse for an assault by the person against whom it exists than such an intent accompanied with a threat to accomplish it. The above instruction authorized the jury to convict the defendant even though he had abandoned the purpose to kill the deceased when he met him, and was assaulted by deceased and had to kill him to save his own life. . . .

For the errors above noted the judgment is reversed and cause remanded. All concur.

AN INTENTIONAL ACT

Vosburg v. Putney

SUPREME COURT OF WISCONSIN, 1891
80 WIS. 523, 50 N.W. 403

The action was brought to recover damages for an assault and battery, alleged to have been committed by the defendant upon the plaintiff on February 20, 1889. The answer is a general denial. At the date of the alleged assault the plaintiff was a little more than fourteen years of age, and the defendant a little less than twelve years of age.

The injury complained of was caused by a kick inflicted by defendant upon the leg of the plaintiff, a little below the knee. The transaction occurred in a school-room in Waukesha, during school hours, both parties being pupils in the school. A former trial of the cause resulted in a verdict and judgment for the plaintiff for $2,800. The defendant appealed from such judgment to this court, and the same was reversed for error, and a new trial awarded.

The case has been again tried in the circuit court, and the trial resulted in a verdict for plaintiff for $2,500. . . .

On the last trial the jury found a special verdict, as follows: "(1) Had the plaintiff during the month of January, 1889, received an injury just above the knee, which became inflamed, and produced pus? *Answer.* Yes. (2) Had such injury on the 20th day of February, 1889, nearly healed at the point of the injury? *A.* Yes. (3) Was the plaintiff, before said 20th of February, lame, as a result of such injury? *A.* No. (4) Had the tibia in the plaintiff's right leg become inflamed or diseased to some extent before he received the blow or kick from the defendant? *A.* No. (5) What was the exciting cause of the injury to the plaintiff's leg? *A.* Kick. (6) Did the defendant, in touching the plaintiff with his foot, intend to do him any harm? *A.* No. (7) At what sum do you assess the damages of the plaintiff? *A.* $2,500."

The defendant moved for judgment in his favor on the verdict, and also for a new trial. The plaintiff moved for judgment on the verdict in his favor. The motions of defendant were overruled, and that of the plaintiff granted. Thereupon judgment for plaintiff for $2,500 damages and costs of suit was duly entered. The defendant appeals from the judgment.

LYON, J. The jury having found that the defendant, in touching the plaintiff with his foot, did not intend to do him any harm, counsel for defendant maintain that the plaintiff has no cause of action, and that defendant's motion for judgment on the special verdict should have been granted. In support of this proposition counsel quote from 2 Greenl. Ev. § 83, the rule that "the intention to do harm is of the essence of an assault." Such is the rule, no doubt, in actions or prosecutions for mere assaults. But this is an action to recover damages for an alleged assault and battery. In such case the rule is correctly stated, in many of the authorities cited by counsel, that plaintiff must show either that the intention was unlawful, or that the defendant is in fault. If the intended act is unlawful, the intention to commit it must necessarily be unlawful. Hence, as applied to this case, if the kicking of the plaintiff by the defendant was an unlawful act, the intention of defendant to kick him was also unlawful.

Had the parties been upon the play-grounds of the school, engaged in the usual boyish sports, the defendant being free from malice, wantonness, or negligence, and intending no harm to plaintiff in what he did, we should hesitate to hold the act of the defendant unlawful, or that he could be held liable in this action. Some consideration is due to the implied license of the play-grounds. But it appears that the injury was inflicted in the school, after it had been called to order by the teacher, and after the regular exercises of the school had commenced. Under these circumstances, no implied license to do the act complained of existed, and such act was a violation of the order and decorum of the school, and necessarily unlawful. Hence we are of the opinion that, under the evidence and verdict, the action may be sustained. . . .

The judgment of the circuit court must be reversed, and the cause will be remanded for a new trial [because of an error in a ruling on an objection to the admission of certain testimony].

AN INTERVENING ACT

PEOPLE v. LEWIS

SUPREME COURT OF CALIFORNIA, 1899
124 CAL. 551, 57 PAC. 470

TEMPLE, J. The defendant was convicted of manslaughter and appeals from the judgment and from an order refusing a new trial. It is his second appeal. The main facts are stated in the decision of the former appeal, 117 Cal. 186, 48 P. 1088. . . .

Defendant and deceased were brothers-in-law, and not altogether friendly, although they were on speaking and visiting terms. On the morning of the homicide the deceased visited the residence of the defendant, was received in a friendly manner, but after a while an altercation arose, as a result of which defendant shot deceased in the abdomen, inflicting a wound that was necessarily mortal. Farrell fell to the ground, stunned for an instant, but soon got up, and went into the house, saying: "Shoot me again; I shall die anyway." His strength soon failed him and he was put to bed. Soon afterwards,—about how long does not appear, but within a very few minutes,—when no other person was present except a lad about 9 years of age, nephew of the deceased, and son of the defendant, the deceased procured a knife, and cut his throat, inflicting a ghastly wound, from the effect of which, according to the medical evidence, he must necessarily have died in five minutes. The wound inflicted by the defendant severed the mesenteric artery, and medical witnesses testified that under the circumstances it was necessarily mortal, and death would ensue within one hour from the effects of the wound alone. Indeed, the evidence was that usually the effect of such a wound would be to cause death in less time than that, but possibly the omentum may have filled the wound, and thus, by preventing the flow of the blood from the body, have stayed its certain effect for a short period. Internal hemorrhage was still occurring, and, with other effects of the gunshot wound, produced intense pain. The medical witnesses thought that death was accelerated by the knife wound. Perhaps some of them considered it the immediate cause of death.

Now, it is contended that this is a case where one languishing from a mortal wound is killed by an intervening cause, and, therefore, deceased was not killed by Lewis. To constitute manslaughter, the defendant must have killed some one, and if, though mortally wounded by the defendant, Farrell actually died from an independent intervening cause, Lewis, at the most, could only be guilty of a felonious attempt. He was as effectually prevented from killing as he would have been if some obstacle had turned aside the bullet from its course and left Farrell unwounded. And they contend that the intervening act was the cause of death, if it shortened the life of Farrell for any period whatever.

The attorney general does not controvert the general proposition here contended for, but argues that the wound inflicted by the defendant was the direct cause of the throat-cutting, and therefore, defendant is criminally responsible for the death. He illustrates his position by supposing a case of one dangerously wounded and whose wounds had been bandaged by a surgeon. He says, suppose through the fever and pain consequent upon the wound the patient becomes frenzied and tears away the bandage and thus accelerates his own death. Would not the defendant be responsible for a homicide? Undoubtedly he would be, for in the case supposed the deceased died from the wound, aggravated, it is true, by the restlessness of the deceased, but still the wound inflicted by the defendant produced death. Whether such is the case here is the question.

The attorney general seems to admit a fact which I do not concede,—that the gunshot wound was not, when Farrell died, then itself directly contributing to the death. I think the jury were warranted in finding that it was. But if the deceased did die from the effect of the knife wound alone, no doubt the defendant would be responsible, if it was made to appear, and the jury could have found from the evidence, that the knife wound was caused by the wound inflicted by the defendant in the natural course of events. If the relation was causal, and the wounded condition of the deceased was not merely the occasion upon which another cause intervened, not produced by the first wound or related to it in other than a casual way, then defendant is guilty of a homicide. But, if the wounded condition only afforded an opportunity for another unconnected person to kill, defendant would not be guilty of a homicide, even though he had inflicted a mortal wound. In such case, I think, it would be true that the defendant was thus prevented from killing.

The case, considered under this view, is further complicated from the fact that it is impossible to determine whether deceased was induced to cut his throat through pain produced by the wound. May it not have been from remorse, or from a desire to shield his brother-in-law? In either case the causal relation between the knife wound and the gunshot wound would seem to be the same. In either case, if defendant had not shot the deceased, the knife wound would not have been inflicted.

Suppose one assaults and wounds another intending to take life, but the wound, though painful, is not even dangerous, and the wounded man knows that it is not mortal, and yet takes his own life to escape pain, would it not be suicide only? Yet, the wound inflicted by the assailant would have the same relation to death which the original wound in this case has to the knife wound. The wound induced the suicide, but the wound was not, in the usual course of things, the cause of the suicide.

Though no case altogether like this has been found, yet, as was to have been expected, the general subject has often been considered. . . . In State v. Scates, 50 N.C. 420, a child was found dead, badly burned, and with a wound from a blow on the head. The burning was admitted by defendant, but the blow was not, and it was not proven who inflicted it. The medical witness thought the burning was the primary cause of death, but the blow may have hastened it. The jury was told that, if it was doubtful which was the immediate cause of death, they must acquit, but if they found that the burning was the primary cause of death, and the blow only hastened it, they could convict. The case was reversed, the appellate court holding that the blow might have been the independent act of another, and, if it hastened the death, it, and not the burning, was the cause of death. In Bush v. Com., 78 Ky. 268, the deceased received a wound not necessarily mortal, and, in consequence, was taken to a hospital, where she took scarlet fever from a nurse, and died of the fever. The court said: "When the disease is a consequence of the wound, although the proximate cause of the death, the person inflicting the wound is guilty, because the death can be traced as a result naturally flowing from the wound, and coming in the natural order of things; but when there is a supervening cause, not naturally intervening by reason of the wound, the death is by visitation of Providence, and not from the act of the party inflicting the wound. . . . If the death was not connected with the wound in the regular chain of causes and consequences, there ought not to be any responsibility." The last case, in my opinion, so far as it goes, correctly states the law. . . .

But why is it that one who inflicts a wound not mortal is guilty of a homicide, if through misconduct of the patient or unskillful treatment gangrene or fever sets in, producing a fatal termination, when, if it can be clearly made to appear that the medicine, and not the wound, was the cause of the death, he is not guilty of a homicide? In each case, if the wound had not been, the treatment would not have been, and the man would not then have died. In each case the wound occasioned the treatment which caused or contributed to the death. The reason, I think, is found in the words advisedly used in the last sentence. In the one case the treatment caused the death, and in the other it merely contributed to it. In one case the treatment aggravated the wound, but the wound thus aggravated produced death. In the other the wound, though the occasion of the treatment, did not contribute to the death, which occurred without any present contribution to the natural effect of the medicine from the wound. Take, for instance, the giving of a dose of morphine, by mistake, sufficient to end life at once. . . .

This case differs from that in this: that here the intervening cause, which it is alleged hastened death, was not medical treatment, designed to be helpful, and which the deceased was compelled to procure because of the wound, but was an act intended to produce death, and did not result from the first wound in the natural course of events. But we have reached the conclusion by a course of argument unnecessarily prolix, except from a desire to fully consider the earnest and able argument of the defendant, that the test is—or at least one test—whether, when the death occurred, the wound inflicted by the defendant did contribute to the event. If it did, although other independent causes also contributed, the causal relation between the unlawful acts of the defendant and the death has been made out. Here, when the throat was cut, Farrell was not merely languishing from a mortal wound; he was actually dying; and after the throat was cut he continued to languish from both wounds. Drop by drop the life current went out from both wounds, and at the very instant of death the gunshot wound was contributing to the event. If the throat-cutting had been by a third person, unconnected with the defendant, he might be guilty; for although a man cannot be killed twice, two persons, acting independently, may contribute to his death and each be guilty of a homicide. A person dying is still in life, and may be killed, but if he is dying from a wound given by another both may properly be said to have contributed to his death. . . .

The court refused to instruct the jury as follows: "If you believe from the evidence that it is impossible to tell whether Will Farrell died from the wound in the throat, or the wound in the abdomen, you are bound to acquit." The instruction was properly refused. It assumed that death must have resulted wholly from one wound or the other, and ignored the proposition that both might have contributed—as the jury could have found from the evidence.

The other points are relatively trivial. I have examined them and cannot see how injury could have resulted, supposing the rulings to have been erroneous. The judgment is affirmed.

We concur: McFarland, J.; Henshaw, J.

A NEGLIGENT ACT

Palsgraf v. Long Island R. R. Co.

court of appeals of new york, 1928
248 n.y. 339, 162 n.e. 99

Cardozo, C. J. Plaintiff was standing on a platform of defendant's railroad after buying a ticket to go to Rockaway Beach. A train stopped at the station, bound for another place. Two men ran forward to catch it. One of the men reached the platform of the car without mishap, though the train was already moving. The other man, carrying a package, jumped aboard the car, but seemed unsteady as if about to fall. A guard on the car, who had held the door open, reached forward to help him in, and another guard on the platform pushed him from behind. In this act, the package was dislodged, and fell upon the rails. It was a package of small size, about fifteen inches long, and was covered by a newspaper. In fact it contained fireworks, but there was nothing in its appearance to give notice of its contents. The fireworks when they fell exploded. The shock of the explosion threw down some scales at the other end of the platform many feet away. The scales struck the plaintiff, causing injuries for which she sues.

The conduct of the defendant's guard, if a wrong in its relation to the holder of the package, was not a wrong in its relation to the plaintiff, standing far away. Relatively to her it was not negligence at all. Nothing in the situation gave notice that the falling package had in it the potency of peril to persons thus removed. Negligence is not actionable unless it involves the invasion of a legally protected interest, the violation of a right. "Proof of negligence in the air, so to speak, will not do." Pollock, Torts

164

(11th Ed.) p. 455; Martin v. Herzog, 228 N.Y. 164, 170, 126 N.E. 814. Cf. Salmond, Torts (6th Ed.) p. 24. . . .

The plaintiff, as she stood upon the platform of the station, might claim to be protected against intentional invasion of her bodily security. Such invasion is not charged. She might claim to be protected against unintentional invasion by conduct involving in the thought of reasonable men an unreasonable hazard that such invasion would ensue. These, from the point of view of the law, were the bounds of her immunity, with perhaps some rare exceptions, survivals for the most part of ancient forms of liability, where conduct is held to be at the peril of the actor. Sullivan v. Dunham, 161 N.Y. 290, 55 N.E. 923, 47 L.A.R. 715, 76 Am. St. Rep. 274. If no hazard was apparent to the eye of ordinary vigilance, an act innocent and harmless, at least to outward seeming, with reference to her, did not take to itself the quality of a tort because it happened to be a wrong, though apparently not one involving the risk of bodily insecurity, with reference to some one else. "In every instance, before negligence can be predicated of a given act, back of the act must be sought and found a duty to the individual complaining, the observance of which would have averted or avoided the injury." McSherry, C. J., in West Virginia Central & P. R. Co. v. State, 96 Md. 652, 666, 54 A. 669, 671 (61 L.R.A. 574). . . .

"The ideas of negligence and duty are strictly correlative." Bowen, L.J., in Thomas v. Quartermaine, 18 Q.B.D. 685, 694. The plaintiff sues in her own right for a wrong personal to her, and not as the vicarious beneficiary of a breach of duty to another.

A different conclusion will involve us, and swiftly too, in a maze of contradictions. A guard stumbles over a package which has been left upon a platform. It seems to be a bundle of newspapers. It turns out to be a can of dynamite. To the eye of ordinary vigilance, the bundle is abandoned waste, which may be kicked or trod on with impunity. Is a passenger at the other end of the platform protected by the law against the unsuspected hazard concealed beneath the waste? If not, is the result to be any different, so far as the distant passenger is concerned, when the guard stumbles over a valise which a truckman or a porter has left upon the walk? The passenger far away, if the victim of a wrong at all, has a cause of action, not derivative, but original and primary. His claim to be protected against invasion of his bodily security is neither greater nor less because the act resulting in the invasion is a wrong to another far removed. In this case, the rights that are said to have been violated, the interests said to have been invaded, are not even of the same order. The man was not injured in his person or even put in danger. The purpose of the act, as well as its effect, was to make his person safe. If there was a wrong to him at all, which may very well be doubted, it was a wrong to a property interest only, the safety of his package. Out of this wrong to property, which threatened injury to nothing else, there has passed, we are told, to the plaintiff by derivation or succession a right of action for the invasion of an interest of another order, the right to bodily security. The diversity of interests emphasizes the futility of the effort to build the plaintiff's right upon the basis of a wrong to some one else. The gain is one of emphasis, for a like result would follow if the interests were the same. Even then, the orbit of the danger as disclosed to the eye of reasonable vigilance would be the orbit of duty. One who jostles one's neighbor in a crowd does not invade the rights of others standing at the outer fringe when the unintended contact casts a bomb upon the ground. The wrongdoer as to them is the man who carries the bomb, not the one who explodes it without suspicion of the danger. Life will have to be made over, and human nature transformed, before prevision so extravagant can be accepted as the norm of conduct, the customary standard to which behavior must conform.

The argument for the plaintiff is built upon the shifting meanings of such words as "wrong" and "wrongful," and shares their instability. What the plaintiff must show is "a wrong" to herself; i.e., a violation of her own right, and not merely a wrong to some one else, nor conduct, "wrongful" because unsocial, but not "a wrong" to any one. We are told that one who drives at reckless speed through a crowded city street is guilty of a negligent act and therefore of a wrongful one, irrespective of the consequences. Negligent the act is, and wrongful in the sense that it is unsocial, but wrongful and unsocial in relation to other travelers, only because the eye of vigilance perceives the risk of damage. If the same act were to be committed on a speedway or a race course, it would lose its wrongful quality. The risk reasonably to be perceived defines the duty to be obeyed and risk imports relation; it is risk to another or to others within the range of apprehension. Seavey, Negligence, Subjective or Objective, 41 H.L. Rv. 6; Boronkay v. Robinson & Carpenter, 247 N.Y. 365, 160 N.E. 400. This does not mean, of course, that one who launches a destructive force is always relieved of liability, if the force, though known to be destructive, pursues an unexpected path. "It was not necessary that the defendant should have had notice of the particular method in which an accident would occur, if the possibility of an accident was clear to the ordinarily prudent eye." Munsey v. Webb, 231 U.S. 150, 156, 34 S. Ct. 44, 45 (58 L. Ed. 162). . . . Some acts, such as shooting are so imminently dangerous to any one who may come within reach of the missile however unexpectedly, as to impose a duty of prevision not far from that of an insurer. Even today, and much oftener in earlier stages of the law, one acts sometimes at one's peril. Jeremiah Smith, Tort and Absolute Liability, 30 H.L. Rv. 328; Street, Foundations of Legal Liability, vol. 1, pp. 77, 78. Under this head, it may be, fall certain cases of what is known as transferred intent, an act willfully dangerous to A resulting by misadventure in injury to B. Talmage v. Smith, 101 Mich. 370, 374, 59 N.W. 656, 45 Am. St. Rep. 414. These cases aside, wrong is defined in terms of the natural or probable, at least when unintentional. Parrot v. Wells-Fargo Co. (The Nitro-Glycerine Case) 15 Wall 524, 21 L. Ed. 206. The range of reasonable apprehension is at times a question for the court, and at times, if varying inferences are possible, a question for the jury. Here, by concession there was nothing in the situation to suggest to the most cautious mind that the parcel wrapped in newspaper would spread wreckage through the station. If the guard had thrown it down knowingly and willfully, he would not have threatened the plaintiff's safety, so far as appearances could warn him. His conduct would not have involved, even then, an unreasonable probability of invasion of her bodily security. Liability can be no greater where the act is inadvertent.

Negligence, like risk, is thus a term of relation. Negligence in the abstract, apart from things related, is surely not a tort, if indeed it is understandable at all. Bowen, L.J., in Thomas v. Quartermaine, 18 Q.B.D. 685, 694. Negligence is not a tort unless it results in the commission of a wrong, and the commission of a wrong imports the violation of a right, in this case, we are told, the right to be protected against interference with one's bodily security. But bodily security is protected, not against all forms of interference or aggression, but only against some. One who seeks redress at all does not make out a cause of action by showing without more that there has been damage to his person. If the harm was not willful, he must show that the act as to him has possibilities of danger so many and apparent as to entitle him to be protected against the doing of it though the harm was unintended. Affront to personality is still the keynote of the wrong. Confirmation of this view will be found in the history and development of the action on the case. Negligence as a basis of civil liability was unknown to mediaeval law. 8 Holdsworth, History of English Law, p. 449; Street, Foundations of Legal Liability, vol. 1, pp. 189, 190. For damage to the person, the sole remedy was trespass, and trespass did not lie in the absence of aggression, and that direct and personal. Holdsworth, op. cit. p. 453; Street, op. cit. vol. 3, pp. 258, 260, vol. 1, pp. 71, 74. Liability for other damage, as where a servant without orders from the master does or omits something to the damage of another, is a plant of later growth. Holdsworth, op. cit. 450, 457; Wigmore, Responsibility for Tortious Acts, vol. 3, Essays in Anglo-American Legal History, 520, 523, 526, 533. When it emerged out of the legal soil, it was thought of as a variant of trespass, an offshoot of the parent stock. This appears in the form of action, which was known as trespass on the case. Holdsworth, op. cit., p. 449; cf. Scott v. Shepard, 2 Wm. Black, 892; Green, Rationale of Proximate Cause, p. 19. The victim does not sue derivatively, or by right of subrogation, to vindicate an interest invaded in the person of another. Thus to view his cause of action is to ignore the fundamental difference between tort and crime. Holland, Jurisprudence (12th Ed.) p. 328. He sues for breach of duty owing to himself.

The law of causation, remote or proximate, is thus foreign to the case before us. The question of liability is always anterior to the question of the measure of the consequences that go with liability. If there is no tort to be redressed, there is no occasion to consider what damage might be recovered if there were a finding of a tort. We may assume, without deciding, that negligence, not at large or in the abstract, but in relation to the plaintiff, would entail liability for any and all consequences, however novel or extraordinary. . . . There is room for argument that a distinction is to be drawn according to the diversity of interests invaded by the act, as where conduct negligent in that it threatens an insignificant invasion of an interest in property results in an unforeseeable invasion of an interest of another order, as, e.g., one of bodily security. Perhaps other distinctions may be necessary. We do not go into the question now. The consequences to be followed must first be rooted in a wrong.

The judgment of the Appellate Division and that of the Trial Term should be reversed, and the complaint dismissed, with costs in all courts.

ANDREWS, J. (dissenting). Assisting a passenger to board a train, the defendant's servant negligently knocked a package from his arms. It fell between the platform and the cars. Of its contents the servant knew and could know nothing. A violent explosion followed. The concussion broke some scales standing a considerable distance away. In falling, they injured the plaintiff, an intending passenger.

Upon these facts, may she recover the damages she has suffered in an action brought against the master? The result we shall reach depends upon our theory as to the nature of negligence. Is it a relative concept—the breach of some duty owing to a particular person or to particular persons? Or, where there is an act which unreasonably threatens the safety of others, is the doer liable for all its proximate consequences, even where they result in injury to one who would generally be thought to be outside the radius of danger? This is not a mere dispute as to words. We might not believe that to the average mind the dropping of the bundle would seem to involve the probability of harm to the plaintiff standing many feet away whatever might be the case as to the owner or to one so near as to be likely to be struck by its fall. If, however, we adopt the second hypothesis, we have to inquire only as to the relation between cause and effect. We deal in terms of proximate cause, not of negligence.

Negligence may be defined roughly as an act or omission which unreasonably does or may affect the rights of others, or which unreasonably fails to protect one's self from the dangers resulting from such acts. Here I confine myself to the first branch of the definition. Nor do I comment on the word "unreasonable." For present purposes it sufficiently describes that average of conduct that society requires of its members.

There must be both the act or the omission, and the right. It is the act itself, not the intent of the actor, that is important. Hover v. Barkhoof, 44 N.Y. 113; Mertz v. Connecticut Co., 217 N.Y. 475, 112 N.E. 166. In criminal law both the intent and the result are to be considered. Intent again is material in tort actions, where punitive damages are sought, dependent on actual malice—not on merely reckless conduct. But here neither insanity nor infancy lessens responsibility. Williams v. Hays, 143 N.Y. 442, 38 N.E. 449, 26 L.R.A. 153, 42 Am. St. Rep. 743.

As has been said, except in cases of contributory negligence, there must be rights which are or may be affected. Often though injury has occurred, no rights of him who suffers have been touched. A licensee or trespasser upon my land has no claim to affirmative care on my part that the land be made safe. Meiers v. Fred Koch Brewery, 229 N.Y. 10, 127 N.E. 491, 13 A.L.R. 633. Where a railroad is required to fence its tracks against cattle, no man's rights are injured should he wander upon the road because such fence is absent. Di Caprio v. New York Cent. R. Co., 231 N.Y. 94, 131 N.E. 746, 16 A.L.R. 940. An unborn child may not demand immunity from personal harm. Drobner v. Peters, 232 N.Y. 220, 133 N.E. 567, 20 A.L.R. 1503.

But we are told that "there is no negligence unless there is in the particular case a legal duty to take care, and this duty must be one which is owed to the plaintiff himself and not merely to others." Salmond, Torts (6th Ed.) 24. This I think too narrow a conception. Where there is the unreasonable act, and some right that may be affected there is negligence whether damage does or does not result. That is immaterial. Should we drive down Broadway at a reckless speed, we are negligent whether we strike an approaching car or miss it by an inch. The act itself is wrongful. It is a wrong not only to those who happen to be within the radius of danger, but to all who might have been there—a wrong to the public at large. Such is the language of the street. Such the language of the courts when speaking of contributory negligence.

Such again and again their language in speaking of the duty of some defendant and discussing proximate cause in cases where such a discussion is wholly irrelevant on any other theory. Perry v. Rochester Lime Co., 219 N.Y. 60, 113 N.E. 529, L.R.A. 1917B, 1058. As was said by Mr. Justice Holmes many years ago:

"The measure of the defendant's duty in determining whether a wrong has been committed is one thing, the measure of liability when a wrong has been committed is another." Spade v. Lynn & B. R. Co., 172 Mass. 488, 491, 52 N.E. 747, 748 (43 L.R.A. 832, 70 Am. St. Rep. 298).

Due care is a duty imposed on each one of us to protect society from unnecessary danger, not to protect A., B., or C. alone.

It may well be that there is no such thing as negligence in the abstract. "Proof of negligence in the air, so to speak, will not do." In an empty world negligence would not exist. It does involve a relationship between man and his fellows, but not merely a relationship between man and those whom he might reasonably expect his act would injure; rather, a relationship between him and those whom he does in fact injure. If his act has a tendency to harm some one, it harms him a mile away as surely as it does those on the scene. We now permit children to recover for the negligent killing of the father. It was never prevented on the theory that no duty was owing to them. A husband may be compensated for the loss of his wife's services. To say that the wrongdoer was negligent as to the husband as well as to the wife is merely an attempt to fit facts to theory. An insurance company paying a fire loss recovers its payment of the negligent incendiary. We speak of subrogation—of suing in the right of the insured. Behind the cloud of words is the fact they hide, that the act, wrongful as to the insured, has also injured the company. Even if it be true that the fault of the father, wife, or insured will prevent recovery, it is because we consider the original negligence not the proximate cause of the injury. Pollock, Torts (12th Ed.) 463.

In the well-known Polemis Case, (1921) 3 K.B. 560, Scrutton, L.J., said that the dropping of a plank was negligent, for it might injure "workman or cargo or ship." Because of either possibility, the owner of the vessel was to be made good for his loss. The act being wrongful, the doer was liable for its proximate results. Criticized and explained as this statement may have been, I think it states the law as it should be and as it is. . . .

The proposition is this: Every one owes to the world at large the duty of refraining from those acts that may unreasonably threaten the safety of others. Such an act occurs. Not only is he wronged to whom harm might reasonably be expected to result, but he also who is in fact injured, even if he be outside what would generally be thought the danger zone. There needs be duty due the one complaining, but this is not a duty to a particular individual because as to him harm might be expected. Harm to some one being the natural result of the act, not only that one alone, but all those in fact injured may complain. We have never, I think, held otherwise. Indeed in the Di Caprio Case we said that a breach of a general ordinance defining the degree of care to be exercised in one's calling is evidence of negligence as to every one. We did not limit this statement to those who might be expected to be exposed to danger. Unreasonable risk being taken, its consequences are not confined to those who might probably be hurt.

If this be so, we do not have a plaintiff suing by "derivation or succession." Her action is original and primary. Her claim is for a breach of duty to herself—not that she is subrogated to any right of action of the owner of the parcel or of a passenger standing at the scene of the explosion.

The right to recover damages rests on additional considerations. The plaintiff's rights must be injured, and this injury must be caused by the negligence. We build a dam, but are negligent as to its foundations. Breaking, it injures property down stream. We are not liable if all this happened because of some reason other than the insecure foundation. But, when injuries do result from our unlawful act, we are liable for the consequences. It does not matter that they are unusual, unexpected, unforeseen, and unforeseeable. But there is one limitation. The damages must be so connected with the negligence that the latter may be said to be the proximate cause of the former.

These two words have never been given an inclusive definition. What is a cause in a legal sense, still more what is a proximate cause, depend in each case upon many considerations, as does the existence of negligence itself. Any philosophical doctrine of causation does not help us. A boy throws a stone into a pond. The ripples spread. The water level rises. The history of that pond is altered to all eternity. It will be altered by other causes also. Yet it will be forever the resultant of all causes combined. Each one will have an influence. How great only omniscience can say. You may speak of a chain, or, if you please, a net. An analogy is of little aid. Each cause brings about future events. Without each the future would not be the same. Each is proximate in the sense it is essential. But that is not what we mean by the word. Nor on the other hand do we mean sole cause. There is no such thing.

Should analogy be thought helpful, however, I prefer that of a stream. The spring, starting on its journey, is joined by tributary after tributary. The river, reaching the ocean, comes from a hundred sources. No man may say whence any drop of water is derived. Yet for a time distinction may be possible. Into the clear creek, brown swamp water flows from the left. Later, from the right comes water stained by its clay bed. The three may remain for a space, sharply divided. But at last inevitably no trace of separation remains. They are so commingled that all distinction is lost.

As we have said, we cannot trace the effect of an act to the end, if end there is. Again, however, we may trace it part of the way. A murder at Serajevo may be the necessary antecedent to an assassination in London twenty years hence. An overturned lantern may burn all Chicago. We may follow the fire from the shed to the last building. We rightly say that the fire started by the lantern caused its destruction.

A cause, but not the proximate cause. What we do mean by the word "proximate" is that, because of convenience, of public policy, of a rough sense of justice, the law arbitrarily declines to trace a series of events beyond a certain point. This is not logic. It is practical politics. Take our rule as to fires. Sparks from my burning haystack set on fire my house and my neighbor's. I may recover from a negligent railroad. He may not. Yet the wrongful act as directly harmed the one as the other. We may regret that the line was drawn just where it was, but drawn somewhere it had to be. We said the act of the railroad was not the proximate cause of our neighbor's fire. Cause it surely was. The words we used were simply indicative of our notions of public policy. Other courts think differently. But somewhere they reach the point where they cannot say the stream comes from any one source.

Take the illustration given in an unpublished manuscript by a distinguished and helpful writer on the law of torts. A chauffeur negligently collides with another car which is filled with dynamite, although he could not know it. An explosion follows. A, walking on the sidewalk nearby, is killed. B, sitting in a window of a building opposite, is cut by flying glass. C, likewise sitting in a window a block away, is similarly injured. And a further illustration: A nursemaid, ten blocks away, startled by the noise, involuntarily drops a baby from her arms to the walk. We are told that C may not recover while A may. As to B it is a question for court or jury. We will all agree that the baby might not. Because, we are again told, the chauffeur had no reason to believe his conduct involved any risk of injuring either C or the baby. As to them he was not negligent.

But the chauffeur, being negligent in risking the collision, his belief that the scope of the harm he might do would be limited is immaterial. His act unreasonably jeopardized the safety of any one who might be affected by it. C's injury and that of the baby were directly traceable to the collision. Without that, the injury would not have happened. C had the right to sit in his office, secure from such dangers. The baby was entitled to use the sidewalk with reasonable safety.

The true theory is, it seems to me, that the injury to C, if in truth he is to be denied recovery, and the injury to the baby, is that their several injuries were not the proximate result of the negligence. And here not what the chauffeur had reason to believe would be the result of his conduct, but what the prudent would foresee, may have a bearing—may have some bearing, for the problem of proximate cause is not to be solved by any one consideration. It is all a question of expediency. There are no fixed rules to govern our judgment. There are simply matters of which we may take account. We have in a somewhat different connection spoken of "the stream of events." We have asked whether that stream was deflected—whether it was forced into new and unexpected channels. Donnelly v. H. C. & A. I. Piercy Contracting Co., 222 N.Y. 210, 118 N.E. 605. This is rather rhetoric than law. There is in truth little to guide us other than common sense.

There are some hints that may help us. The proximate cause, involved as it may be with many other causes, must be, at the least, something without which the event would not happen. The court must ask itself whether there was a natural and continuous sequence between cause and effect. Was the one a substantial factor in producing the other? Was there a direct connection between them, without too many intervening causes? Is the effect of cause on result not too attenuated? Is the cause likely, in the usual judgment of mankind, to produce the result? Or, by the exercise of prudent foresight, could the result be foreseen? Is the result too remote from the cause, and here we consider remoteness in time and space. Bird v. St. Paul & M. Ins. Co., 224 N.Y. 47, 120 N.E. 86, 13 A.L.R. 875, where we passed upon the construction of a contract—but something was also said on this subject. Clearly we must so consider, for the greater distance either in time or space, the more surely do other causes intervene to affect the result. When a lantern is overturned, the firing of a shed is a fairly direct consequence. Many things contribute to the spread of the conflagration—the force of the wind, the direction and width of streets, the character of intervening structures, other factors. We draw an uncertain and wavering line, but draw it we must as best we can.

Once again, it is all a question of fair judgment, always keeping in mind the fact that we endeavor to make a rule in each case that will be practical and in keeping with the general understanding of mankind.

Here another question must be answered. In the case supposed, it is said, and said correctly, that the chauffeur is liable for the direct effect of the explosion, although he had no reason to suppose it would follow a collision. "The fact that the injury occurred in a different manner than that which might have been expected does not prevent the chauffeur's negligence from being in law the cause of the injury." But the natural results of a negligent act—the results which a prudent man would or should foresee—do have a bearing upon the decision as to proximate cause. We have said so repeatedly. What should be foreseen? No human foresight would suggest that a collision itself might injure one a block away. On the contrary, given an explosion, such a possibility might be reasonably expected. I think the direct connection, the foresight of which the courts speak, assumes prevision of the explosion, for the immediate results of which, at least, the chauffeur is responsible.

It may be said this is unjust. Why? In fairness he should make good every injury flowing from his negligence. Not because of tenderness toward him we say he need not answer for all that follows his wrong. We look back to the catastrophe, the fire kindled by the spark, or the explosion. We trace the consequences, not indefinitely, but to a certain point. And to aid us in fixing that point we ask what might ordinarily be expected to follow the fire or the explosion.

This last suggestion is the factor which must determine the case before us. The act upon which defendant's liability rests is knocking an apparently harmless package onto the platform. The act was negligent. For its proximate consequences the defendant is liable. If its contents were broken, to the owner; if it fell upon and crushed a passenger's foot, then to him; if it exploded and injured one in the immediate vicinity, to him also as to A in the illustration. Mrs. Palsgraf was standing some distance away. How far cannot be told from the record—apparently 25 or 30 feet, perhaps less. Except for the explosion, she would not have been injured. We are told by the appellant in his brief, "It cannot be denied that the explosion was the direct cause of the plaintiff's injuries." So it was a substantial factor in producing the result—there was here a natural and continuous sequence—direct connection. The only intervening cause was that, instead of blowing her to the ground, the concussion smashed the weighing machine which in turn fell upon her. There was no remoteness in time, little in space. And surely, given such an explosion as here, it needed no great foresight to predict that the natural result would be to injure one on the platform at no greater distance from its scene than was the plaintiff. Just how no one might be able to predict. Whether by flying fragments, by broken glass, by wreckage of machines or structures no one could say. But injury in some form was most probable.

Under these circumstances I cannot say as a matter of law that the plaintiff's injuries were not the proximate result of the negligence. That is all we have before us. The court refused to so charge. No request was made to submit the matter to the jury as a question of fact, even would that have been proper upon the record before us.

The judgment appealed from should be affirmed, with costs.

POUND, LEHMAN, and KELLOGG, JJ., concur with CARDOZO, C.J.

ANDREWS, J., dissents in opinion in which CRANE and O'BRIEN, JJ., concur.

Judgment reversed, etc.

A FIRST CASE

Hinish v. Meier & Frank Co.

supreme court of oregon, 1941
166 or. 482, 113 p.2d 438

Lusk, Justice. This is an action to recover damages caused by the defendants' invasion of the plaintiff's right of privacy.

The Circuit Court sustained a demurrer to the complaint, and, the plaintiff refusing to amend, entered judgment for the defendants from which this appeal is taken.

The complaint alleges: The defendant, Meier & Frank Company, Inc., is an Oregon Corporation engaged in the general mercantile business, as a part of which it maintains an optical department. The defendant, Kenneth C. Braymen, is the manager of the optical department.

On February 28, 1939, the defendants, without plaintiff's knowledge or consent, signed his name to the following telegram which they caused to be sent to the Governor of the State of Oregon:

"Governor Charles A. Sprague

1939 Feb 28 PM 9 36

"There is no demand for Optical Bill Seventy except by those who are financially interested in its passing. It is not a bill set out by the people. I urge you to veto it.

"George Hinish 2810 NE 49 Ave."

It is alleged that Bill Seventy referred to in this message was a bill passed by the Oregon legislative assembly, which, had it been approved by the Governor and become a law, would have prevented the defendant Meier & Frank Company, Inc., from continuing to engage in the business of fitting and selling optical glasses to the public.

It is further alleged that the plaintiff is a Classified Civil Service Employee of the United States Government, that as such he is prohibited by statute and the rules duly promulgated by the United States Civil Service Commission from engaging in political activities, and that the defendants, by sending the said telegram, jeopardized plaintiff's position and his right to receive a pension upon reaching the age of retirement.

It is alleged that the plaintiff suffered mental anguish as a result of defendants' wrongful act, and damages are sought in the sum of $20,000, of which the sum of $10,000 is punitive damages.

The case presents to this Court for the first time the question whether there is such a thing in this state as a legal right of privacy, for breach of which an action for damages will lie. This right, first brought forcefully to the attention of the profession in the year 1890 by an article in the Harvard Law Review by Louis D. Brandeis (later Mr. Justice Brandeis) and Samuel D. Warren ("The Right to Privacy," 4 Harv. L. Rev. 193), is said to be one that inheres in an "inviolate personality." In the language of Judge Cooley: "The right to one's person may be said to be a right of complete immunity; To be let alone." Cooley on Torts, 4th Ed. 34, § 18.

Where this right has been invaded, as, for example, by using the name or photograph of a person without his authority, for advertising or commercial purposes, or by parading a person's intimate, private affairs before the public gaze, unjustifiably and against his will, some of the courts of this country have thought that no legal redress could be granted, largely because the right was unknown to the common law, and to recognize it would be judicial legislation. No one, however, has had the hardihood to excuse as ethically or morally defensible practices which, becoming increasingly common and in many instances more and more offensive and injurious, under modern social conditions and through the use of modern scientific inventions, give sharper point to the demand that in such cases courts discharge the function for which they exist, of administering justice and affording redress for wrongs committed. . . .

Dean Pound, writing in 1915, said upon this subject:

"It is a modern demand, growing out of the conditions of life in the crowded communities of today, and presents difficult problems. The interest is clear. Such publicity with respect to private matters of purely personal concern is an injury to personality. It impairs the mental peace and comfort of the individual and may produce suffering much more acute than that produced by a mere bodily injury. . . . But while the law is slow in recognizing this interest as something to be secured in and of itself, it would seem that the aggressions of a type of unscrupulous journalism, the invasions of privacy by reporters in competition for a 'story,' the activities of photographers, and the temptation to advertisers to sacrifice private feelings to their individual gain call upon the law to do more in the attempt to secure this interest than merely take incidental account of infringements of it. A man's feelings are as much a part of his personality as his limbs. The actions that protect the latter from injury may well be made to protect the former by the ordinary process of legal growth. The problems are rather to devise suitable redress and to limit the right in view of other interests involved." "Interests of Personality," 28 Harv. L. Rev. 362. . . .

As to names, it is the general rule (although, as we have observed, there is authority to the contrary) that a person has no such exclusive right to the use of his own name as to prevent the assumption of its use by another. But it is different when one's own name is used in such a way as to amount to unfair competition. In connection with questions of that kind, a man's name is said to be his own property. . . .

By analogy to this principle, there ought to be little difficulty today in deciding a question such as that involved in the Roberson case in favor of the one asserting the exclusive right to the use of his own picture as against appropriation by another for the purpose of advertising his wares; for selling one's likeness to be so used is today a business in itself. Faces, some faces, at any rate, have a recognized commercial value. The face of the plaintiff in the Roberson case must have had such value, else the defendants would not have gone to the trouble and expense of reproducing and distributing broadcast her likeness. If it was of value to the defendants, why not let her, even though she preferred not to, capitalize upon it? Said Judge Gray in his dissenting opinion in the Roberson case:

"Property is not, necessarily, the thing itself which is owned; it is the right of the owner in relation to it. The right to be protected in one's possession of a thing or in one's privileges, belonging to him as an individual, or secured to him as a member of the commonwealth, is property, and as such entitled to the protection of the law."

But we deem it unnecessary to search for a right of property, or a contract, or a relation of confidence. The question is whether a right of privacy, distinct and of itself and not incidental to some other long recognized right, is to be accepted by the courts and a violation of the right held actionable. We are called upon, as Mr. Justice Holmes says somewhere, "to exercise the sovereign prerogative of choice" between the view that the courts for want of a precedent are impotent to grant redress for injury resulting from conduct which universal opinion in a state of civilized society would unhesitatingly condemn as indecent and outrageous, and the view that the common law, with its capacity for growth and expansion and its adaptability to the needs and requirements of changing conditions, contains within itself the resources of principle upon which relief in such a case can be founded. As the court said in Clark v. Associated Retail Credit Men, 70 App. D.C. 183, 105 F.2d 62, 64: "We cannot evade this duty; for unless we establish a right in the plaintiff we establish a privilege or immunity in the defendant."

Our consideration of the subject leads us to the conclusion that natural justice and the needs of the society in which we live should prevail over objections based upon the novelty of the asserted cause of action. It is time that fictions be abandoned and the real character of the injury be frankly avowed. When Brandeis and Warren wrote in 1890, that it was the unseemly intrusions of a portion of the press into the privacy of the home that was emphasized as the main source of evil; since then motion pictures and the radio have been perfected and have taken their places among our great industries, while instantaneous photography today accomplishes miracles scarcely dreamed of fifty years ago. Thus, the potentialities for this character of wrong are now greatly multiplied. A decision against the right of privacy would be nothing less than an invitation to those so inclined who control these instrumentalities of communication, information, and education, to put them to base uses, with complete immunity, and without regard to the hurt done to the sensibilities of individuals whose private affairs might be exploited, whether out of malice or for selfish purposes.

We should not be deterred by fear of being accused of judicial legislation. Much of our law is judge-made, and there are those who think that it is the best law. Cardozo, "The Growth of the Law," p. 133. The common law's capacity to discover and apply remedies for acknowledged wrongs without waiting on legislation is one of its cardinal virtues. The so-called "family purpose doctrine," approved by this court in McDowell v. Hurner, 142 Or. 611, 13 P.2d 600, 20 P.2d 395, 88 A.L.R. 578, is a creation of the courts, and so, as Mr. Justice Bailey points out in the opinion in that case, are the defenses of fellow-servant, assumption of risk and contributory negligence. Courts cannot, of course, as Sir Frederick Pollock says in "The Expansion of the Common Law," p. 49, "lay down any rule they choose." He continues, however: "They may supplement and enlarge the law as they find it, or rather they must do so from time to time, as the novelty of questions coming before them may require; but they must not reverse what has been settled."

The opinion of the court in the Roberson case, after an exaggerated statement, as we view it, of what is claimed for the right of privacy, dwelt upon the absurd consequences which it was conceived would follow from the acceptance of the doctrine. "The attempts to logically apply the principle," it was said, "will necessarily result not only in a vast amount of litigation, but in litigation bordering upon the absurd." It was not stated that the litigation then before the court was absurd. It may be doubted whether any court today would render the decision that the New York court did in that case, and there is reason to believe that the accuracy of Justice Cobb's prediction, above quoted, as to the attitude of the American Bar toward that decision may already have been demonstrated. Be that as it may, all judicial decisions, as Mr. Justice Holmes once said, "are a series of points tending to fix a point in a line." 2 Holmes, Pollock Letters, 28. When a legal principle is pushed to an absurdity, the principle is not abandoned, but the absurdity avoided. The courts are competent, we think, to deal with difficulties of the sort suggested, and case by case, through the traditional process of inclusion and exclusion, gradually to develop the fullness of the principle and its limitations. That there are difficulties may be conceded. They arise especially in that class of cases where the complaint is founded on unwanted publicity and are well illustrated by the recent case of Sidis v. F-R Publishing Corp., 2 Cir., 113 F.2d 806, 809, where the action was brought by a quondam infant prodigy, once much in the public eye, who had sought out for himself a life of obscurity from which he was rudely lifted by a magazine article. He sued the publishers of the magazine. The court held, rightly as we think, that since the plaintiff's subsequent history "was still a matter of public concern" and the article possessed "considerable popular news interest," the plaintiff's right of privacy had not been invaded. In such cases, other interests, such, for example, as the freedom of the press, are involved, and the courts must needs proceed cautiously. We are not embarrassed by questions of that kind here, and can do nothing for their discussion until they arise.

The objection is urged that the law does not give redress for mental anguish alone, and that no other damage is alleged in the complaint in the instant case. The rule invoked is the law in this state. . . . But it is well settled that where the wrongful act constitutes an infringement of a legal right, mental suffering may be recovered for, if it is a direct, proximate and natural result of the wrongful act. . . . Violation of the right of privacy is a wrong of that character.

The damages may be difficult of ascertainment, but not more so than in actions for malicious prosecutions, breach of promise of marriage, or alienation of affections, and in many cases of libel, slander and assault. The law has never denied recovery to one entitled to damages simply because of uncertainty as to the extent of his injury and the amount which would properly compensate him.

It remains only to say that the complaint plainly states a cause of action for breach of the plaintiff's right of privacy. If the facts are as alleged, the defendants appropriated to themselves for their own purposes, without the plaintiff's consent and against his will, his name, his personality and whatever influence he may have possessed, and injected them into a political controversy in which, as far as appears, he had no interest. This they had no legal right to do, and on account of their wrong the plaintiff is entitled to recover nominal damages at least, and any additional damages for injury to his feelings that he may be able to prove, besides punitive damages if there was actual malice. He is not entitled to damages, however, on the theory that the defendants' acts endangered his position or his retirement rights as an employe of the government, since, although it possibly would have been a violation of the United States Civil Service Rules for the plaintiff to have sent the telegram himself, he did not in fact do so, and it cannot be assumed that he would have been penalized for misconduct of which he was not guilty.

It is, perhaps, needless to add that, the case being here on demurrer, our decision is necessarily based upon the assumption that the allegations of the complaint are true. What defense there may be to the charge remains to be seen.

The judgment is reversed, and the cause is remanded with directions to overrule the demurrer to the complaint, and for further proceedings.

Notes

1. The cause of action in *Hinish v. Meier & Frank Co.* is described as "an invasion of a right of privacy." The "act" is the signing of another's name to a telegram which was sent without the consent or knowledge of the plaintiff. The recognition of the right of privacy made it a "legal act," i.e., one for which the defendant could be held liable. Suppose the existence of the legal right had been denied. What sort of "act" would it be then? What grounds are there for calling it a moral (or immoral) act? Do you agree with the judge that "natural justice and the needs of the society" require its recognition? If the right of privacy is a genuinely moral right, are those courts which deny it legal status acting immorally?

2. The main point of Judge Cardozo's opinion in *Palsgraf v. Long Island R. R. Co.* is that the conduct of the guard, though negligent with respect to the passenger possibly, was not so with respect to the plaintiff. Since there was no foreseeable hazard to her, no duty of care was owed to her. In other words, Cardozo emphasizes the notion of "duty" as a basis of finding negligence. Judge Andrews, on the other hand, emphasizes the notion of "causation." He reasons that if the defendant's act unreasonably endangers the rights of others, no matter whose, then the defendant is responsible for all its proximate consequences. Both agree that negligence is a type of conduct rather than a state of mind. The issue between them is only whether a "negligent act" is a relative concept. Since Cardozo fails to discover the requisite relation to the plaintiff, doesn't it follow that on his view there simply was no "act" at all? Does this make sense? What then did the guard "do"? On the other hand, Andrews finds an act which was wrongful (negligent) to "anybody" who might be affected by it—a "wrong to the public at large." Does this make any better sense? Did the guard do something to the public at large? Are there such abstract or general acts?

3. Compare the case of *People v. Lewis* with that of *Watson v. Kentucky & Indiana Bridge & R. R. Co.* (Chapter 2). In the latter, the judge said that if Duerr was malicious in throwing the lighted match in the presence of gasoline fumes, then the defendant could not be "bound to anticipate the criminal acts of others by which damage is inflicted and hence is not liable therefor." However, such an intentional act was not found, and the judgment in favor of the Railroad Co. was reversed. Suppose it had been found that the knife wound inflicted by the de-

ceased in *People v. Lewis* was an intentional act of suicide. Would this intentional and intervening act have excused the defendant? If not, explain the difference in the two cases. Compare also the relative difficulty in establishing the existence of an intention in the respective cases.

4. What's the difference between an "accident" and an "act"? Cf. *Vosburg v. Putney*. Why did the judge in that case conclude that the intention of the defendant was "unlawful" even though the jury found that he didn't intend to do the other boy any harm? Are several senses of "intention" being employed in this case? To what law or kind of law is the judge referring when he speaks of the act as an "unlawful" one?

5. The case of *State v. Rider* makes clear the policy of the law not to hold persons responsible merely for their thoughts. Some moral philosophers would make persons (morally) responsible only for their thoughts and intentions. Does this indicate a basic and irreconcilable difference between the spheres of law and morals?

Does it make sense to talk of "mental acts"? Does it make any more sense to talk of exclusively "physical acts"?

6. In law and in morals, we are often held responsible for our omissions as well as for our commissions. Cf. *Kimble v. MacKintosh Hemphill Co.* Also, just as we are not held responsible for all that we do, so we are not held responsible for all that we do not do. Is the problem of responsibility the same in both cases then, or are there special problems in regard to omissions? For instance, is there a difference between "doing nothing" and "not doing something"? Suppose a person stands by while another commits suicide. Is this an act, an omission, or neither?

5

LEGAL NORMS

A first condition for making a legal judgment of responsibility is the finding of an act. The act must then be shown to be related to a legal norm; that is to say, it must be shown to fall within the class of human acts of which the law takes cognizance. Thus, if someone breaks a promise to himself, no doubt he "did" something, but not something with which the law concerns itself. On the other hand, if he attempts suicide, or finds a hidden treasure, these acts are among those which are related to certain "legal norms."

The term "legal norm" covers quite a variety of different things. It denotes *concepts,* such as the concept of possession; *rules,* such as the rule that the finder of lost property has a right to it against all except the true owner; *standards,* such as the general requirement that one who engages in an activity which creates a risk of harm to others must exercise reasonable care. It denotes other legal bases for decision such as *principles* and *maxims,* as well. Their functions in legal reasoning are considerably different, as the cases will suggest, but what they all have in common, at the very least, is a reference to those types of human behavior to which legal responsibility may be ascribed.

It cannot be taken for granted, however, that in making a judgment of legal responsibility the tasks of both finding an act and relating or applying a legal norm are wholly separate processes. At times they appear to be, but at other times they do not. For example, to prove that A acted negligently with respect to B, it is as necessary to find that A violated a relevant rule or standard as it is to find that A did something which caused B's injury. Sometimes these matters are established separately; in some cases, establishing the one establishes the other, or, as was the case in *Palsgraf v. Long Island R. R. Co.* (Chapter 4), the failure to prove that A violated a standard of care with respect to the plaintiff was sufficient to warrant the claim that there was no act relative to the plaintiff.

One's theory of an act (as discussed in the last chapter) has an important bearing upon how one views the relationship between the two processes. If, for instance, a person adopts the traditional theory of an act as a volition plus an overt physical movement, no doubt he will attempt to analyze the problem of making and justifying a legal judgment by asking two distinct questions: (1) what is the act? and (2) what legal norm is this act related to or subsumed under?

Whether this approach will be useful in analyzing all the cases is questionable. As we saw in the previous chapter, this theory of an act is suggested by some of the cases but not by others. Some of the cases lend themselves to the quite different theory that an act is an item of behavior which is "rule governed," as a chess move, for example, is describable only by reference to the relevant chess rules. On this latter theory, the finding of an act cannot be viewed as logically distinct from the process of relating a norm.

But whether these processes are logically distinct or not, for the purpose of analysis at least they may be dealt with separately. If they are in fact distinct, there is no problem. If they are in fact logically identical, then even the same process may be viewed from different perspectives and this in itself is instructive. The "perspective" of the last chapter, it may then be said, is the perspective of an "act." In this chapter, the perspective on the process of making and justifying a judgment of legal responsibility is the perspective of "norms," their kinds, and how they function is legal reasoning.

The case of *Durfee v. Jones* illustrates the function of legal concepts, specifically the following: "possession," "ownership," "lost" and "mislaid" property. A blacksmith is entrusted with an old safe and is authorized to sell it for the owner. Upon examining it he finds some money secreted within the lining. Is he entitled to keep the money by "right of possession," or does the owner of the safe, merely by virtue of that ownership, have a "right of prior possession"? Which rule applies depends on the application of the concept of possession. Did the owner of the safe, who was quite unaware of its contents until they were found, ever in fact possess the money? In a similar way it is argued by the defendant that the money was lost property, and that with regard to such cases the controlling rule is "finders keepers." A different rule seems indicated if the property was merely "mislaid." It becomes clear that the chief function of legal concepts is to provide a basis for the selection of certain relevant rules.

In *Hynes v. New York R. Co.*, a boy is killed while about to dive into the Harlem River from a plank attached to the defendant's property. He is struck by a crossarm and some electric wires falling from a nearby pole which the defendant had failed to keep in good repair. The defendant claims that the boy was a "trespasser," and that therefore he owed the boy no duty of care. He insists that the concept of trespasser as related to the facts of this case so dictates this conclusion that no other is possible in either logic or law. The lower court apparently agreed. Judge Cardozo does not see it that way. He admits that the victim was a trespasser in a technical sense (the board was affixed to the defendant's land), but he also finds that he can equally be regarded as a "user of the public ways" (the river was a public waterway). The different concepts give rise to two competitive rules: (1) "Landowners are not bound to regulate their conduct in contemplation of the presence of trespassers intruding upon private structures," and (2) "Landowners *are* bound to regulate their conduct in contemplation of the presence of travelers upon the adjacent public ways." The choice of the latter rule as the controlling norm is then based on considerations other than the applicable concepts and rules themselves.

"Rules" are not easily distinguished from "standards." The two expressions are commonly used synonymously, both in law and in morals. Yet, in ordinary discourse and in legal cases, rules tend to have characteristics somewhat different from standards. For example, rules tend to be more specific in their reference to fact situations than do standards. Furthermore, the fact situations to which rules relate tend to be more or less typical or uniform. Standards, being more abstractly expressed, are more applicable to "atypical" or extraordinary situations.

This difference is well illustrated by two decisions, one by Justice Holmes in *Baltimore & Ohio R. R. Co. v. Goodman,* and another by Justice Cardozo in *Pokora v. Wabash Ry. Co.* Both involve the same type of fact situation—a truck driver is struck by a train while attempting to cross its tracks. The issue is whether the driver contributed to the injury by his own negligence. Justice Holmes lays down the rule that under these circumstances the driver should "stop and look" and if necessary get out of his vehicle to view the situation before proceeding. Justice Cardozo doubts the advisability of such a detailed prescription and urges that the eccentricities of each situation must be taken into account before allowing the jury to apply a general "standard of reasonable care." These two opinions, especially Justice Cardozo's, raise serious questions about the utility of attempting to reduce standards to rules as bases of judgment.

Such then are some of the kinds of norms to which judges appeal in passing their judgments. It is to be noted that neither concepts, rules, nor standards, in themselves determine the wrongfulness of a given act, or a person's responsibility for it. A rule, for example, which states that

X owes a duty to Y only initiates the query whether defendant A and plaintiff B are "substitution instances" of the variables X and Y, such that a duty exists which A has failed to fulfill, and for which act he has no excuse or justification. These latter substantive questions must of course be answered before responsibility can be assigned. The primary role of the legal norm is to supply a rational basis for the judgment of wrong and/or responsibility. It is, in this sense, a formal requirement of legal judgment.

Erie Railroad Co. v. Tompkins raises a somewhat different issue regarding the bases of legal judgment from those brought out in the preceding cases. It reveals not only how many different kinds of law there are, but also how many different bodies or codes of law there are, or are thought to be: statutory, common, local, general, substantive, procedural, federal, state, and even "transcendental." The list could be extended. A judge is sometimes required to make a choice not merely between rules, but between whole bodies of rules on which to rest his judgment. What considerations must then be taken into account? Justice Brandeis bases his decision in *Erie Railroad Co. v. Tompkins* largely on the demand for "equal protection of the law." It is relevant to ask whether this constitutional requirement isn't a moral requirement as well.

The final case in this chapter, *Rochin v. California,* comes perhaps closer than any of the others to raising the question whether there are not times when the legal norm is itself an independent moral norm. The Due Process Clause of the Fourteenth Amendment is spoken of as "a summarized constitutional guarantee" of respect for those personal immunities which are "so rooted in the traditions and conscience of our people as to be ranked as fundamental." They are called "standards of justice," not to be confused with the judges' "own merely personal and private notions," nor, on the other hand, derided as a "resort to a revival of 'natural law.'" They are "canons of decency and fairness which express the nations of justice of English-speaking peoples."

The concurring opinion of Justice Black protests this interpretation of the Due Process Clause. He asks, for example, why the Court "should consider only the notions of English-speaking peoples to determine what are immutable and fundamental principles of justice." Or again, "What avenues of investigation are open to discover 'canons' of conduct so universally favored that this Court should write them into the Constitution?"

Rochin v. California also suggests questions about the ethics of the judgment process itself, and the moral legitimacy of persuasion based on wrongfully obtained evidence. These issues are further considered in Chapter 6.

LEGAL CONCEPTS

Durfee v. Jones

supreme court of rhode island, 1877

11 r.i. 588, 23 am. dec. 528

Assumpsit, heard by the court, jury trial being waived.

Durfee, C.J. The facts in this case are briefly these: In April 1874, the plaintiff bought an old safe and soon afterwards instructed his agent to sell it again. The agent offered to sell it to the defendant for ten dollars, but the defendant refused to buy it. The agent then left it with the defendant, who was a blacksmith, at his shop for sale for ten dollars, authorizing him to keep his books in it until it was sold or reclaimed. The safe was old-fashioned, of sheet-iron, about three feet square, having a few pigeon-holes and a place for books, and back of the place for books a large crack in the lining. The defendant shortly after the safe was left, upon examining it, found secreted between the sheet-iron exterior and the wooden lining a roll of bills amounting to $165, of the denomination of the national bank bills which have been current for the last ten or twelve years. Neither the plaintiff nor the defendant knew the money was there before it was found. The owner of the money is still unknown. The defendant informed the plaintiff's agent that he had found it, and offered it to him for the plaintiff; but the agent declined it, stating that it did not belong to either himself or the plaintiff and advised the defendant to deposit it where it would be drawing interest until the rightful owner appeared. The plaintiff was then out of the city. Upon his return, being informed of the finding, he immediately called on the defendant and asked for the money, but the defendant refused to give it to him. He then, after taking advice, demanded the return of the safe and its contents, precisely as they existed when placed in the defendant's hands. The defendant promptly gave up the safe, but retained the money. This plaintiff brings this action to recover it or its equivalent.

The plaintiff does not claim that he acquired, by purchasing the safe, any right to the money in the safe as against the owner; for he bought the safe alone, not the safe and its contents. See Merry v. Green, 7 M. & W. 623. But he claims that as between himself and the defendant his is the better right. The defendant, however, has the possession, and therefore it is for the plaintiff, in order to succeed in his action, to prove his better right.

The plaintiff claims that he is entitled to have the money by right of prior possession. But the plaintiff never had any possession of the money, except, unwittingly, by having possession of the safe which contained it. Such possession, if possession it can be called, does not of itself confer a right. The case at bar is in this view like Bridges v. Hawkesworth, 15 Jur. 1079; 21 L.J.Q.B. 75, A.D. 1851; 7 Eng. L. & Eq. 424. In that case, the plaintiff while in the defendant's shop on business, picked up from the floor a parcel containing bank notes. He gave them to the defendant for the owner if he could be found. The owner could not be found, and it was held that the plaintiff as finder was entitled to them, as against the defendant as owner of the shop in which they were found. "The notes," said the court, "never were in custody of the defendant nor within the protection of his house, before they were found, as they would have been if they had been intentionally deposited there." The same in effect may be said of the notes in the case at bar; for though they were originally deposited in the safe by design, they were not so deposited in the safe, after it became the plaintiff's safe, so as to be in the protection of the safe as his safe, or as to affect him with any responsibility for them. The case at bar is also in this respect like Tatum v. Sharpless, 6 Phila. 18. There it was held, that a conductor who found money which had been lost in a railroad car was entitled to it as against the railroad company.

The plaintiff also claims that the money was not lost but designedly left where it was found, and that therefore as owner of the safe he is entitled to its custody. He refers to cases in which it has been held, that money or other property voluntarily laid down and forgotten is not in legal contemplation lost, and that of such money or property the owner of the shop or place where it is left is the proper custodian rather than the person who happens to discover it first. State v. McCann, 19 Mo. 249; Lawrence v. The State, 1 Humph. 228; McAvoy v. Medina, 11 Allen, 549. It may be questioned whether this distinction has not been pushed to an extreme. See Kincaid v. Eaton, 98 Mass. 139. But, however that may be, we think the money here, though designedly left in the safe, was probably not designedly put in the crevice or interspace where it was found, but that, being left in the safe, it probably slipped or was accidentally shoved into the place where it was found without the knowledge of the owner, and so was lost, in the strictest sense of the word. The money was not simply deposited and forgotten, but deposited and lost by reason of a defect or insecurity in the place of deposit.

The plaintiff claims that the finding was a wrongful act on the part of the defendant, and that therefore he is entitled to recover the money or to have it replaced. We do not so regard it. The safe was left with the defendant for sale. As seller he would properly examine it under an implied permission to do so, to qualify him the better to act as seller. Also under the permission to use it for his books, he would have the right to inspect it to see if it was a fit depository. And finally, as a possible purchaser he might examine it, for though he had once declined to purchase, he might on closer examination change his mind. And the defendant, having found in the safe something which did not belong there, might, we think, properly remove it. He certainly would not be expected either to sell the safe to another, or to buy it himself without first removing it. It is not pretended that he used any violence or did any harm to the safe. And it is evident that the idea that any trespass or tort had been committed did not even occur to the plaintiff's agent when he was first informed of the finding.

The general rule undoubtedly is, that the finder of lost property is entitled to it against all the world except the real owner, and that ordinarily the place where it is found does not make any difference. We can not find anything in the circumstances of the case at bar to take it out of this rule.

We give the defendant judgment for costs.

COMPETITIVE RULES

Hynes v. New York Central R. Co.

COURT OF APPEALS OF NEW YORK, 1921
231 N.Y. 229, 131 N.E. 898

CARDOZO, J. On July 8, 1916, Harvey Hynes, a lad of six-teen, swam with two companions from the Manhattan to the Bronx side of the Harlem river or United States Ship canal, a navigable stream. Along the Bronx side of the river was the right of way of the defendant, the New York Central railroad, which operated its trains at that point by high tension wires, strung on poles and crossarms. Projecting from the defendant's bulkhead above the waters of the river was a plank or springboard from which boys of the neighborhood used to dive. One end of the board had been placed under a rock on the defendant's land, and nails had been driven at its point of contact with the bulkhead. Measured from this point of contact the length behind was five feet; the length in front eleven. The bulkhead itself was about three and a half feet back of the pier line as located by the gov-ernment. From this it follows that for seven and a half feet the springboard was beyond the line of the defendant's property, and above the public waterway. Its height measured from the stream was three feet at the bulkhead, and five feet at its outermost extremity. For more than five years swimmers had used it as a diving board without protest or obstruction.

On this day Hynes and his companions climbed on top of the bulkhead intending to leap into the water. One of them made the plunge in safety. Hynes followed to the front of the springboard, and stood poised for his dive. At that moment a crossarm with electric wires fell from the defendant's pole. The wires struck the diver, flung him from the shattered board, and plunged him to his death below. His mother, suing as administratrix, brings this action for her damages. Thus far the courts have held that Hynes at the end of the springboard above the public waters was a trespasser on the defendant's land. They have thought it immaterial that the board itself was a trespass, an encroachment on the public ways. They have thought it of no significance that Hynes would have met the same fate if he had been below the board and not above it. The board, they have said, was annexed to the defendant's bulkhead. By force of such annexation, it was to be reckoned as a fixture, and thus constructively, if not actually, an extension of the land. The defendant was under a duty to use reasonable care that bathers swimming or standing in the water should not be electrocuted by wires falling from its right of way. But to bathers diving from the springboard, there was no duty, we are told, unless the injury was the product of mere willfulness or wantonness, no duty of active vigilance to safeguard the impending structure. Without wrong to them, crossarms might be left to rot; wires highly charged with electricity might sweep them from their stand, and bury them in the subjacent waters. In climbing on the board, they became trespassers and outlaws. The conclusion is defended with much subtlety of reasoning, with much insistence upon its inevitableness as a merely logical deduction. A majority of the court are unable to accept it as the conclusion of the law.

We assume, without deciding, that the springboard was a fixture, a permanent improvement of the defendant's right of way. Much might be said in favor of another view. We do not press the inquiry, for we are persuaded that the rights of the bathers do not depend upon these nice distinctions. Liability would not be doubtful, we are told, had the boy been diving from a pole, if the pole had been vertical. The diver in such a situation would have been separated from the defendant's freehold. Liability, it is said, has been escaped because the pole was horizontal. The plank when projected lengthwise was an extension of the soil. We are to concentrate our gaze on the private ownership of the board. We are to ignore the public ownership of the circumambient spaces of water and of air. Jumping from a boat or a barrel, the boy would have been a bather in the river. Jumping from the end of a springboard, he was no longer, it is said, a bather, but a trespasser on a right of way.

Rights and duties in systems of living law are not built upon such quicksands.

Bathers in the Harlem river on the day of this disaster were in the enjoyment of a public highway, entitled to reasonable protection against destruction by the defendant's wires. They did not cease to be bathers entitled to the same protection while they were diving from encroaching objects or engaging in the sports that are common among swimmers. Such acts were not equivalent to an abandonment of the highway, a departure from its proper uses, a withdrawal from the waters, and an entry upon land. A plane or private right had been interposed between the river and the air, but public ownership was unchanged in the space below it and above. The defendant does not deny that it would have owed a duty to this boy if he had been leaning against the springboard with his feet upon the ground. He is said to have forfeited protection as he put his feet upon the plank. Presumably the same result would follow if the plank had been a few inches above the surface of the water instead of a few feet. Duties are thus supposed to arise and to be extinguished in alternate zones or strata. Two boys walking in the country or swimming in a river stop to rest for a moment along side of the road or the margin of the stream. One of them throws himself beneath the overhanging branches of a tree. The other perches himself on a bough a foot or so above the ground (Hoffman v. Armstrong, 48 N.Y. 201). Both are killed by falling wires. The defendant would have us say that there is a remedy for the representatives of one, and none for the representatives of the other. We may be permitted to distrust the logic that leads to such conclusions.

The truth is that every act of Hynes from his first plunge into the river until the moment of his death, was in the enjoyment of the public waters, and under cover of the protection which his presence in those waters gave him. The use of the springboard was not an abandonment of his rights as bather. It was a mere by-play, an incident, subordinate and ancillary to the execution of his primary purpose, the enjoyment of the highway. The by-play, the incident, was not the *cause* of the disaster.

Hynes would have gone to his death if he had been below the springboard or beside it (Laidlaw v. Sage, 158 N.Y. 73, 97). The wires were not stayed by the presence of the plank. They followed the boy in his fall, and overwhelmed him in the waters. The defendant assumes that the identification of the ownership of a fixture with ownership of land is complete in every incident. But there are important elements of difference. Title to the fixture, unlike title to the land, does not carry with its rights of ownership usque ad coelum. There will hardly be denial that a cause of action would have arisen if the wires had fallen on an aeroplane proceeding above the river, though the location of the impact would be identified as the space above the springboard. The most that the defendant can fairly ask is exemption from liability where the use of the fixture is itself the efficient peril. That would be the situation, for example, if the weight of the boy upon the board had caused it to break and thereby throw him into the river. There is no such causal connection here between his position and his injuries. We think there was no moment when he was beyond the pale of the defendant's duty—the duty of care and vigilance in the storage of destructive forces.

This case is a striking instance of the dangers of "a jurisprudence of conceptions" (Pound, Mechanical Jurisprudence, 8 Columbia Law Review, 605, 608, 610), the extension of a maxim or a definition with relentless disregard of consequences to a "dryly logical extreme." The approximate and relative become the definite and absolute. Landowners are not bound to regulate their conduct in contemplation of the presence of trespassers intruding upon private structures. Landowners *are* bound to regulate their conduct in contemplation of the presence of travelers upon the adjacent public ways. There are times when there is little trouble in marking off the field of exemption and immunity from that of liability and duty. Here structures and ways are so united and commingled, superimposed upon each other, that the fields are brought together. In such circumstances, there is little help in pursuing general maxims to ultimate conclusions. They have been framed alio intuitu. They must be reformulated and readapted to meet exceptional conditions. Rules appropriate to spheres which are conceived of as separate and distinct cannot, both, be enforced when the spheres become concentric. There must then be readjustment or collision. In one sense, and that a highly technical and artificial one, the diver at the end of the springboard is an intruder on the adjoining lands. In another sense, and one that realists will accept more readily, he is still on public waters in the exercise of public rights. The law must say whether it will subject him to the rule of the one field or of the other, of this sphere or of that. We think that considerations of analogy, of convenience, of policy, and of justice, exclude him from the field of the defendant's immunity and exemption, and place him in the field of liability and duty. . . .

The judgment of the Appellate Division and that of the Trial Term should be reversed, and a new trial granted, with costs to abide the event.

HOGAN, POUND, and CRANE, J.J., concur.

HISCOCK, C.J., and CHASE and McLAUGHLIN, J.J., dissent. Judgments reversed, etc.

RULES VERSUS STANDARDS

Baltimore & Ohio R.R. v. Goodman

SUPREME COURT OF THE UNITED STATES, 1927
275 U.S. 66, 48 SUP. CT. 24

MR. JUSTICE HOLMES delivered the opinion of the Court.

This is a suit brought by the widow and administratrix of Nathan Goodman against the petitioner for causing his death by running him down at a grade crossing. The defence is that Goodman's own negligence caused the death. At the trial, the defendant asked the Court to direct a verdict for it, but the request, and others looking to the same direction, were refused, and the plaintiff got a verdict and a judgment which was affirmed by the Circuit Court of Appeals. 10 F.(2d) 58.

Goodman was driving an automobile truck in an easterly direction and was killed by a train running southwesterly across the road at a rate of not less than sixty miles an hour. The line was straight, but it is said by the respondent that Goodman "had no practical view" beyond a section house two hundred and forty-three feet north of the crossing until he was about twenty feet from the first rail, or, as the respondent argues, twelve feet from danger, and then the engine was still obscured by the section house. He had been driving at the rate of ten or twelve miles an hour, but had cut down his rate to five or six miles at about forty feet from the crossing. It is thought that there was an emergency in which, so far as appears, Goodman did all that he could.

We do not go into further details as to Goodman's precise situation, beyond mentioning that it was daylight and that he was familiar with the crossing, for it appears to us plain that nothing is suggested by the evidence to relieve Goodman from responsibility for his own death. When a man goes upon a railroad track he knows that he goes to a place where he will be killed if a train comes upon him before he is clear of the track. He knows that he must stop for the train, not the train stop for him. In such circumstances it seems to us that if a driver cannot be sure otherwise whether a train is dangerously near he must stop and get out of his vehicle, although obviously he will not often be required to do more than to stop and look. It seems to us that if he relies upon not hearing the train or any signal and takes no further precaution he does so at his own risk. If at the last moment Goodman found himself in an emergency it was his own fault that he did not reduce his speed earlier or come to a stop. It is true as said in Flannelly v. Delaware & Hudson Co., 225 U.S. 597, 603, that the question of due care very generally is left to the jury. But we are dealing with a standard of conduct, and when the standard is clear it should be laid down once for all by the Courts. See Southern Pacific Co. v. Berkshire, 254 U.S. 415, 417, 419.

Judgment reversed.

STANDARDS VERSUS RULES

Pokora v. Wabash Ry. Co.

supreme court of the united states, 1934
292 u.s. 98, 54 sup. ct. 580

Mr. Justice Cardozo delivered the opinion of the Court.

John Pokora, driving his truck across a railway grade crossing in the city of Springfield, Ill., was struck by a train and injured. Upon the trial of his suit for damages, the District Court held that he had been guilty of contributory negligence, and directed a verdict for the defendant. The Circuit Court of Appeals (one judge dissenting) affirmed [66 F.2d 166], resting its judgment on the opinion of this court in B. & O. R. Co. v. Goodman, 275 U.S. 66, 48 S. Ct. 24, 25, 72 L. Ed. 167, 56 A.L.R. 645. A writ of certiorari brings the case here.

Pokora was an ice dealer, and had come to the crossing to load his truck with ice. The tracks of the Wabash Railway are laid along Tenth street, which runs north and south. There is a crossing at Edwards street running east and west. Two ice depots are on opposite corners of Tenth and Edwards streets; one at the northeast corner, the other at the southwest. Pokora, driving west along Edwards street, stopped at the first of these corners to get his load of ice, but found so many trucks ahead of him that he decided to try the depot on the other side of the way. In this crossing of the railway, the accident occurred.

The defendant has four tracks on Tenth street; a switch track on the east, then the main track, and then two switches. Pokora, as he left the northeast corner where his truck had been stopped, looked to the north for approaching trains. He did this at a point

about ten or fifteen feet east of the switch ahead of him. A string
of box cars standing on the switch, about five to ten feet from
the north line of Edwards street, cut off his view of the tracks beyond him to the north. At the same time he listened. There was
neither bell nor whistle. Still listening, he crossed the switch, and
reaching the main track was struck by a passenger train coming from the north at a speed of twenty-five to thirty miles an
hour. . . .

The argument is made, however, that our decision in B. &
O. R. Co. v. Goodman, supra, is a barrier in the plaintiff's path,
irrespective of the conclusion that might commend itself if the
question were at large. There is no doubt that the opinion in that
case is correct in its result. Goodman, the driver, traveling only
five or six miles an hour, had, before reaching the track, a clear
space of eighteen feet within which the train was plainly visible.
With that opportunity, he fell short of the legal standard of duty
established for a traveler when he failed to look and see. This was
decisive of the case. But the court did not stop there. It added a
remark, unnecessary upon the facts before it, which has been a
fertile source of controversy. "In such circumstances it seems to
us that if a driver cannot be sure otherwise whether a train is
dangerously near he must stop and get out of his vehicle, although
obviously he will not often be required to do more than to stop
and look."

There is need at this stage to clear the ground of brushwood
that may obscure the point at issue. We do not now inquire into
the existence of a duty to stop, disconnected from a duty to get
out and reconnoitre. The inquiry, if pursued, would lead us into
the thickets of conflicting judgments. Some courts apply what is
often spoken of as the Pennsylvania rule, and impose an unyield-
ing duty to stop, as well as to look and listen, no matter how clear
the crossing or the tracks on either side. . . .

Other courts, the majority, adopt the rule that the traveler
must look and listen, but that the existence of a duty to stop
depends upon the circumstances, and hence generally, even if not
invariably, upon the judgment of the jury. . . . The subject has
been less considered in this court, but in none of its opinions is
there a suggestion that at any and every crossing the duty to stop
is absolute, irrespective of the danger. Not even in B. & O. R. Co.

v. Goodman, supra, which goes farther than the earlier cases, is there support for such a rule. To the contrary, the opinion makes it clear that the duty is conditioned upon the presence of impediments whereby sight and hearing become inadequate for the traveler's protection. . . .

Choice between these diversities of doctrine is unnecessary for the decision of the case at hand. Here the fact is not disputed that the plaintiff did stop before he started to cross the tracks. If we assume that by reason of the box cars, there was a duty to stop again when the obstructions had been cleared, that duty did not arise unless a stop could be made safely after the point of clearance had been reached. See, e.g., Dobson v. St. Louis-S.F. Ry. Co., supra. For reasons already stated, the testimony permits the inference that the truck was in the zone of danger by the time the field of vision was enlarged. No stop would then have helped the plaintiff if he remained seated on his truck, or so the triers of the facts might find. His case was for the jury, unless as a matter of law he was subject to a duty to get out of the vehicle before it crossed the switch, walk forward to the front, and then, afoot, survey the scene. We must say whether his failure to do this was negligence so obvious and certain that one conclusion and one only is permissible for rational and candid minds. . . .

Standards of prudent conduct are declared at times by courts, but they are taken over from the facts of life. To get out of a vehicle and reconnoitre is an uncommon precaution, as everyday experience informs us. Besides being uncommon, it is very likely to be futile, and sometimes even dangerous. If the driver leaves his vehicle when he nears a cut or curve, he will learn nothing by getting out about the perils that lurk beyond. By the time he regains his seat and sets his car in motion, the hidden train may be upon him. . . . Often the added safeguard will be dubious though the track happens to be straight, as it seems that this one was, at all events as far as the station, above five blocks to the north. A train traveling at a speed of thirty miles an hour will cover a quarter of a mile in the space of thirty seconds. It may thus emerge out of obscurity as the driver turns his back to regain the waiting car, and may then descend upon him suddenly when his car is on the track. Instead of helping himself by getting out, he might do better to press forward with all his faculties alert. So a train at a neighboring station, apparently at rest and harmless, may be transformed in a few seconds into an instrument of destruction. At times the course of safety may be different. One can figure to oneself a roadbed so level and unbroken that getting out will be a gain. Even then the balance of advantage depends on many circumstances and can be easily disturbed. Where was Pokora to leave his truck after getting out to reconnoitre? If he was to leave it on the switch, there was the possibility that the box cars would be shunted down upon him before he could regain his seat. The defendant did not show whether there was a locomotive at the forward end, or whether the cars were so few that a locomotive could be seen. If he was to leave his vehicle near the curb, there was even stronger reason to believe that the space to be covered in going back and forth would make his observations worthless. One must remember that while the traveler turns his eyes in one direction, a train or a loose engine may be approaching from the other.

Illustrations such as these bear witness to the need for caution in framing standards of behavior that amount to rules of law. The need is the more urgent when there is no background of experience out of which the standards have emerged. They are then, not the natural flowerings of behavior in its customary forms, but rules artificially developed, and imposed from without. Extraordinary situations may not wisely or fairly be subjected to tests or regulations that are fitting for the commonplace or normal. In default of the guide of customary conduct, what is suitable for the traveler caught in a mesh where the ordinary safeguards fail him is for the judgment of a jury. . . . The opinion in Goodman's Case has been a source of confusion in the federal courts to the extent that it imposes a standard for application by the judge, and has had only wavering support in the courts of the states. We limit it accordingly.

The judgment should be reversed, and the cause remanded for further proceedings in accordance with this opinion.

It is so ordered.

GENERAL LAW

Erie Railroad Co. v. Tompkins

SUPREME COURT OF THE UNITED STATES, 1938
304 U.S. 64, 58 SUP. CT. 817

Certiorari to the Circuit Court of Appeals for the Second Circuit.

Certiorari, 302 U.S. 671, to review the affirmance of a judgment recovered against the railroad company in an action for personal injuries. The accident was in Pennsylvania. The action was in New York, jurisdiction being based on diversity of citizenship.

MR. JUSTICE BRANDEIS delivered the opinion of the Court.*

The question for decision is whether the oft-challenged doctrine of Swift v. Tyson shall now be disapproved.

Tompkins, a citizen of Pennsylvania, was injured on a dark night by a passing freight train of the Erie Railroad Company while walking along its right of way at Hughestown in that State. He claimed that the accident occurred through negligence in the operation, or maintenance, of the train; that he was rightfully on the premises as licensee because on a commonly used beaten footpath which ran for a short distance alongside the tracks; and that he was struck by something which looked like a door projecting from one of the moving cars. To enforce that claim he brought an action in the federal court for southern New York, which had jurisdiction because the company is a corporation of that State. It denied liability; and the case was tried by a jury.

* Footnotes by the Court are omitted, as are the minority opinions.

The Erie insisted that its duty to Tompkins was no greater than that owed to a trespasser. It contended, among other things, that its duty to Tompkins, and hence its liability, should be determined in accordance with the Pennsylvania law; that under the law of Pennsylvania, as declared by its highest court, persons who use pathways along the railroad right of way—that is a longitudinal pathway as distinguished from a crossing—are to be deemed trespassers; and that the railroad is not liable for injuries to undiscovered trespassers resulting from its negligence, unless it be wanton or wilful. Tompkins denied that any such rule had been established by the decisions of the Pennsylvania courts; and contended that, since there was no statute of the State on the subject, the railroad's duty and liability is to be determined in federal courts as a matter of general law.

The trial judge refused to rule that the applicable law precluded recovery. The jury brought in a verdict of $30,000; and the judgment entered thereon was affirmed by the Circuit Court of Appeals, which held, 90 F. 2d 603, 604, that it was unnecessary to consider whether the law of Pennsylvania was as contended, because the question was one not of local, but of general, law and that "upon questions of general law the federal courts are free, in the absence of a local statute, to exercise independent judgment as to what the law is; and it is well settled that the question of the responsibility of a railroad for injuries caused by its servants is one of general law. . . . Where the public has made open and notorious use of a railroad right of way for a long period of time and without objection, the company owes to persons on such permissive pathway a duty of care in the operation of its trains. . . . It is likewise generally recognized law that a jury may find that negligence exists toward a pedestrian using a permissive path on the railroad right of way if he is hit by some object projecting from the side of the train."

The Erie had contended that application of the Pennsylvania rule was required, among other things, by § 34 of the Federal Judiciary Act of September 24, 1789, c. 20, 28 U. S. C. § 725, which provides:

"The laws of the several States, except where the Constitution, treaties, or statutes of the United States otherwise require or provide, shall be regarded as rules of decision in trials at common law, in the courts of the United States, in cases where they apply."

Because of the importance of the question whether the federal court was free to disregard the alleged rule of the Pennsylvania common law, we granted certiorari.

First. Swift v. Tyson, 16 Pet. 1, 18, held that federal courts exercising jurisdiction on the ground of diversity of citizenship need not, in matters of general jurisprudence, apply the unwritten law of the State as declared by its highest court; that they are free to exercise an independent judgment as to what the common law of the State is—or should be; . . .

The Court in applying the rule of § 34 to equity cases, in Mason v. United States, 260 U.S. 545, 559, said: "The statute, however, is merely declarative of the rule which would exist in the absence of the statute." The federal courts assumed, in the broad field of "general law," the power to declare rules of decision which Congress was confessedly without power to enact as statutes. Doubt was repeatedly expressed as to the correctness of the construction given § 34, and as to the soundness of the rule which it introduced. But it was the more recent research of a competent scholar, [Charles Warren, "New Light on the History of the Federal Judiciary Act of 1789," (1923) 37 Harv. L. Rev. 49] who examined the original document, which established that the construction given to it by the Court was erroneous; and that the purpose of the section was merely to make certain that, in all matters except those in which some federal law is controlling, the federal courts exercising jurisdiction in diversity of citizenship cases would apply as their rules of decision the law of the State, unwritten as well as written.

Criticism of the doctrine became widespread after the decision of Black & White Taxicab Co. v. Brown & Yellow Taxicab Co., 276 U.S. 518. There, Brown and Yellow, a Kentucky corporation owned by Kentuckians, and the Louisville and Nashville Railroad, also a Kentucky corporation, wished that the former should have the exclusive privilege of soliciting passenger and baggage transportation at the Bowling Green, Kentucky, railroad station; and that the Black and White, a competing Kentucky corporation, should be prevented from interfering with that privilege. Knowing that such a contract would be void under the common law of Kentucky, it was arranged that the Brown and

Yellow reincorporate under the law of Tennessee, and that the contract with the railroad should be executed there. The suit was then brought by the Tennessee corporation in the federal court for western Kentucky to enjoin competition by the Black and White; an injunction issued by the District Court was sustained by the Court of Appeals; and this Court, citing many decisions in which the doctrine of Swift v. Tyson had been applied, affirmed the decree.

Second. Experience in applying the doctrine of Swift v. Tyson, had revealed its defects, political and social; and the benefits expected to flow from the rule did not accrue. Persistence of state courts in their own opinions on questions of common law prevented uniformity; and the impossibility of discovering a satisfactory line of demarcation between the province of general law and that of local law developed a new well of uncertainties.

On the other hand, the mischievous results of the doctrine had become apparent. Diversity of citizenship jurisdiction was conferred in order to prevent apprehended discrimination in state courts against those not citizens of the State. Swift v. Tyson introduced grave discrimination by non-citizens against citizens. It made rights enjoyed under the unwritten "general law" vary according to whether enforcement was sought in the state or in the federal court; and the privilege of selecting the court in which the right should be determined was conferred upon the non-citizen. Thus, the doctrine rendered impossible equal protection of the law. In attempting to promote uniformity of law throughout the United States, the doctrine had prevented uniformity in the administration of the law of the State.

The discrimination resulting became in practice far-reaching. This resulted in part from the broad province accorded to the so-called "general law" as to which federal courts exercised an independent judgment. In addition to questions of purely commercial law, "general law" was held to include the obligations under contracts entered into and to be performed within the State, the extent to which a carrier operating within a State may stipulate for exemption from liability for his negligence or that of his employee; the liability for torts committed within the State upon persons resident or property located there, even where the question of liability depended upon the scope of a property right conferred by the State; and the right to exemplary or punitive damages. Furthermore, state decisions construing local deeds, mineral conveyances, and even devises of real estate were disregarded.

In part the discrimination resulted from the wide range of persons held entitled to avail themselves of the federal rule by resort to the diversity of citizenship jurisdiction. Through this jurisdiction individual citizens willing to remove from their own State and become citizens of another might avail themselves of the federal rule. And, without even change of residence, a corporate citizen of the State could avail itself of the federal rule by re-incorporating under the laws of another State, as was done in the Taxicab case.

The injustice and confusion incident to the doctrine of Swift v. Tyson have been repeatedly urged as reasons for abolishing or limiting diversity of citizenship jurisdiction. Other legislative relief has been proposed. If only a question of statutory construction were involved, we should not be prepared to abandon a doctrine so widely applied throughout nearly a century. But the unconstitutionality of the course pursued has now been made clear and compels us to do so.

Third. Except in matters governed by the Federal Constitution or by Acts of Congress, the law to be applied in any case is the law of the State. And whether the law of the State shall be declared by its Legislature in a statute or by its highest court in a decision is not a matter of federal concern. There is no federal general common law. Congress has no power to declare substantive rules of common law applicable in a State whether they be local in their nature or "general," be they commercial law or a part of the law of torts. And no clause in the Constitution purports to confer such a power upon the federal courts. . . .

The fallacy underlying the rule declared in Swift v. Tyson is made clear by Mr. Justice Holmes [Kuhn v. Fairmont Coal Co., 215 U.S. 349, 370-372; Black & White Taxicab Co. v. Brown & Yellow Taxicab Co., 276 U.S. 518, 532-536]. The doctrine rests upon the assumption that there is "a transcendental body of law outside of any particular State but obligatory within it unless and until changed by statute," that federal courts have the power to use their judgment as to what the rules of common law are; and that in the federal courts "the parties are entitled to an independent judgment on matters of general law": "but law in the sense in which courts speak of it today does not exist without some definite authority behind it. The common law so far as it is enforced in a State, whether called common law or not, is not the common law generally but the law of that State existing by the authority of that State without regard to what it may have been in England or anywhere else. . . .

"The authority and only authority is the State, and if that be so, the voice adopted by the State as its own [whether it be of its Legislature or of its Supreme Court] should utter the last word."

Thus the doctrine of Swift v. Tyson is, as Mr. Justice Holmes said, "an unconstitutional assumption of powers by courts of the United States which no lapse of time or respectable array of opinion should make us hesitate to correct." In disapproving that doctrine we do not hold unconstitutional § 34 of the Federal Judiciary Act of 1789 or any other Act of Congress. We merely declare that in applying the doctrine this Court and the lower courts have invaded rights which in our opinion are reserved by the Constitution to the several States.

Fourth. The defendant contended that by the common law of Pennsylvania as declared by its highest court in Falchetti v. Pennsylvania R. Co., 307 Pa. 203; 160 A. 859, the only duty owed to the plaintiff was to refrain from wilful or wanton injury. The plaintiff denied that such is the Pennsylvania law. In support of their respective contentions the parties discussed and cited many decisions of the Supreme Court of the State. The Circuit Court of Appeals ruled that the question of liability is one of general law; and on that ground declined to decide the issue of the state law. As we hold this was error, the judgment is reversed and the case remanded to it for further proceedings in conformity with our opinion.

Reversed.

THE DUE PROCESS CLAUSE

Rochin v. California

supreme court of the united states, 1952
342 u.s. 165, 96 l. ed. 183, 25 a.l.r.2d 1396,
72 sup. ct. 205

Certiorari to the District Court of Appeal for the Second
Appellate District of California.

Mr. Justice Frankfurter delivered the opinion of the
Court.*

Having "some information that [the petitioner here] was
selling narcotics," three deputy sheriffs of the County of Los
Angeles, on the morning of July 1, 1949, made for the two-story
dwelling house in which Rochin lived with his mother, common-
law wife, brothers and sisters. Finding the outside door open, they
entered and then forced open the door to Rochin's room on the
second floor. Inside they found petitioner sitting partly dressed
on the side of the bed, upon which his wife was lying. On a
"night stand" beside the bed the deputies spied two capsules.
When asked "Whose stuff is this?" Rochin seized the capsules and
put them in his mouth. A struggle ensued, in the course of which
the three officers "jumped upon him" and attempted to extract
the capsules. The force they applied proved unavailing against
Rochin's resistance. He was handcuffed and taken to a hospital.
At the direction of one of the officers a doctor forced an emetic
solution through a tube into Rochin's stomach against his will.
This "stomach pumping" produced vomiting. In the vomited

* Footnotes by the Court are omitted.

matter were found two capsules which proved to contain morphine.

Rochin was brought to trial before a California Superior Court, sitting without a jury on the charge of "possessing a preparation of morphine" in violation of the California Health and Safety Code, 1947, § 11,500. Rochin was convicted and sentenced to sixty days' imprisonment. The chief evidence against him was the two capsules. They were admitted over petitioner's objection, although the means of obtaining them was frankly set forth in the testimony by one of the deputies, substantially as here narrated.

On appeal, the District Court of Appeal affirmed the conviction, despite the finding that the officers "were guilty of unlawfully breaking into and entering defendant's room and were guilty of unlawfully assaulting and battering defendant while in the room," and "were guilty of unlawfully assaulting, battering, torturing and falsely imprisoning the defendant at the alleged hospital." 101 Cal. App.2d 140, 143, 225 P.2d 1, 3. One of the three judges, while finding that "the record in this case reveals a shocking series of violations of constitutional rights," concurred only because he felt bound by decisions of his Supreme Court. These, he asserted, "have been looked upon by law enforcement officers as an encouragement, if not an invitation, to the commission of such lawless acts." *Ibid.* The Supreme Court of California denied without opinion Rochin's petition for a hearing. Two justices dissented from this denial, and in doing so expressed themselves thus: ". . . a conviction which rests upon evidence of incriminating objects obtained from the body of the accused by physical abuse is as invalid as a conviction which rests upon a verbal confession extracted from him by such abuse. . . . Had the evidence forced from the defendant's lips consisted of an oral confession that he illegally possessed a drug . . . he would have the protection of the rule of law which excludes coerced confessions from evidence. But because the evidence forced from his lips consisted of real objects the People of this state are permitted to base a conviction upon it. [We] find no valid ground of distinction between a verbal confession extracted by physical abuse and a confession wrested from defendant's body by physical abuse." 101 Cal. App.2d 143, 149-150, 225 P.2d 913, 917-918.

This Court granted certiorari, 341 U.S. 939, because a serious question is raised as to the limitations which the Due Process Clause of the Fourteenth Amendment imposes on the conduct of criminal proceedings by the States.

In our federal system the administration of criminal justice is predominantly committed to the care of the States. The power to define crimes belongs to Congress only as an appropriate means of carrying into execution its limited grant of legislative powers. U.S. Const., Art. I, § 8, cl. 18. Broadly speaking, crimes in the United States are what the laws of the individual States make them, subject to the limitations of Art. I, § 10, cl. 1, in the original Constitution, prohibiting bills of attainder and *ex post facto* laws, and of the Thirteenth and Fourteenth Amendments.

These limitations, in the main, concern not restrictions upon the powers of the States to define crime, except in the restricted area where federal authority has preempted the field, but restrictions upon the manner in which the States may enforce their penal codes. Accordingly, in reviewing a State criminal conviction under a claim of right guaranteed by the Due Process Clause of the Fourteenth Amendment, from which is derived the most far-reaching and most frequent federal basis of challenging State criminal justice, "we must be deeply mindful of the responsibilities of the States for the enforcement of criminal laws, and exercise with due humility our merely negative function in subjecting convictions from state courts to the very narrow scrutiny which the Due Process Clause of the Fourteenth Amendment authorizes." Malinski v. New York, 324 U.S. 401, 412, 418. Due Process of law, "itself a historical product," Jackman v. Rosenbaum Co., 260 U.S. 22, 31, is not to be turned into a destructive dogma against the States in the administration of their systems of criminal justice.

However, this Court too has its responsibility. Regard for the requirements of the Due Process Clause "inescapably imposes upon this Court an exercise of judgment upon the whole course of the proceedings [resulting in a conviction] in order to ascertain whether they offend those canons of decency and fairness which express the notions of justice of English-speaking peoples even toward those charged with the most heinous offenses." Malinski v. New York, supra, at 416-417. These standards of justice are not authoritatively formulated anywhere as though they were specifics. Due process of law is a summarized constitutional guarantee of respect for those personal immunities which, as Mr. Justice Cardozo twice wrote for the Court, are "so rooted in the traditions and conscience of our people as to be ranked as fundamental," Snyder v. Massachusetts, 291 U.S. 97, 105, or are "implicit in the concept of ordered liberty." Palko v. Connecticut, 302 U.S. 319, 325.

The Court's function in the observance of this settled conception of the Due Process Clause does not leave us without adequate guides in subjecting State criminal procedures to constitutional judgment. In dealing not with the machinery of government but with human rights, the absence of formal exactitude, or want of fixity of meaning, is not an unusual or even regrettable attribute of constitutional provisions. . . .

The vague contours of the Due Process Clause do not leave judges at large. We may not draw on our merely personal and private notions and disregard the limits that bind judges in their judicial function. Even though the concept of due process of law is not final and fixed, these limits are derived from considerations that are fused in the whole nature of our judicial process. See Cardozo, The Nature of the Judicial Process; The Growth of the Law; The Paradoxes of Legal Science. These are considerations deeply rooted in reason and in the compelling traditions of the legal profession. The Due Process Clause places upon this Court the duty of exercising a judgment, within the narrow confines of judicial power in reviewing State convictions, upon interests of society pushing in opposite directions.

Due process of law thus conceived is not to be derided as resort to a revival of "natural law." To believe that this judicial exercise of judgment could be avoided by freezing "due process of law" at some fixed stage of time or thought is to suggest that the most important aspect of constitutional adjudication is a function for inanimate machines and not for judges, for whom the independence safeguarded by Article III of the Constitution was designed and who are presumably guided by established standards of judicial behavior. Even cybernetics has not yet made that haughty claim. To practice the requisite detachment and to achieve sufficient objectivity no doubt demands of judges the habit of self-discipline and self-criticism, incertitude that one's own views are incontestable and alert tolerance toward views not shared. But these are precisely the presuppositions of our judicial process. They are precisely the qualities society has a right to expect from those entrusted with ultimate judicial power.

Restraints on our jurisdiction are self-imposed only in the sense that there is from our decisions no immediate appeal short of impeachment or constitutional amendment. But that does not make due process of law a matter of judicial caprice. The faculties of the Due Process Clause may be indefinite and vague, but the mode of their ascertainment is not self-willed. In each case "due process of law" requires an evaluation based on a disinterested inquiry pursued in the spirit of science, on a balanced order of facts exactly and fairly stated, on the detached consideration of conflicting claims, see Hudson County Water Co. v. McCarter, 209 U.S. 349, 355, on a judgment not *ad hoc* and episodic but duly mindful of reconciling the needs both of continuity and of change in a progressive society.

Applying these general considerations to the circumstances of the present case, we are compelled to conclude that the proceedings by which this conviction was obtained do more than offend some fastidious squeamishness or private sentimentalism about combatting crime too energetically. This is conduct that shocks the conscience. Illegally breaking into the privacy of the petitioner, the struggle to open his mouth and remove what was there, the forcible extraction of his stomach's contents—this course of proceeding by agents of government to obtain evidence is bound to offend even hardened sensibilities. They are methods too close to the rack and the screw to permit of constitutional differentiation.

It has long since ceased to be true that due process of law is heedless of the means by which otherwise relevant and credible evidence is obtained. This was not true even before the series of recent cases enforced the constitutional principle that the States may not base convictions upon confessions, however much verified, obtained by coercion. These decisions are not arbitrary exceptions to the comprehensive right of States to fashion their own rules of evidence for criminal trials. They are not sports in our constitutional law but applications of a general principle. They are only instances of the general requirement that States in their prosecutions respect certain decencies of civilized conduct. Due process of law, as a historic and generative principle, precludes defining, and thereby confining, these standards of conduct more precisely than to say that convictions cannot be brought about by methods that offend "a sense of justice." See Mr. Chief Justice Hughes, speaking for a unanimous Court in Brown v. Mississippi, 297 U.S. 278, 285-286. It would be a stultification of the responsibility which the course of constitutional history has cast upon this Court to hold that in order to convict a man the police cannot extract by force what is in his mind but can extract what is in his stomach.

To attempt in this case to distinguish what lawyers call "real evidence" from verbal evidence is to ignore the reasons for excluding coerced confessions. Use of involuntary verbal confessions in State criminal trials is constitutionally obnoxious not only because of their unreliability. They are inadmissible under the Due Process Clause even though statements contained in them may be independently established as true. Coerced confessions offend the community's sense of fair play and decency. So here, to sanction the brutal conduct which naturally enough was condemned by the court whose judgment is before us, would be to afford brutality the cloak of law. Nothing would be more calculated to discredit law and thereby to brutalize the temper of a society.

In deciding this case we do not heedlessly bring into question decisions in many States dealing with essentially different, even if related, problems. We therefore put to one side cases which have arisen in the State courts through use of modern methods and devices for discovering wrongdoers and bringing them to book. It does not fairly represent these decisions to suggest that they legalize force so brutal and so offensive to human dignity in securing evidence from a suspect as is revealed by this record. Indeed the California Supreme Court has not sanctioned this mode of securing a conviction. It merely exercised its discretion to decline a review of the conviction. All the California judges who have expressed themselves in this case have condemned the conduct in the strongest language.

We are not unmindful that hypothetical situations can be

conjured up, shading imperceptibly from the circumstances of this case and by gradations producing practical differences despite seemingly logical extensions. But the Constitution is "intended to preserve practical and substantial rights, not to maintain theories." Davis v. Mills, 194 U.S. 451, 457.

On the facts of this case the conviction of the petitioner has been obtained by methods that offend the Due Process Clause. The judgment below must be

Reversed.

MR. JUSTICE MINTON took no part in the consideration or decision of this case.

MR. JUSTICE BLACK, concurring.

Adamson v. California, 332 U.S. 46, 68-123, sets out reasons for my belief that state as well as federal courts and law enforcement officers must obey the Fifth Amendment's command that "No person . . . shall be compelled in any criminal case to be a witness against himself." I think a person is compelled to be a witness against himself not only when he is compelled to testify, but also when as here, incriminating evidence is forcibly taken from him by a contrivance of modern science. Cf. Boyd v. United States, 116 U.S. 616; Counselman v. Hitchcock, 142 U.S. 547, 562; Bram v. United States, 168 U.S. 532; Chambers v. Florida, 309 U.S. 227. California convicted this petitioner by using against him evidence obtained in this manner, and I agree with MR. JUSTICE DOUGLAS that the case should be reversed on this ground.

In the view of a majority of the Court, however, the Fifth Amendment imposes no restraint of any kind on the states. They nevertheless hold that California's use of this evidence violated the Due Process Clause of the Fourteenth Amendment. Since they hold as I do in this case, I regret my inability to accept their interpretation without protest. But I believe that faithful adherence to the specific guarantees in the Bill of Rights insures a more permanent protection of individual liberty than that which can be afforded by the nebulous standards stated by the majority.

What the majority hold is that the Due Process Clause empowers this Court to nullify any state law if its application "shocks the conscience," offends "a sense of justice" or runs coun-

ter to the "decencies of civilized conduct." The majority emphasize that these statements do not refer to their own consciences
or to their senses of justice and decency. For we are told that "we
may not draw on our merely personal and private notions"; our
judgment must be grounded on "considerations deeply rooted in
reason and in the compelling traditions of the legal profession."
We are further admonished to measure the validity of state practices, not by our reason, or by the traditions of the legal profession, but by "the community's sense of fair play and decency";
by the "traditions and conscience of our people"; or by "those
canons of decency and fairness which express the notions of justice of English-speaking peoples." These canons are made necessary, it is said, because of "interests of society pushing in opposite
directions."

If the Due Process Clause does vest this Court with such un-
limited power to invalidate laws, I am still in doubt as to why we
should consider only the notions of English-speaking peoples to
determine what are immutable and fundamental principles of
justice. Moreover, one may well ask what avenues of investigation
are open to discover "canons" of conduct so universally favored
that this Court should write them into the Constitution? All we
are told is that the discovery must be made by an "evaluation
based on a disinterested inquiry pursued in the spirit of science,
on a balanced order of facts."

Some constitutional provisions are stated in absolute and un-
qualified language such, for illustration, as the First Amendment
stating that no law shall be passed prohibiting the free exercise of
religion or abridging the freedom of speech or press. Other constitutional provisions do require courts to choose between competing policies, such as the Fourth Amendment which, by its
terms necessitates a judicial decision as to what is an "unreasonable" search or seizure. There is, however, no express constitutional language granting judicial power to invalidate *every* state
law of *every* kind deemed "unreasonable" or contrary to the
Court's notion of civilized decencies; yet the constitutional philosophy used by the majority has, in the past, been used to deny a
state the right to fix the price of gasoline, Williams v. Standard
Oil Co., 278 U.S. 235; and even the right to prevent bakers from
palming off smaller for larger loaves of bread, Jay Burns Baking

Co. v. Bryan, 264 U.S. 504. These cases, and others, show the extent to which the evanescent standards of the majority's philosophy have been used to nullify state legislative programs passed to suppress evil economic practices. What paralyzing role this same philosophy will play in the future economic affairs of this country is impossible to predict. Of even graver concern, however, is the use of the philosophy to nullify the Bill of Rights. I long ago concluded that the accordion-like qualities of this philosophy must inevitably imperil all the individual liberty safeguards specifically enumerated in the Bill of Rights. Reflection and recent decisions of this Court sanctioning abridgment of the freedom of speech and press have strengthened this conclusion.

MR. JUSTICE DOUGLAS, concurring.

The evidence obtained from this accused's stomach would be admissible in the majority of states where the question has been raised. So far as the reported cases reveal, the only states which would probably exclude the evidence would be Arkansas, Iowa, Michigan, and Missouri. Yet the Court now says that the rule which the majority of the states have fashioned violates the "decencies of civilized conduct." To that I cannot agree. It is a rule formulated by responsible courts with judges as sensitive as we are to the proper standards for law administration.

As an original matter it might be debatable whether the provision in the Fifth Amendment that no person "shall be compelled in any criminal case to be a witness against himself" serves the ends of justice. Not all civilized legal procedures recognize it. But the choice was made by the Framers, a choice which sets a standard for legal trials in this country. The Framers made it a standard of due process for prosecutions by the Federal Government. If it is a requirement of due process for a trial in the federal courthouse, it is impossible for me to say it is not a requirement of due process for a trial in the state courthouse. That was the issue recently surveyed in Adamson v. California, 332 U.S. 46. The Court rejected the view that compelled testimony should be excluded and held in substance that the accused in a state trial can be forced to testify against himself. I disagree. Of course an accused can be compelled to be present at the trial, to stand, to sit, to turn this way or that, and to try on a cap or a coat. See

Holt v. United States, 218 U.S. 245, 252-253. But I think that words taken from his lips, capsules taken from his veins are all inadmissible provided they are taken from him without his consent. They are inadmissible because of the command of the Fifth Amendment.

That is an unequivocal, definite and workable rule of evidence for state and federal courts. But we cannot in fairness free the state courts from that command and yet excoriate them from flouting the "decencies of civilized conduct" when they admit the evidence. That is to make the rule turn not on the Constitution but on the idiosyncrasies of the judges who sit here.

The damage of the view sponsored by the Court in this case may not be conspicuous here. But it is part of the same philosophy that produced Betts v. Brady, 316 U.S. 455, denying counsel to an accused in a state trial against the command of the Sixth Amendment, and Wolf v. Colorado, 338 U.S. 25, allowing evidence obtained as a result of a search and seizure that is illegal under the Fourth Amendment to be introduced in a state trial. It is part of the process of erosion of civil rights of the citizen in recent years.

Notes

1. The majority opinion in *Rochin v. California* suggests that the Due Process Clause of the U. S. Constitution does not have its authority as law merely because it is mentioned or written therein. It is said to be based on certain standards of justice "not authoritatively formulated anywhere as though they were specifics." On the other hand, Justice Frankfurter eschews the idea that this conception entails a "resort to a revival of 'natural law.'" What then is the status of the Due Process Clause? What is wrong with treating it as a kind of "natural law"?

2. It is sometimes maintained that there are not only different kinds, but also different codes, of moral rules, e.g., codes of professional ethics, codes of business practice, personal or private codes of morality, as opposed to public rules of conduct. Can these be reconciled? Are some codes "higher" than others, some "primary" and others "secondary"? By what criterion or by what authority should one choose between one set and another in making his moral decisions?

3. Compare the treatment and application of the standard of reasonable care in *Pokora v. Wabash Ry. Co.* with the same or similar standard referred to in *Palsgraf v. Long Island R. R. Co.* (Chapter 4), *Kimble v. MacKintosh Hemphill Co.* (Chapter 4), *Tedla v. Ellman* (Chapter 3), *Marengo v. Roy* (Chapter 1) and *Wagner v. International Ry. Co.* (Chapter 1). Is it possible to get a composite picture of "the reasonable man"? How does it compare with Aristotle's "man of practical wisdom"? (Cf. *Nicomachean Ethics,* 1107a, 1140a)

4. Justice Holmes, in *Baltimore & Ohio R. R. v. Goodman,* appears only to be trying to solve, in part, the problem of applying a rule or standard, by specifying the factual circumstances to which it is to be applied, then and in the future. Seven years later, Justice Cardozo objects to such exact specification because "extraordinary situations may not wisely or fairly be subjected to tests or regulations that are fitting for the commonplace or normal." Yet, what is more common-place or normal than the crossing of railroad tracks? Is there no hope of being able to specify the factual conditions for the application of a rule in advance? If not, of what value is the rule as a guide to conduct?

5. In *Hynes v. New York Central R. Co.,* Judge Cardozo makes use of "considerations of analogy, of convenience, of policy, and of justice" to

decide between two competitive rules. Exactly what does he have in mind? What is his objection to a "merely logical deduction"? Is a "conclusion of the law" so very different? Is his own reasoning illogical?

6. It is decided in *Durfee v. Jones* that the money was "lost" rather than "mislaid." Suppose it had been decided otherwise. Might it have made no difference, either in the rule applied or in the outcome of the case? Describe the process of reasoning which would have allowed the application of another rule.

6

THE MEANS AND LIMITS
OF PERSUASION

Some philosophers claim that there can be no genuine arguments
regarding value judgments. They contend that judgments of the form,
"X is good" or "What Y did was wrong," are simply not statements of
the sort which can meaningfully be said to be either true or false. Thus,
the denials, "X is not good" or "What Y did was not wrong" do not, in
a strict logical sense, contradict the former assertions. What appears to
be a dispute over value judgments, they say, turns out on examination
to be only a dispute over certain underlying facts, or if not that, merely
a conflict of different attitudes.

Other philosophers disagree. They insist either that value judgments are as factual as any other kind, or else they hold some form of
the view that although value judgments are not strictly speaking factual,
they do permit valid inferences when coupled with relevant descrip-
tive judgments. On both these latter views, genuine moral dispute is
possible.

A reading of the following cases is not likely to settle this particular
philosophical debate. Nevertheless, they should throw some light on
what all ethical theorists agree is involved in almost every serious dispute
over value judgments, namely, a disagreement over relevant facts. Certainly it can hardly be denied that facts are a consideration, if not the
only one, in holding a person responsible for his acts. What has been
too little realized perhaps is that a dispute over the facts in a moral
context is often no small matter, and that it is misleading to characterize it as a "mere dispute over facts." Often it makes all the difference.
This at least is one of the lessons to be learned from examining the way
judges deal with the factual or evidential aspects of issues involving the
placement of responsibility.

The law of evidence, however, is something quite different from what the average layman takes it to be. There are at least two misconceptions. First, it is assumed that by "evidence" the lawyer means all the available facts that are relevant to the settlement of an issue. Second, it is assumed that the aim of procuring and presenting evidence at a trial is solely the ascertainment of the truth or falsity of some disputed proposition.

The modern theory of evidence, as contrasted with the older modes of trial, such as trial by combat or trial by ordeal, does regard only that which is relevant, in the logical sense, as evidence, but from this it does not follow that all that is relevant is admitted as evidence. The complex set of rules which constitute this branch of law is best understood as determining among probative matters which classes of things shall not be admitted for consideration by a court. Thus, hearsay and testimony regarding a man's character are often excluded, not because they are irrelevant, since many times they are very relevant, but for a variety of other reasons. Among the reasons for such exclusions are the following: too much expenditure of time and money would be involved; admission would create undue prejudice or mislead the jury; certain fundamental social relationships would be threatened; the civil liberties of witnesses would be compromised. These are but a few of the limits imposed upon the body of available relevant facts which constitute admissible evidence.

The general purpose of these limitations is fairly clear. The primary aim of a trial is achieving justice and preventing injustice. Ascertaining the truth regarding a disputed matter is a subsidiary goal. Indeed, there are times when the actual truth is simply irrelevant, e.g., in the case where a defendant is estopped (prevented) from denying or retracting a deliberate falsehood or misrepresentation of fact which he has made and upon which another has relied. Furthermore, it must be realized that the deliberate exclusion of much that is relevant for either practical reasons or reasons of justice, plus the fact that the court must make its judgment only on the basis of the evidence actually presented before it during the trial, preclude the possibility of a final, or even scientifically satisfactory, determination of the truth.

The most that can be expected of legal evidence, as far as the determination of the truth is concerned, is that it will produce a reasonable and, hopefully, a true belief or conviction in the mind of the judge or jury. Legal "evidence" is therefore quite commonly and appropriately defined as "the means of persuasion," and legal "proof," as distinguished from argument, as the "final persuasive effect" of the evidence upon the judge or jurors. The latter admits of degrees—proof "beyond a reasonable doubt" in criminal cases, and proof "by a preponderance of the evidence" in civil cases.

The case of *Rochin v. California* in the previous chapter and the case of *People v. Zackowitz* in this chapter indicate two of the types of evidence which, though relevant, are treated as inadmissible. Evidence acquired by (illegal) force, and testimony regarding a man's character.

Worth v. Worth raises specific questions regarding the evidential status of presumptions and the burden of proof. The law abounds with presumptions, e.g., the presumption of innocence in criminal cases, the presumption of falsity in defamation suits, the presumption of good faith in contractual and other cases, and the presumption of death after an unexplained absence of seven years in insurance and other types of cases. Many legal questions have arisen regarding the evidential status of presumptions, however. One is whether a presumption is itself evidence or a "substitute" for evidence, or only a procedural rule of law which shifts the burden of proving the contrary to the other party. Another question is whether the presumption is rebutted simply by the introduction of evidence which makes it an issue for the jury, or whether it continues in effect until a sufficient quantity of contrary evidence is produced to convince the jury that the presumption is false or that it is no more probable than its denial.

Although the legal situation differs from the moral situation in that the latter lacks a forum in which methods of dealing with matters of evidence can be legislated or authoritatively controlled, it is nevertheless true that in the "forum of one's own conscience" such procedures need to be taken into account. Certainly moral judgments are often made in the context of what may be called "moral presumptions." Indeed, many of the presumptions of the law, e.g., innocence, good faith, are at the same time moral presumptions. Their status in moral argument needs to be clarified. So too does the notion of "burden of proof," that is, if evidence is to be thought at all relevant to moral disputes.

The next three cases make clear, in different ways, a point which reflective persons do not need to be reminded of, but which should be stressed because of its importance. The point is that "facts" are, more often than not, the products of interpretation. So-called neutral facts are sometimes colored by deep human emotions or by general views of the nature of society and government. Such is found to be the case in *Baumgartner v. United States,* where the appellant is charged with being a "Nazi" and so stands a chance of losing his naturalized citizenship.

Warmke v. Commonwealth involves a different type of inference, but nonetheless one which seeks to establish a fact. A woman is charged with the manslaughter of her infant child. The body was never found, so the corpus delicti is absent and has to be established almost entirely by circumstantial evidence.

In *Muller v. Oregon,* the fact put in evidence, or rather, taken judicial notice of, is that a woman's health is endangered by working longer than ten hours a day. This case involves the famous "Brandeis brief," which incorporates a sociological study using scientific methods as a way of establishing fact.

All three cases are illustrative of the issue regarding the admissibility or inadmissibility of logically relevant evidence. The last two mentioned, however, also illustrate another consideration of ethical significance, namely, the fact that although judges do sometimes admit "general knowledge" as a basis for finding of fact, they do so with considerably more hesitation than they do in admitting circumstantial evidence.

Woods v. Lancet, in a sense, summarizes all the questions raised in Part II, and adds another. It suggests the following: What is an act? Are there grounds for a cause of action? To what legal norm may one appeal in the absence of legislation and precedent? Where the case is novel or relatively unprecedented, what is to count as "proper evidence"? Where proof is particularly difficult, should a right of action even be recognized? Should theoretical difficulties be weighed as heavily as practical or procedural difficulties?

The last point suggests, for the moral philosopher, the question of "moral certainty." Must we always await the appearance of conclusive evidence before we recognize a claim of right or undertake to assign responsibility?

INCOMPETENT EVIDENCE

People v. Zackowitz

COURT OF APPEALS OF NEW YORK, 1930
254 N.Y. 192, 172 N.E. 466

CARDOZO, C. J. On November 10, 1929, shortly after midnight, the defendant in Kings county shot Frank Coppola and killed him without justification or excuse. A crime is admitted. What is doubtful is the degree only.

Four young men, of whom Coppola was one, were at work repairing an automobile in a Brooklyn street. A woman, the defendant's wife, walked by on the opposite side. One of the men spoke to her insultingly, or so at least she understood him. The defendant, who had dropped behind to buy a newspaper, came up to find his wife in tears. He was told she had been insulted, though she did not then repeat the words. Enraged, he stepped across the street and upbraided the offenders with words of coarse profanity. He informed them, so the survivors testify, that "if they did not get out of there in five minutes, he would come back and bump them all off." Rejoining his wife, he walked with her to their apartment house located close at hand. He was heated with liquor which he had been drinking at a dance. Within the apartment he induced her to tell him what the insulting words had been. A youth had asked her to lie with him, and had offered her $2. With rage aroused again, the defendant went back to the scene of the insult and found the four young men still working at the car. In a statement to the police, he said that he had armed himself at the apartment with a .25-caliber automatic pistol. In his testimony at the trial he said that this pistol had been in his pocket all the evening. Words and blows followed, and then a shot. The defendant kicked Coppola in the stomach. There is evidence that Coppola went for him with a wrench. The pistol came from the pocket, and from the pistol a single shot, which did its deadly work. The defendant walked away and at the corner met his wife who had followed him from the home. The two took a taxicab to Manhattan, where they spent the rest of the night at the dwelling of a friend. On the way the defendant threw his pistol into the river. He was arrested on January 7, 1930, about two months following the crime.

At the trial the vital question was the defendant's state of mind at the moment of the homicide. Did he shoot with a deliberate and premeditated design to kill? Was he so inflamed by drink or by anger or by both combined that, though he knew the nature of his act, he was the prey to sudden impulse, the fury of the fleeting moment? People v. Caruso, 246 N.Y. 437, 446, 159 N.E. 390. If he went forth from his apartment with a preconceived design to kill, how is it that he failed to shoot at once? How reconcile such a design with the drawing of the pistol later in the heat and rage of an affray? These and like questions the jurors were to ask themselves and answer before measuring the defendant's guilt. Answers consistent with guilt in its highest grade can reasonably be made. Even so, the line between impulse and deliberation is too narrow and elusive to make the answers wholly clear. The sphygmograph records with graphic certainty the fluctuations of the pulse. There is no instrument yet invented that records with equal certainty the fluctuations of the mind. At least, if such an instrument exists it was not working at midnight in the Brooklyn street when Coppola and the defendant came together in a chance affray. With only the rough and ready tests supplied by their experiences of life, the jurors were to look into the workings of another's mind, and discover its capacities and disabilities, its urges and inhibitions, in moments of intense excitement. Delicate enough and subtle is the inquiry, even in the most favorable conditions, with every warping influence excluded. There must be no blurring of the issues by evidence illegally admitted and carrying with it in its admission an appeal to prejudice and passion.

Evidence charged with that appeal was, we think, admitted

here. Not only was it admitted, and this under objection and exception, but the changes were rung upon it by prosecutor and judge. Almost at the opening of the trial the people began the endeavor to load the defendant down with the burden of an evil character. He was to be put before the jury as a man of murderous disposition. To that end they were allowed to prove that at the time of the encounter and at that of his arrest he had in his apartment, kept there in a radio box, three pistols and a tear-gas gun. There was no claim that he had brought these weapons out at the time of the affray, no claim that with any of them he had discharged the fatal shot. He could not have done so, for they were all of different caliber. The end to be served by laying the weapons before the jury was something very different. The end was to bring persuasion that here was a man of vicious and dangerous propensities, who because of those propensities was more likely to kill with deliberate and premeditated design than a man of irreproachable life and amiable manners. Indeed, this is the very ground on which the introduction of the evidence is now explained and defended. The district attorney tells us in his brief that the possession of the weapons characterized the defendant as "a desperate type of criminal," a "person criminally inclined." The dissenting opinion, if it puts the argument less bluntly, leaves the substance of the thought unchanged. "Defendant was presented to the jury as a man having dangerous weapons in his possession, making a selection therefrom and going forth to put into execution his threats to kill." The weapons were not brought by the defendant to the scene of the encounter. They were left in his apartment where they were incapable of harm. In such circumstances, ownership of the weapons, if it has any relevance at all, has relevance only as indicating a general disposition to make use of them thereafter, and a general disposition to make use of them thereafter is without relevance except as indicating a "desperate type of criminal," a criminal affected with a murderous propensity.

We are asked to extenuate the error by calling it an incident; what was proved may have an air of innocence if it is styled the history of the crime. The virus of the ruling is not so easily extracted. Here was no passing reference to something casually brought out in the narrative of the killing, as if an admission had been proved against the defendant that he had picked one weapon out of several. Here in the forefront of the trial, immediately following the statement of the medical examiner, testimony was admitted that weapons, not the instrument of the killing, had been discovered by the police in the apartment of the killer; and the weapons with great display were laid before the jury, marked as exhibits, and thereafter made the subject of animated argument. Room for doubt there is none that in the thought of the jury, as in that of the district attorney, the tendency of the whole performance was to characterize the defendant as a man murderously inclined. The purpose was not disguised. From the opening to the verdict, it was flaunted and avowed.

If a murderous propensity may be proved against a defendant as one of the tokens of his guilt, a rule of criminal evidence, long believed to be of fundamental importance for the protection of the innocent, must be first declared away. Fundamental hitherto has been the rule that character is never an issue in a criminal prosecution unless the defendant chooses to make it one. Wigmore, Evidence, vol. 1, §§ 55, 192. In a very real sense a defendant starts his life afresh when he stands before a jury, a prisoner at the bar. There has been a homicide in a public place. The killer admits the killing, but urges self-defense and sudden impulse. Inflexibly the law has set its face against the endeavor to fasten guilt upon him by proof of character or experience predisposing to an act of crime. Wigmore, Evidence, vol. 1, §§ 57, 192; People v. Molineux, 168 N.Y. 264, 61 N.E. 286, 62 L.R.A. 193. The endeavor has been often made, but always it has failed. At times, when the issue has been self-defense, testimony has been admitted as to the murderous propensity of the deceased, the victim of the homicide. People v. Druse, 103 N.Y. 655, 8 N.E. 733; People v. Rodawald, 177 N.Y. 408, 70 N.E. 1; Wigmore, Evidence, vol. 1, § 63, 246, but never of such a propensity on the part of the killer. The principle back of the exclusion is one, not of logic, but of policy. Wigmore, vol. 1, §§ 57, 194; People v. Richardson, 222 N.Y. 103, 109, 110, 118 N.E. 514. There may be cogency in the argument that a quarrelsome defendant is more likely to start a quarrel than one of milder type, a man of dangerous mode of life more likely than a shy recluse. The law is not blind to this, but equally it is not blind to the peril to the innocent if character is accepted as probative of crime. "The natural and inevitable tendency of the tribunal—whether judge or jury—is to give excessive weight to the vicious record of crime thus exhibited, and either to allow it to bear too strongly on the present charge, or to take the proof of it as justifying a condemnation irrespective of guilt of the present charge." Wigmore, Evidence, vol. 1, § 194, and cases cited.

A different question would be here if the pistols had been bought in expectation of this particular encounter. They would then have been admissible as evidence of preparation and design. Wigmore, Evidence, vol. 1, § 238; People v. Scott, 153 N.Y. 40, 46 N.E. 1028. A different question would be here if they were so connected with the crime as to identify the perpetrator, if he had dropped them, for example, at the scene of the affray. People v. Hill, 198 N.Y. 64, 91 N.E. 272. They would then have been admissible as tending to implicate the possessor (if identity was disputed), no matter what the opprobrium attached to his possession. Different, also, would be the question if the defendant had been shown to have gone forth from the apartment with all the weapons on his person. To be armed from head to foot at the very moment of an encounter may be a circumstance worthy to be considered, like acts of preparation generally, as a proof of preconceived design. There can be no such implication from the ownership of weapons which one leaves behind at home.

The endeavor was to generate an atmosphere of professional criminality. It was an endeavor the more unfair in that, apart from the suspicion attaching to the possession of these weapons, there is nothing to mark the defendant as a man of evil life. He was not in crime as a business. He did not shoot as a bandit shoots in the hope of wrongful gain. He was engaged in a decent calling, an optician regularly employed, without criminal associates. If his own testimony be true, he had gathered these weapons together as curios, a collection that interested and amused him. Perhaps his explanation of their ownership is false. There is nothing stronger than mere suspicion to guide us to an answer. Whether the explanation be false or true, he should not have been driven by the people to the necessity of offering it. Brought to answer a specific charge, and to defend himself against it, he was placed in a position where he had to defend himself against another, more general and sweeping. He was made to answer to the charge, pervasive and poisonous even if insidious and covert, that he was a man of murderous heart, of criminal disposition.

The argument is made that the evidence, if incompetent when admitted, became competent thereafter when the defendant took the stand. By taking the stand he subjected himself like any other witness to cross-examination designed to shake belief in his veracity by exhibiting his ways of life. . . . Cross-examination brought out the fact that he had no license for a pistol. That fact disclosed, the prosecution was at liberty to prove the possession of the weapons in an attempt to impeach his credibility, since possession was a felony. All this may be true, but the evidence was not offered or admitted with such an end in view. It was received at a time when there was nothing to show that the defendant was without a license, and without suggestion that any such evidence would be brought into the case thereafter. The jury were not told that the possession of the weapons had significance only in so far as possession without a license had a tendency to cast a shadow on the defendant's character, and so impair the faith to be given to his word. . . . They were told in effect through the whole course and tenor of the trial that irrespective of any license, the mere possession of the weapons was evidence of a murderous disposition, which, apart from any bearing upon the defendant's credibility as a witness, was evidence of guilt. Here is no case of a mere technical departure from the approved order of proof. If the evidence had been received for the purpose of impeachment merely, the people would have been bound by the answer of the witness as to the time and purpose of the purchase, and would not have been permitted to contradict him. Stokes v. People, 53 N.Y. 164, 176, 13 Am. Rep. 492; People v. De Garmo, supra. Here is a case where evidence offered and received as probative of an essential element of the crime, used for that purpose, and for no other, repeatedly throughout the trial, is now about to be viewed as if accepted at a later stage and accepted for a purpose unmentioned and unthought of. This is not justice in accordance with the forms of law. "The practice of calling out evidence for one purpose, apparently innocent, and using it for another, which is illegal, is improper; and, if it is clear and manifest that the avowed object is colorable merely, its admission is error." Coleman v. People, 55 N.Y. 81, 88. Even more plainly is it a perversion to call out evidence for an avowed object manifestly illegal, and use it later on appeal as if admitted at another stage in aid of another purpose innocent and lawful.

The judgment of conviction should be reversed, and a new trial ordered.

[The dissenting opinion of Judge Pound is omitted.]

LEHMAN, KELLOGG, and O'BRIEN, JJ., concur with CARDOZO, C.J.

POUND, J., dissents in opinion in which CRANE and HUBBS, JJ., concur.

Judgment reversed, etc.

PRESUMPTIONS AND BURDEN OF PROOF

WORTH v. WORTH

SUPREME COURT OF WYOMING, 1935
48 WYO. 441, 49 P.2D 649

BLUME, JUSTICE. This is an action for alienation of affection by a daughter-in-law against her parents-in-law. The plaintiff is the wife of Harold Worth, son of G. M. Worth and Kate Worth, defendants herein. Plaintiff sued to recover the sum of $35,000 from the defendants. The case was tried to a jury, who returned a verdict for plaintiff in the sum of $10,000. Judgment was entered for that amount, and the defendants have appealed. A few brief facts, to elucidate the opinion herein, are as follows:

The defendants, parents of Harold, had a ranch south of Wheatland. Plaintiff, then 22 years of age, was married to Harold, then about 24 years of age, on December 3, 1927. He had been married before and divorced. At the time of the marriage he was working at the mines at Sunrise; the plaintiff was teaching. The young folks moved in with the defendants in the spring of 1928. Everything was harmonious for some time, but plaintiff claims that commencing with the summer or fall of 1928, she was subjected to a systematic unfavorable treatment at the hands of the parents; that they attempted to keep Harold on the farm, when she (plaintiff) felt that it would be better for them to live at some other place. According to her testimony, a bad scene between her and the defendants, particularly Mr. Worth, took place in the summer of 1929. As a result of this and other unfavorable treatment, she went, so she states, to her own folks in Nebraska in the fall of 1929. A few weeks later she joined her husband on a homestead, where they stayed until the severe weather drove them back to the home of the defendants. They were both there until about February, when another scene, this time with Mrs. Worth, drove plaintiff, so she testified, out again, never to return. She again went to Nebraska, where she stayed till spring, when she joined her husband on the so-called Salliday place, some thirteen miles from the place of defendants. Subsequent facts, and testimony specially considered, will be mentioned later.*

[During the summer of 1930, while plaintiff and her husband were living at the Salliday place, some thirteen miles away from the home of the parents, the plaintiff became pregnant, and she and her husband apparently agreed that she should go to Nebraska and stay there until after her confinement, which was not expected until March, 1931. She went some time in November. Late in December she received a letter from a Mrs. Rich, a friend, advising her to return if she expected to keep her husband. She met Mrs. Rich in Cheyenne and drove with her to Wheatland, where she arrived on December 30, 1930. The next day she went to the post office and was handed a bunch of letters addressed to her husband by another woman, with whom, apparently, Harold had illicit relations. Plaintiff tried to find Harold, but did not succeed for a day or so. The testimony is not clear at this point. Harold was or had been in Denver with this other woman. The day following the finding of the letters, plaintiff consulted an attorney, and on January 2, 1931, filed a complaint for separate maintenance. On January 13, she filed a criminal complaint against Harold. What became of that does not appear. In March of that year Harold took his wife to Cheyenne to be confined there, and went to see her again on the following Sunday, and during these trips the couple were apparently friendly and planned for the future. Plaintiff seemingly left Cheyenne and went to Wheatland a few days thereafter without any knowledge of Harold, who, again on a visit to Cheyenne, found her gone. The parties apparently have been separated ever since. . . .]

1. The defendants asked the court to give the following instruction C: "You are instructed that in an alienation suit by the wife against the husband's parents, the law recognizes the right of the parents to advise and counsel their son in respect to his

* Included in the following paragraph.

domestic affairs, and that the law presumes that counsel and advice given by a parent to a son is given in good faith and from proper motives and honest impulses, and that the burden is upon the plaintiff to establish to your satisfaction by a preponderance of all the evidence that such counsel and advice was not given in good faith, but was given through malicious motives directed against her, and unless she has established such facts to your reasonable satisfaction, you will find for the defendants."

Another instruction, named B, was asked. This was like or similar to the asked instruction C, except that it contained the further statement reading: "You are instructed that there is a wide distinction between an action by a husband or wife against the parents of either, and one against some stranger who invades the domestic circle and separates husband and wife." It is not necessary to decide whether this additional instruction should have been given. The court refused to give either of the instructions asked, but aside from the usual instruction on the burden of proof, gave its instruction No. 7, reading as follows: "The Court instructs the jury that the defendants, being the parents of plaintiff's husband, had the right to receive their son into their home, also the right to counsel and advise him regarding his relations to the plaintiff, in good faith, on reasonable grounds and in the honest desire to promote his welfare and happiness, and they are not responsible for doing any of these things unless they acted not in good faith as above-defined, but wrongfully and maliciously; but the law does not justify or excuse parents in willfully and maliciously interfering in the domestic affairs of their married children."

Defendants claim that the refusal to give instruction C asked by them is error. . . .

Counsel for plaintiff claims that instruction No. 7 given by the court subserved all the purposes of the case. That instruction told the jury that parents have certain rights. That, however, clearly falls short of the thought that the conduct and statements of the defendants must be presumed to have been in good faith until the contrary has been shown. . . . Counsel further claims that the instruction asked is incorrect in not expressing the fact that the presumption exists only until the contrary is shown. It does not so state directly; but it does indirectly, and sufficiently shows, we think, that the presumption is not a conclusive one, but is rebuttable, and while it might have been more specific, it cannot be held to be so defective that it should be wholly rejected on that account. Wallace v. Fidelity Phoenix Fire Ins. Co., 135 Kan. 133, 9 P.2d 621; First Nat. Bank v. Commercial Assurance Co., 33 Or. 43, 52 P. 1050.

It is further contended by plaintiff that it was not proper to give an instruction on presumption, that it disappeared upon the introduction of evidence, and that this showed malice. Originally presumptions of all kinds were but inferences, based on human experience, but some of them, by reason of constantly treating them as rules of law, have from time to time been raised to the position of presumptions of law, or as sometimes called "mandatory presumptions." Watkins v. Prudential Ins. Co., 315 Pa. 497, 173 A. 644, 95 A.L.R. 869; Ward v. Metropolitan Life Ins. Co., 66 Conn. 227, 33 A. 902, 904, 50 Am. St. Rep. 80; 5 N. Car. Law Review, 297. We take it that we are here dealing with the latter. Questions relating to presumptions have given rise to considerable discussion since the memorable work of Thayer (Preliminary Treatise on Evidence, 1898). While formerly it was thought by many that they are evidence, the authorities now generally are to the contrary. Doubting Thomases, however, still remain. Cases cited in 8 Columbia Law Review, 128; Smellie v. Southern Pac. Co., Cal. Sup., 287 P. 343. A recent note on the subject may be found in 95 A.L.R. 878. We have had occasion to consider the general subject in Hildebrand v. Chicago, B. & Q. R. R., on rehearing, 45 Wyo. 175, 17 P.2d 651, where we held that a presumption disappears when, and only when, it is met by evidence adequate to dissipate it.

The question whether or not an instruction on presumptions should be given has been little discussed in its fundamental aspects, although, as stated in 5 N. Car. Law Review, which seems to be borne out by the reported cases, "the practice of apprising the jury of presumptions is followed constantly in many states." Thus it was stated in an early Missouri case to "let the jury be so told" of such presumptions. Glover's Adm'rs v. Duhle, 19 Mo. 360. And the Alabama court stated in 1885 that there was no objection to give proper instructions thereon or on anything else which is a matter of law. Westbrook v. Fulton, 79 Ala. 510. But the practice above mentioned has been questioned in later years. Instructions on inferences have at times been condemned. 64 C.J. 527. So, too, it has been held, particularly in negligence cases, that when all the detailed evidence is before the jury, an instruction on presumptions is improper. 64 C.J. 604; 45 C.J. 1362, 1363; cases cited in Hildebrand v. Chicago, B.&Q.R.R., supra. We expressly reserved a decision on that point in the case just mentioned. Among the cases holding that an instruction is improper are a number from Missouri. We find it stated that "the law is well settled in this state that it is reversible error to instruct the jury as to the existence of a presumption where evidence was introduced to rebut it." McCune v. Daniels (Mo. App.) 251 S.W. 458, 461. This, to say the least, is disconcerting in the face of the decision of Cornelius v. Cornelius, supra, which holds, in language which is unmistakable, and at length, that it is error not to give an instruction on the presumption in favor of parents in a case such as we have here. The decision has never been overruled, nor distinguished. It is apparent, accordingly, that if this opinion is to be of any value in the future as a guidepost, either of security or danger, we must give the subject more than a cursory examination, without heeding the clamor for short opinions.

All authorities agree, we think, that a presumption must be dissipated by adequate evidence. And there cannot be much dispute as to the duty of the court either when there is no contrary evidence, or the evidence is such that the presumption must be said to be rebutted as a matter of law. The case at bar does not fall within either of these classes. The only class of cases which interest us here is that lying between the two extremes—the cases of doubt. And the crux of the question is as to who shall be the arbiter in such case as to the sufficiency of the evidence produced contrary to the presumption. Is it the trial judge, or is it the jury? . . .

In an article in 5 North Carolina Law Review, 1927, Charles T. McCormick, professor of law of North Carolina University, treats of "Charges on Presumptions and Burden of Proof." He asks the question whether an instruction on presumptions should always or never be given. He takes a middle course; that ordinarily the matter should be left to the discretion of the trial judge; but that in some cases, in order that a presumption be effectuated, an instruction thereon should be given. Edmund M. Morgan, professor of law of Harvard University, in 47 Harvard Law Review, 59, treats of "Instructing the Jury upon Presumptions and Burden of Proof," and states in part as follows: "A presumption, then, will utterly fail of its purpose as to any issue to be decided by the jury if it vanishes upon the mere introduction of evidence which makes the issue one for the jury; it will best justify its existence if it persists until the evidence persuades the jury that the presumed fact does not exist or at least, that its non-existence is equally as probable as its existence. There is no difficulty in framing or applying an instruction which will enable it to perform this most desirable office. Consequently, one of the two views should be adopted. . . . The conclusion then is that most presumptions should, where applicable at all, continue to operate unless and until the evidence persuades the trier (of fact) at least that the non-existence of the presumed fact is as probable as its existence."

In view of the confusing state of the law on the subject before us, we have thought it advisable not to draw any unnecessary conclusions and to limit ourselves as much as possible to the exact presumption here involved. In the case at bar, not only was substantially all of the testimony of the plaintiff that of interested witnesses, but none of it, as already indicated, necessarily required the inference of malice, notwithstanding the vigorous claim of counsel for the plaintiff to the contrary. Two incidents are claimed to be of importance. We cannot go into details. One, involving Mr. Worth—the so-called swimming episode—would warrant the conclusion that if the statements made by him in that connection are true, they were but the outburst of temporary anger, caused to a large extent by the fact that plaintiff told Mr. Worth that her going swimming without her husband was none of his business, and that she called him a liar and refused to apologize for it. The other incident, involving Mrs. Worth, could be construed as one of those unfortunate incidents which, proverbially, take place between mother-in-law and daughter-in-law.

The presumption of good faith in this case, operating as it did in favor of the defendant, could not subserve the purpose of shifting the burden of going forward with the evidence, since the burden to show the contrary of good faith was on plaintiff in any event, so that, if that is the only function of a presumption in all cases, defendants could derive no possible benefit from it here. A similar situation was considered in the case of Lisbon v. Lyman, 49 N.H. 553, 563. It was there held that an instruction, that the presumption should be taken into account, as one of the elements of evidence was erroneous. We have no occasion here to question that holding. But the court apparently further held that a presumption in such situation is of no value whatever. In New London Water Commissioners v. Robbins, 82 Conn. 623, 640, 74 A. 938, 945, the court considered two presumptions operating in favor of the defendants, one against fraud and one regarding the performance of governmental duties. The court in discussing presumptions stated: "When such a presumption is advanced in favor of one upon whom the burden of proof does not rest, it really adds nothing to the duty or burden of the other party, since the latter is already under the obligation to present proof in support of his contention, and the presumption only reiterates that obligation." However, the court had instructed that "fraud and bad faith was not to be presumed," so that we are not certain just what the court had in mind.

It is not, we think, quite correct to say that the "presumption only reiterates" the obligation of the burden of proof. An instruction that the burden to prove malice is on the plaintiff states the duty resting on the latter. An instruction that the jury must start out with the assumption that the defendants were in good faith states a benefit or privilege conferred upon the defendants by the law. It at least makes that benefit clear and brings it home to the jury—which, after all, is the one important point in a jury trial. It is, in fact, a distinct thought which, particularly if pressed home to the jury by counsel, may often be of value. And that it should be of value is unquestionably the intent of the law. If what is said in the Connecticut case is correct, it is apparent that the presumption, created by law specially in favor of parties situated as the defendants herein, would, so far as the jury is concerned, be but a phantom. It is hardly possible that a presumption such as we are dealing with here can be of that nature. It is not a procedural rule; it is based upon reason; upon the strong love usual in parents for their children. By giving merely the ordinary instruction, and refusing that on presumption [the judge] would not even call attention to the inference, which, as a matter of reason (Wigmore, supra, § 2491), remains to be considered in any event no matter how we view a presumption. If our reasoning herein is faulty, and logic requires that the presumption herein be considered as a phantom, then we should feel warranted in appealing herein to the statement made by us in First Nat. Bank v. Ford, 30 Wyo. 110, 216 P. 691, 696, 31 A.L.R. 1441, that "logic in law must to some extent be tempered by considerations of public policy and justice." We find it stated that, in order that parents may be held liable for alienation of affection, their interference must be aggravated, Miller v. Levine, 130 Me. 153, 154 A. 174; that the evidence of malice must be clear, Cramer v. Cramer, supra; Spiry v. Spiry, 47 S.D. 500, 199 N.W. 778; that the presumption which arises in favor of parents in such case is strong, Spiry v. Spiry, supra; Miller v. Levine, supra; that the measure of proof must be exceedingly high, Hall v. Hall, 174 Cal. 718, 164 P. 390; that it must be stronger than in other cases, Russell v. Pace, 241 App. Div. 833, 271 N.Y.S. 251; 13 R.C.L. 1474. Mr. Thayer, Ev., 336, and Appx. B, p. 576, would say, when such expressions occur, that the presumption is accompanied by a rule relating to the weight of the evidence. Perhaps so. Nevertheless, reason dictates that an important presumption, intended to benefit parents in a material way, should not be kept hidden from the jury. The instruction on the burden of proof given herein was the ordinary instruction on that subject. It put the case upon the exact level of any other case. But the law puts it on a different level. In fact, Indiana, New York, and Illinois, in the present year, outlawed actions of this nature entirely as against public policy. Michigan Law Review, vol. 33, p. 997. We think, therefore, that the requested instruction, or the fundamental ideas contained therein, should have been given to the jury. It is not necessary, however, to decide, and we do not decide, that the failure to do so, standing by itself, would be sufficient to reverse the case. . . .

Reversed and remanded.

FINDING OF FACT

Baumgartner v. United States

SUPREME COURT OF THE UNITED STATES, 1944
322 U.S. 665, 88 L. ED. 1525, 64 SUP. CT. 1240

MR. JUSTICE FRANKFURTER delivered the opinion of the Court.*

On September 26, 1932, the United States District Court for the Western District of Missouri entered its order admitting Baumgartner to citizenship and issued a certificate of naturalization to him. Almost ten years later, on August 21, 1942, the United States brought this suit under § 338 of the Nationality Act of 1940 (54 Stat. 1137, 1158, 8 U.S.C. § 738) to set aside the naturalization decree and cancel the certificate. The District Court entered a decree for the Government, 47 F. Supp. 622, which the Circuit Court of Appeals for the Eighth Circuit, with one judge dissenting, affirmed. 138 F.2d 29. We brought the case here because it raises important issues in the proper administration of the law affecting naturalized citizens. . . .

As a condition to receiving his American citizenship, Baumgartner, like every other alien applying for that great gift, was required to declare an oath that he renounced his former allegiance, in this case to the German Reich, and that he would "support and defend the Constitution and laws of the United States of America against all enemies, foreign and domestic," and that he would "bear true faith and allegiance to the same." That he did not truly and fully renounce his allegiance to Germany

---

* Footnotes by the Court are omitted.

and that he did not in fact intend to support the Constitution and laws of the United States and give them true faith and allegiance, are the charges of fraud and illegality on which his citizenship is claimed forfeit.

As is true of the determination of all issues of falsity and fraud, the case depends on its own particular facts. But the division of opinion among the judges below makes manifest that facts do not assess themselves and that the decisive element is the attitude appropriate for judgment of the facts in a case like this. The two lower courts have sustained the Government's claim that expressions by Baumgartner, in conversations with others and in the soliloquies of a diary, showed that he consciously withheld complete renunciation of his allegiance to Germany and entertained reservations in his oath of allegiance to this country, its Constitution and its laws. What follows is a fair summary of the evidence on which this finding rests, putting the Government's case in its most favorable light.

Baumgartner was born in Kiel, Germany, on January 20, 1895, and brought up in modestly comfortable circumstances. He received a classical high-school education, which he completed in time to enter the German army in 1914. He was commissioned a second lieutenant in 1917, and shortly thereafter he was captured by the British and confined in England until November, 1919. Upon his return to Germany, Baumgartner studied at the University of Darmstadt, from which he was graduated in 1925 as an electrical engineer. Thereupon he was employed by a public utility company until January, 1927, when he left for the United States. Shortly before Baumgartner had married, and his wife followed him to this country later in the same year.

For about three months, Baumgartner stayed with friends in Illinois, and then came to Kansas City, Missouri, where he was employed by the Kansas City Power and Light Company. He continued in its employ down to the time of this suit. The man to whom he reported to work testified that after about two days on the job, Baumgartner began to discuss the political scene in Germany, to express a lack of enthusiasm for the then German Government, and to extol the virtues of Hitler and his movement. Baumgartner spoke so persistently about the superiority of German people, the German schools, and the engineering work of the

Germans, that he aroused antagonism among his co-workers and was transferred to a different section of the plant.

There was testimony that in 1933 or 1934 Mrs. Baumgartner's mother visited this country, and that after this visit, Baumgartner, beginning in 1934, "praised the work that Hitler was doing over there in bringing Germany back, on repeated occasions." Evidence of statements made by Baumgartner over a period of about seven years beginning in 1933 indicated oft-repeated admiration for the Nazi Government, comparisons between President Roosevelt and Adolf Hitler which led to conclusions that this country would be better off if run as Hitler ran Germany, "that regimentation, as the Nazis, formed it [sic] was superior to the democracy," and that "the democracy of the United States was a practical farce." One witness of German extraction testified that Baumgartner told him he was "a traitor to my country because of the witness's condemnation of Hitler. Baumgartner made public speeches on at least three occasions before business-men's groups, clubs, and the like, in which he told of the accomplishments of the Nazi Government and indicated that "he would be glad to live under the regime of Hitler."

During 1937 and 1938, Baumgartner conducted a Sunday school class, and former students testified that the discussion in class turned to Germany very frequently, that Baumgartner indicated that his students could get a fairer picture of conditions in Germany from the German radio, and that Germany was justified in much of what it was doing. The school superintendent also testified that he had received complaints that Baumgartner was preaching Naziism.

In 1938 Baumgartner resigned from the Country Club Congregational Church in Kansas City because he objected to the injection of politics into the sermons. In May of the next year his wife and their three children, who had been born in Kansas City, went to Germany to visit Mrs. Baumgartner's parents. One witness testified that Baumgartner explained this trip in part by saying that "he wanted the children to be brought up in German schools," and when war broke out in September, 1939, Mrs. Baumgartner cabled for money to return but Baumgartner could not raise the necessary funds and felt that his family would be as safe in Germany as here. Baumgartner remarked that he wanted his wife to come back from Germany, when she did, on a German boat. One of Baumgartner's neighbors testified that in a conversation in December, 1939, Baumgartner, asked about his thirteen-year-old daughter then in Germany, said sarcastically: "Edith has done a very un-American thing, she has joined the Nazi Youth Movement."

There was testimony that Baumgartner justified the German invasions in the late 1930's and announced, when Dunkerque fell, that "Today I am rejoicing." One witness testified that Baumgartner told him that he "belonged to an order called the so-called 'Bund,'" and the diary which Baumgartner kept from December 1, 1938, to the summer of 1941 reveals that he attended a meeting of the German Vocational League where the German national anthem was sung and "everyone naturally arose and assumed the usual German stance with the arm extended to give the National Socialist greeting." Other diary entries reflect violent anti-semitism, impatience at the lack of pro-German militancy of German-Americans, and approval of Germans who have not "been Americanized, that is, ruined." Finally, Baumgartner replied in the affirmative to the trial judge's question: "was your attitude towards the principles of the American government in 1932 when you took the oath the same as it has been ever since?"

That the concurrent findings of two lower courts are persuasive proof in support of their judgments is a rule of wisdom in judicial administration. In reaffirming its importance we mean to pay more than lip service. But the rule does not relieve us of the task of examining the foundation for findings in a particular case. The measure of proof requisite to denaturalize a citizen was before this Court in Schneiderman v. United States, 320 U.S. 118. It was there held that proof to bring about a loss of citizenship must be clear and unequivocal. We cannot escape the conviction that the case made out by the Government lacks that solidity of proof which leaves no troubling doubt in deciding a question of such gravity as is implied in an attempt to reduce a person to the status of alien from that of citizen.

The phrase "finding of fact" may be a summary characterization of complicated factors of varying significance for judgment. Such a "finding of fact" may be the ultimate judgment on a mass of details involving not merely an assessment of the trustworthiness of witnesses but other appropriate inferences that may be drawn from living testimony which elude print. The conclusiveness of a "finding of fact" depends on the nature of the materials on which the finding is based. The finding even of a so-called "subsidiary fact" may be a more or less difficult process varying according to the simplicity or subtlety of the type of "fact" in controversy. Finding so-called ultimate "facts" more clearly implies the application of standards of law. And so the "finding of fact" even if made by two courts may go beyond the determination that should not be set aside here. Though labeled "finding of fact," it may involve the very basis on which judgment of fallible evidence is to be made. Thus, the conclusion that may appropriately be drawn from the whole mass of evidence is not always the ascertainment of the kind of "fact" that precludes consideration by this Court. See, e.g., Beyer v. LeFevre, 186 U.S. 114. Particularly is this so where a decision here for review cannot escape broadly social judgments—judgments lying close to opinion regarding the whole nature of our Government and the duties and immunities of citizenship. Deference properly due to the findings of a lower court does not preclue the review here of such judgments. This recognized scope of appellate review is usually differentiated from the review of ordinary questions of fact by being called review of a question of law, but that is often not an illuminating test and is never self-executing. Suffice it to say that emphasis on the importance of "clear, unequivocal, and convincing" proof, see Schneiderman v. United States, supra, at 125, on which to rest the cancellation of a certificate of naturalization would be lost if the ascertainment by the lower courts whether that exacting standard of proof had been satisfied on the whole record were to be deemed a "fact" of the same order as all other "facts," not open to review here.

The gravamen of the Government's complaint and of the findings and opinions below is that Baumgartner consciously withheld allegiance to the United States and its Constitution and laws; in short, that Baumgartner was guilty of fraud. To prove such intentional misrepresentation evidence calculated to establish only the objective falsity of Baumgartner's oath was adduced. Nothing else was offered to show that Baumgartner was aware of a conflict between his views and the new political allegiance he assumed. But even if objective falsity as against perjurious falsity of the oath is to be deemed sufficient under § 338 (a) of the Nationality Act of 1940 to revoke an admission to citizenship, it is our view that the evidence does not measure up to the standard of proof which must be applied to this case.

We come then to a consideration of the evidence in the context in which that evidence is to be judged. Congress alone has been entrusted by the Constitution with the power to give or withhold naturalization and to that end "to establish a uniform Rule of Naturalization." Art. I, § 8, Clause 4. In exercising its power, Congress has authorized the courts to grant American citizenship only if the alien has satisfied the conditions imposed by Congress for naturalization. . . . From the earliest days of the Republic, Congress has required as a condition of citizenship that an alien renounce his foreign allegiance and swear allegiance to this country and its Constitution. Act of January 29, 1795, 1 Stat. 414. By this requirement Congress has not used meaningless words. Nor, on the other hand, has it thereby expressed a narrow test or formula susceptible of almost mechanical proof, as is true of other prerequisites for naturalization—period of residence, documentation of arrival, requisite number of sponsoring witnesses and the like. Allegiance to this Government and its laws, is a compendious phrase to describe those political and legal institutions that are the enduring features of American political society. . . .

The denial of application for citizenship because the judicial mind has not been satisfied that the test of allegiance has been met, presents a problem very different from the revocation of the naturalization certificate once admission to the community of American citizenship has been decreed. No doubt the statutory procedure for naturalization (§ 334, Nationality Act of 1940), and § 338, with which we are here concerned, "were designed to afford cumulative protection against fraudulent or illegal naturalization." United States v. Ness, 245 U.S. 319, 327. But relaxation in the vigor appropriate for scrutinizing the intensity of the allegiance to this country embraced by an applicant before admitting him to citizenship is not to be corrected by meagre standards for disproving such allegiance retrospectively. New relations and new interests flow, once citizenship has been granted. All that should not be undone unless the proof is compelling that that which was granted was obtained in defiance of Congressional authority. Non-fulfilment of specific conditions, like time of residence or the required number of supporting witnesses, are easily established, and when established leave no room for discretion because Congress has left no area of discretion. But where the claim of "illegality" really involves issues of belief or fraud, proof is treacherous and objective judgment, even by the most disciplined minds, precarious. That is why denaturalization on this score calls for weighty proof, especially when the proof of a false or fraudulent oath rests predominantly not upon contemporaneous evidence but is established by later expressions of opinion argumentatively projected, and often through the distorting and self-deluding medium of memory, to an earlier year when qualifications for citizenship were claimed, tested and adjudicated. . . .

The insufficiency of the evidence to show that Baumgartner did not renounce his allegiance to Germany in 1932 need not be labored. Whatever German political leanings Baumgartner had in 1932, they were to Hitler and Hitlerism, certainly not to the Weimar Republic. Hitler did not come to power until after Baumgartner forswore his allegiance to the then German nation.

Views attributed to Baumgartner as to the superiority of German people, schools, engineering techniques, and the virtues of Hitler, expressed in 1927, when he began to work in Kansas City, are the only direct evidence introduced to show that before he was naturalized in 1932, his attitude precluded his truly or honestly taking an oath of allegiance to the United States, its Constitution and its laws. And his statement at the trial that his attitude toward the principles of the American Government was the same in 1932 as it was at the time of the trial, is hardly significant. For Baumgartner professed loyalty at the trial, denied or explained the few disturbing statements attributed to him by others, and reconciled suspicious diary entries in ways that do not preclude the validity of his oath of allegiance. In short, the weakness of the proof as to Baumgartner's state of mind at the time he took the oath of allegiance can be removed, if at all, only by a presumption that disqualifying views expressed after naturalization were accurate representations of his views when he took the oath. The logical validity of such a presumption is at best dubious even were the supporting evidence less rhetorical and more conclusive. Baumgartner was certainly not shown to have been a party Nazi, and there is only the statement of one witness that Baumgartner had told him that he was a member of the Bund, to hint even remotely that Baumgartner was associated with any group for the systematic agitation of Nazi views or views hostile to this Government. On the contrary, Baumgartner's diary, on which the Government mainly relies, reveals that when in 1939 he attended a meeting of the German Vocational League at which the Nazi salute was given, it was apparently his only experience with this group, and he went "Since I wanted to see what sort of an organization this Vocational League was."

And so we conclude that the evidence as to Baumgartner's attitude after 1932 affords insufficient proof that in 1932 he had knowing reservations in forswearing his allegiance to the Weimar Republic and embracing allegiance to this country so as to warrant the infliction of the grave consequences involved in making an alien out of a man ten years after he was admitted to citizenship. The evidence in the record before us is not sufficiently compelling to require that we penalize a naturalized citizen for the expression of silly or even sinister-sounding views which native-born citizens utter with impunity. The judgment must accordingly be reversed and the case remanded to the District Court for further proceedings not inconsistent with this opinion.

Reversed.

[The separate opinion by MR. JUSTICE MURPHY is omitted.]

CIRCUMSTANTIAL EVIDENCE

Warmke v. Commonwealth

court of appeals of kentucky, 1944
297 ky. 649, 180 s.w.2d 872

FULTON, CHIEF JUSTICE. This appeal is from a manslaughter sentence of nine years imposed on the appellant in connection with the death of her infant child. The sole ground urged for reversal was that the corpus delicti was not sufficiently shown.

The appellant resided in Utica, a village in Davies County. Some weeks prior to July 8, 1943 she went to Louisville and there gave birth to an illegitimate child. On July 8, 1943, she traveled to Cloverport, in Breckenridge County, by bus arriving about 8 o'clock p.m. It was raining very hard and she went into a drug store for shelter. A. T. Couch, an employee of the store, loaned her a coat in which to wrap her baby. She went out leaving her suitcase in the store. She called Couch by telephone about 10:30, requesting him to come to the store so that she might get her suitcase. When she met Couch at the store she did not have the baby but returned the borrowed coat. Early the next morning she went to the home of a kinswoman, Mrs. Pate. The town marshal, having learned that the baby was missing, went to Mrs. Pate's home and questioned the appellant. She told him that after she left the drug store she started to cross a railroad trestle near the town in an effort to get to the home of a friend and that while she was crossing a train approached and she crawled over on the ties and accidentally dropped the baby. The town marshal and a highway patrolman then took the appellant to the trestle and she pointed out where the baby had been dropped. There was a creek under the trestle at this point. It was flooded and the current was swift. A baby's cap was found on the bank of the creek and the appellant exclaimed, "There is my little baby's cap." The baby's body was never found.

When the officers returned to town with the appellant she told them, after some questioning, that she purposely threw the baby into the creek because she was unable to face the humiliation of going home with an illegitimate child.

On the trial she repudiated the confession she had made to the officers and testified that she dropped the baby accidentally, in the manner she first told the officers. She testified that she was scared and excited and didn't remember saying she dropped the baby purposely. She said that after she dropped the baby she wandered around all night barefooted and in a dazed condition and that in the morning she put on her shoes and stockings and went to Mrs. Pate's. She gave as a reason for stopping off at Cloverport that it was her father's home town and that she desired to talk to a friend, Mrs. Atwill, and obtain advice. She did not see Mrs. Atwill but says that she was looking for her house when she dropped the baby and that thereafter she remembered nothing until early morning.

It is axiomatic that the corpus delicti must be shown. The term means the body of the offense, the substance of the crime. Proof of the corpus delicti in homicide cases involves two principal facts, namely, that the person is dead and that he died as a result of the injury alleged to have been received. In short, there must be proof of a death and proof that such death was caused by the criminal agency of the accused. Higgins v. Com., 142 Ky. 647, 134 S.W. 1135; 13 R.C.L. 730.

But the law does not subscribe to the rigid formula that the body must be found or seen after death. The death may be established by circumstantial evidence. 26 Amer. Juris. 376. As said in 13 R.C.L. 737, the death may be shown "by proof of criminal violence adequate to produce death and which accounts for the disappearance of the body. In short, the body must be found or there must be proof of death which the law deems to be equivalent to direct evidence that it was found."

We think there was sufficient proof of the death of the baby in the case before us. It was dropped, either purposely or accidentally, by the appellant from the railroad trestle into the flooded creek below and was never found. It seems beyond the bounds of possibility that the baby survived this ordeal and was never thereafter heard of. At least, we think the evidence was ample to justify the jury's finding that death ensued.

It is argued for the appellant, however, that the corpus delicti must be established by evidence other than the confession of the accused out of court and that there was no other evidence here. The soundness of the legal proposition thus advanced may be admitted. There must be proof of the component elements of the corpus delicti, a death and the criminal agency of the accused, by proof in addition to the confession of the accused made out of court. Criminal Code of Practice, Sec. 240; Moseby v. Com., Ky., 113 S.W. 850, Com. v. Burgess, 91 S.W. 266. But, as indicated above, the appellant testified that the baby was dropped into the creek. Thus there was proof of the death independent of the appellant's confession made out of court.

The remaining question is whether there was proof, in addition to the appellant's confession made out of court, of her criminal agency in causing the death. Her agency in causing the death was admitted from the witness stand. Was there evidence, independent of her confession out of court, that this agency was criminal? We think there was an abundance of such evidence. Such independent evidence may be circumstantial as well as direct.

Circumstances pointing clearly to the fact that the appellant purposely dropped the baby from the trestle may be thus summarized. She had an impelling motive, concealment of the birth of the illegitimate child. Her reason for going to Cloverport instead of her home is rather vague and unsatisfactory. This reason was that she decided to consult her friend, Mrs. Atwill, yet she never did so. She eventually wound up at Mrs. Pate's and not at Mrs. Atwill's. But most illuminating of all is her failure to notify any one that she had dropped the baby from the trestle, if it was dropped accidentally. She accounts for this by saying she was in a dazed condition, nevertheless she called Mr. Couch by telephone to come to the drug store so that she might get her suitcase. She returned the coat to him. She had borrowed this coat to wrap the baby in. It is singular that she would have accidentally dropped the baby without dropping the coat. It is even more singular that she never notified Mrs. Pate, her kinswoman, the next morning of the loss of the baby. These circumstances and the justifiable inferences to be drawn from them, amply warranted the jury in finding that the dropping of the baby from the trestle was purposely, and not accidentally, done by the appellant.

Affirmed.

JUDICIAL NOTICE AND
GENERAL KNOWLEDGE

MULLER V. OREGON

SUPREME COURT OF THE UNITED STATES, 1908
208 U.S. 412, 52 L. ED. 551

MR. JUSTICE BREWER delivered the opinion of the Court:

On February 19, 1903, the legislature of the state of Oregon passed an act (Session Laws 1903, p. 148) the first section of which is in these words:

"Sec. 1. That no female (shall) be employed in any mechanical establishment, or factory, or laundry in this state more than ten hours during any one day. The hours of work may be so arranged as to permit the employment of females at any time so that they shall not work more than ten hours during the twenty-four hours of any one day."

Sec. 3 made a violation of the provisions of the prior sections a misdemeanor subject to a fine of not less than $10 nor more than $25. On September 18, 1905, an information was filed in the circuit court of the state for the county of Multnomah, charging that the defendant "on the 4th day of September, A.D. 1905, in the county of Multnomah and state of Oregon, then and there being the owner of a laundry, known as the Grand Laundry, in the city of Portland, and the employer of females therein, did then and there unlawfully permit and suffer one Joe Haselbock, he, the said Joe Haselbock, then and there being an overseer, superintendent, and agent of said Curt Muller, in the said Grand Laundry, to require a female, to wit, one Mrs. E. Gotcher, to work more than ten hours in said laundry on said 4th day of September, A.D. 1905, contrary to the statutes in such cases made and provided, and against the peace and dignity of the state of Oregon."

A trial resulted in a verdict against the defendant, who was sentenced to pay a fine of $10. The supreme court of the state affirmed the conviction (48 Or. 252, 85 Pac. 855), whereupon the case was brought here on writ of error.

The single question is the constitutionality of the statute under which the defendant was convicted, so far as it affects the work of a female in a laundry. That it does not conflict with any provisions of the state Constitution is settled by the decision of the supreme court of the state. The contentions of the defendant, now plaintiff in error, are thus stated in his brief:

"(1) Because the statute attempts to prevent persons *sui juris* from making their own contracts, and thus violates the provisions of the 14th Amendment, as follows:

" 'No state shall make or enforce any law which shall abridge the privileges or immunities of citizens of the United States; nor shall any state deprive any person of life, liberty, or property, without due process of law; nor deny to any person within its jurisdiction the equal protection of the laws.'

"(2) Because the statute does not apply equally to all persons similarly situated, and is class legislation.

"(3) The statute is not a valid exercise of the police power. The kinds of work prescribed are not unlawful, nor are they declared to be immoral or dangerous to the public health; nor can such a law be sustained on the ground that it is designed to protect women on account of their sex. There is no necessary or reasonable connection between the limitation prescribed by the act and the public health, safety, or welfare."

It is the law of Oregon that women, whether married or single, have equal contractual and personal rights with men. As said by Chief Justice Wolverton, in First Nat. Bank v. Leonard, 36 Or. 390, 396, 59 Pac. 873, 874, after a review of the various statutes of the state upon the subject:

"We may therefore say with perfect confidence that, with these three sections upon the statute book, the wife can deal, not only with her separate property, acquired from whatever source, in the same manner as her husband can with property belonging to him, but that she may make contracts and incur liabilities, and the same may be enforced against her, the same as if she were a *feme sole*. There is now no residuum of civil disability resting upon her which is not recognized as existing against the husband. The current runs steadily and strongly in the direction of the emancipation of the wife, and the policy, as disclosed by all recent legislation upon the subject in this state, is to place her upon the same footing as if she were a *feme sole,* not only with respect to her separate property, but as it affects her right to make binding contracts; and the most natural corollary to the situation is that the remedies for the enforcement of liabilities incurred are made coextensive and coequal with such enlarged conditions."

It thus appears that, putting to one side the elective franchise, in the matter of personal and contractual rights, they stand on the same plane as the other sex. Their rights in these respects can no more be infringed than the equal rights of their brothers. We held in Lochner v. New York, 198 U.S. 45, 49 L. Ed. 937, 25 Sup. Ct. Rep. 539, that a law providing that no laborer shall be required or permitted to work in bakeries more than sixty hours in a week or ten hours in a day was not, as to men, a legitimate exercise of the police power of the state, but an unreasonable, unnecessary, and arbitrary interference with the right and liberty of the individual to contract in relation to his labor, and as such was in conflict with, and void under, the Federal Constitution. That decision is invoked by plaintiff in error as decisive of the question before us. But this assumes that the difference between the sexes does not justify a different rule respecting a restriction of the hours of labor.

In patent cases counsel are apt to open the argument with a discussion of the state of the art. It may not be amiss, in the present case, before examining the constitutional question, to notice the course of legislation, as well as expressions of opinion from other than judicial sources. In the brief filed by Mr. Louis D. Brandeis for the defendant in error is a very copious collection of all these matters, an epitome of which is found in the margin.†

[The following legislation of the states imposes restrictions

† Included here in the following bracketed paragraphs.

in some form or another upon the hours of labor that may be required of women: Massachusetts: 1874, Rev. Laws 1902, chap. 106, § 24; Rhode Island: 1885, Acts and Resolves 1902, chap. 994, p. 73; Louisiana: 1886, Rev. Laws 1904, vol. 1, § 4, p. 989; Connecticut: 1887, Gen. Stat. Revision 1902, § 4691; Maine: 1887, Rev. Stat. 1903, chap. 40, § 48; New Hampshire: 1887, Laws 1907, chap. 94, p. 95; Maryland: 1888, Pub. Gen. Laws 1903, art. 100, § 1; Virginia: 1890, Code 1904, title 51A, chap. 178A, § 3657b; Pennsylvania: 1897, Laws 1905, No. 226, p. 352; New York: 1899, Laws 1907, chap. 507, § 77, subdiv. 3, p. 1078; Nebraska: 1899, Comp. Stat. 1905, § 7955, p. 1986; Washington: Stat. 1901, chap. 68, § 1, p. 118; Colorado: Acts 1903, chap. 138, § 3, p. 310; New Jersey: 1892, Gen. Stat. 1895, p. 2350, §§ 66, 67; Oklahoma: 1890, Rev. Stat. 1903, chap. 25, art. 58, § 729; North Dakota: 1877, Rev. Code 1905, § 9440; South Dakota: 1877, Rev. Code (Penal Code, § 764), p. 1185; Wisconsin, 1867, Code 1898, § 1728; South Carolina: Acts 1907, No. 233.

[In foreign legislation Mr. Brandeis calls attention to these statutes: Great Britain, 1844: Law 1901, 1 Edw. VII, chap. 22. France, 1848: Act Nov. 2, 1892, and March 30, 1900. Switzerland, Canton of Glarus, 1948: Federal Law 1877, art. 2, § 1. Austria, 1855; Acts 1897, art. 96a, §§ 1-3. Holland, 1889; art. 5, § 1. Italy, June 19, 1902, art. 7. Germany, Laws 1891.

[Then follow extracts from over ninety reports of committees, bureaus of statistics, commissioners of hygiene, inspectors of factories, both in this country and in Europe, to the effect that long hours of labor are dangerous for women, primarily because of their special physical organization. The matter is discussed in these reports in different aspects, but all agree as to the danger. It would, of course, take too much space to give these reports in detail. Following them are extracts from similar reports discussing the general benefits of short hours from an economic aspect of the question. In many of these reports individual instances are given tending to support the general conclusion. Perhaps the general scope and character of all these reports may be summed up in what an inspector for Hanover says: "The reasons for the reduction of the working day to ten hours—(a) the physical organization of women, (b) her maternal functions, (c) the rearing and education of the children, (d) the maintenance of the home—are all so important and so far-reaching that the need for such reduction need hardly be discussed."]

While there have been but few decisions bearing directly upon the question, the following sustain the constitutionality of such legislation; Com. v. Hamilton Mfg. Co. 120 Mass. 383; Weham v. State, 65 Neb. 394, 400, 406, 58 L.R.A. 825, 91 N.W. 421; State v. Buchanan, 29 Wash. 602, 59 L.R.A. 342, 92 Am. St. Rep. 930, 70 Pac. 52; Com. v. Beatty, 15 Pa. Super. Ct. 5, 17; against them is the case of Ritchie v. People, 155 Ill. 98, 29 L.R.A. 79, 46 Am. St. Rep. 315, 40 N.E. 454.

The legislation and opinions referred to in the margin may not be, technically speaking, authorities, and in them is little or no discussion of the constitutional question presented to us for determination, yet they are significant of a widespread belief that woman's physical structure, and the functions she performs in consequence thereof, justify special legislation restricting or qualifying the conditions under which she should be permitted to toil. Constitutional questions, it is true, are not settled by even a consensus of present public opinion, for it is the peculiar value of a written constitution that it places in unchanging form limitations upon legislative action, and thus gives a permanence and stability to popular government which otherwise would be lacking. At the same time, when a question of fact is debated and debatable, and the extent to which a special constitutional limitation goes is affected by the truth in respect to that fact, a widespread and long-continued belief concerning it is worthy of consideration. We take judicial cognizance of all matters of general knowledge.

It is undoubtedly true, as more than once declared by this court, that the general right to contract in relation to one's business is part of the liberty of the individual, protected by the 14th Amendment to the Federal Constitution; yet it is equally well settled that this liberty is not absolute and extending to all contracts, and that a state may, without conflicting with the provisions of the 14th Amendment, restrict in many respects the individual's power of contract. Without stopping to discuss at length the extent to which a state may act in this respect, we refer to the following cases in which the question has been considered:

Allgeyer v. Louisiana, 165 U.S. 578, 41 L. Ed. 832, 17 Sup. Ct. Rep. 427; Holden v. Hardy, 169 U.S. 366, 42 L. Ed. 780, 18 Sup. Ct. Rep. 383; Lochner v. New York, supra.

That woman's physical structure and the performance of maternal functions place her at a disadvantage in the struggle for subsistence is obvious. This is especially true when the burdens of motherhood are upon her. Even when they are not, by abundant testimony of the medical fraternity continuance for a long time on her feet at work, repeating this from day to day, tends to injurious effects upon the body, and, as healthy mothers are essential to vigorous offspring, the physical well-being of woman becomes an object of public interest and care in order to preserve the strength and vigor of the race.

Still again, history discloses the fact that woman has always been dependent upon man. He established his control at the outset by superior physical strength, and this control in various forms, with diminishing intensity, has continued to the present. As minors, though not to the same extent, she has been looked upon in the courts as needing especial care that her rights may be preserved. Education was long denied her, and while now the doors of the schoolroom are opened and her opportunities for acquiring knowledge are great, yet even with that and the consequent increase of capacity for business affairs it is still true that in the struggle for subsistence she is not an equal competitor with her brother. Though limitations upon personal and contractual rights may be removed by legislation, there is that in her disposition and habits of life which will operate against a full assertion of those rights. She will still be where some legislation to protect her seems necessary to secure a real equality of right. Doubtless there are individual exceptions, and there are many respects in which she has an advantage over him; but looking at it from the viewpoint of the effort to maintain an independent position in life, she is not upon an equality. Differentiated by these matters from the other sex, she is properly placed in a class by herself, and legislation designed for her protection may be sustained, even when like legislation is not necessary for men, and could not be sustained. It is impossible to close one's eyes to the fact that she still looks to her brother and depends upon him. Even though all restrictions on political, personal, and contractual rights were taken away, and she stood, so far as statutes are concerned, upon an absolutely equal plane with him, it would still be true that she is so constituted that she will rest upon and look to him for protection: that her physical structure and a proper discharge of her maternal functions—having in view not merely her own health, but the well-being of the race—justify legislation to protect her from the greed as well as the passion of man. The limitations which this statute places upon her contractual powers, upon her right to agree with her employer as to the time she shall labor, are not imposed solely for her benefit, but also largely for the benefit of all. Many words cannot make this plainer. The two sexes differ in structure of body, in the functions to be performed by each, in the amount of physical strength, in the capacity for long-continued labor, particularly when done standing, the influence of vigorous health upon the future well-being of the race, the self-reliance which enables one to assert full rights, and in the capacity to maintain the struggle for subsistence. This difference justifies a difference in legislation, and upholds that which is designed to compensate for some of the burdens which rest upon her.

We have not referred in this discussion to the denial of the elective franchise in the state of Oregon, for while that may disclose a lack of political equality in all things with her brother, that is not of itself decisive. The reason runs deeper, and rests in the inherent difference between the two sexes, and in the different functions in life which they perform.

For these reasons, and without questioning in any respect the decision in Lochner v. New York, we are of the opinion that it cannot be adjudged that the act in question is in conflict with the Federal Constitution, so far as it respects the work of a female in a laundry, and the judgment of the Supreme Court of Oregon is affirmed.

DIFFICULTY OF PROOF

Woods v. Lancet

court of appeals of new york, 1951
303 n.y. 349, 102 n.e.2d 691

Desmond, J. The complaint served on behalf of this infant plaintiff alleges that, while the infant was in his mother's womb during the ninth month of her pregnancy, he sustained, through the negligence of defendant, such serious injuries that he came into this world permanently maimed and disabled. Defendant moved to dismiss the complaint as not stating a cause of action, thus taking the position that its allegations, though true, gave the infant no right to recover damages in the courts of New York. The Special Term granted the motion and dismissed the suit, citing Drobner v. Peters (232 N.Y. 220, 133 N.E. 567). In the Appellate Division one Justice voted for reversal with an opinion in which he described the obvious injustice of the rule, noted a decisional trend (in other States and Canada) toward giving relief in such cases, and suggested that since Drobner v. Peters (supra) was decided thirty years ago by a divided vote, our court might well re-examine it.

The four Appellate Division Justices who voted to affirm the dismissal below, wrote no opinion except that one of them stated that, were the question an open one and were he not bound by Drobner v. Peters (supra), he would hold that "when a pregnant woman is injured through negligence and the child subsequently born suffers deformity or other injury as a result, recovery therefor may be allowed to the child, provided the causal relation between the negligence and the damage to the child be established by competent medical evidence." (278 App. Div. 913.) It will hardly be disputed that justice (not emotionalism or sentimentality) dictates the enforcement of such a cause of action. The trend in decisions of other courts, and the writing of learned commentators, in the period since Drobner v. Peters was handed down in 1921, is strongly toward making such a recovery possible. The precise question for us on this appeal is: shall we follow Drobner v. Peters, or shall we bring the common law of this State, on this question, into accord with justice? I think, as New York's court of last resort, we should make the law conform to right.

Drobner v. Peters (supra), like the present case, dealt with the sufficiency of a complaint alleging prenatal injuries, tortiously inflicted on a nine-month foetus, viable at the time and actually born later. There is, therefore, no material distinction between that case and the one we are passing on now. However, Drobner v. Peters must be examined against a background of history and of the legal thought of its time and of the thirty years that have passed since it was handed down. Early British and American common law gives no definite answer to our question, so it is not profitable to go back farther than Dietrich v. Northampton (138 Mass. 4), decided in 1884, with an opinion by JUSTICE HOLMES, and, apparently, the first American case. Actually that was a death case, since the five-month infant, prematurely born, survived for a few minutes after birth. The principal ground asserted by the Massachusetts Supreme Court (138 Mass., at p. 17) for a denial of recovery was that "the unborn child was a part of the mother at the time of the injury" and that "any damage to it which was not too remote to be recovered for at all was recoverable by her" (the mother). A few years later (1890), in Ireland, the Queen's Bench Division, in a very famous holding, refused to allow a suit to be brought on behalf of a child born deformed as the result of an accident in defendant's railway coach, two of the Justices taking the ground that the infant plaintiff was not *in esse* at the time of the wrong, and the other two regarding the suit as one on the contract of carriage with no duty of care owing by the carrier to the unborn infant whose presence was unknown to defendant (Walker v. Great Northern Ry. of Ireland, 28 L.R. Ir. 69). . . . There were, in the early years of this century, rejections of such suits by other courts, with various fact situations involving before-birth traumas . . . and, quite recently, Massachusetts has reaffirmed the Dietrich rule (Bliss v. Passanesi, 326 Mass. 461, 95 N.E.2d 206). . . .

In Drobner v. Peters (supra), this court, finding no precedent for maintaining the suit, adopted the general theory of Dietrich v. Northampton (supra), taking into account, besides the lack of authority to support the suit, the practical difficulties of proof in such cases, and the theoretical lack of separate human existence of an infant *in utero*. It is not unfair to say that the basic reason for Drobner v. Peters was absence of precedent. However, since 1921, numerous and impressive precedents have been developed. In California (Scott v. McPheeters, 33 Cal. App. 2d 629, 92 P.2d 678) the Court of Appeal allowed the suit—reliance was there put on a California statute but that statute was not directly in point, since it directed only that "a child conceived, but not yet born, is to be deemed an existing person, so far as may be necessary for its interests in the event of its subsequent birth." That California statute merely codified an accepted and ancient common-law rule (see Stedfast v. Nicoll, 3 Johns. Cas. 18, 23, 24) which, for some reason, has not, at least in our court, been applied to prepartum injuries tortiously inflicted. In 1949, the Ohio Supreme Court (Williams v. Marion R. T., Inc., 152 Ohio St. 114, 87 N.E.2d 334, rule reaffirmed by the same court in Jasinsky v. Potts, 153 Ohio St. 529, 92 N.E.2d 809) and Minnesota's highest tribunal (Verkennes v. Corniea, 229 Minn. 365, 38 N.W.2d 838), and in 1951 the Court of Appeals of Maryland (Damasiewicz v. Gorsuch, —— Md. ——, 79 S.2d 550) and the Supreme Court of Georgia (Trucker v. Carmichael, 208 Ga. 201, 65 S.E.2d 909) upheld the right of an infant to bring an action like the one we are here examining, without statutory authorization. . . . Of law review articles on the precise question there is an ample supply (see 20 Minn. L. Rev. 321-322; 34 Minn. L. Rev. 65-66; 48 Mich. L. Rev. 539-541; 35 Cornell L.Q. 648-654; 1951 Wis. L. Rev. 518-528; 50 Mich. L. Rev. 166-167). They justify the statement in Prosser on Torts, at page 190, that: "All writers who have discussed the problem have joined in condemning the existing rule, in maintaining that the unborn child in the path of an automobile is as much a person in the street as the mother, and urging that recovery should be allowed upon proper proof."

What, then, stands in the way of a reversal here? Surely, as an original proposition, we would, today, be hard put to it to find a sound reason for the old rule. Following Drobner v. Peters (supra) would call for an affirmance but the chief basis for that holding (lack of precedent) no longer exists. And it is not a very strong reason, anyhow, in a case like this. Of course, rules of law on which men rely in their business dealings should not be changed in the middle of the game, but what has that to do with bringing to justice a tort-feasor who surely has no moral or other right to rely on a decision of the New York Court of Appeals? Negligence law is common law, and the common law has been molded and changed and brought up-to-date in many another case. Our court said, long ago, that it had not only the right, but the duty to re-examine a question where justice demands it (Rumsey v. New York & N.E.R.R. Co., 133 N.Y. 79, 85, 86, 30 N.E. 654, 655, and see Klein v. Maravelas, 219 N.Y. 383, 114 N.E. 809). That opinion notes that CHANCELLOR KENT, more than a century ago, had stated that upwards of a thousand cases could then be pointed out in the English and American reports " 'which had been overruled, doubted or limited in their application,' " and that the great chancellor had declared that decisions which seem contrary to reason " 'ought to be examined without fear, and revised without reluctance, rather than to have the character of our law impaired, and the beauty and harmony of the system destroyed by the perpetuity of error.' " And JUSTICE SUTHERLAND, writing for the Supreme Court in Funk v. United States (290 U.S. 371, 382, 54 S. Ct. 212, 215, 78 L. Ed. 369), said that while legislative bodies have the power to change old rules of law, nevertheless, when they fail to act, it is the duty of the court to bring the law into accordance with present day standards of wisdom and justice rather than "with some outworn and antiquated rule of the past." No reason appears why there should not be the same approach when traditional common-law rules of negligence result in injustice (see Hagopian v. Samuelson, 236 App. Div. 491, 492, 260 N.Y.S. 24, 25, and see JUSTICE STONE's article on "The Common Law in the United States," 50 Harv. L. Rev., pp. 4-7).

The sum of the argument against plaintiff here is that there is no New York decision in which such a claim has been enforced. Winfield's answer to that (see U. of Toronto L.J. article, supra,

p. 29) will serve: "if that were a valid objection, the common law would now be what it was in the Plantagenet period." And we can borrow from our British friends another mot: "When these ghosts of the past stand in the path of justice clanking their mediaeval chains the proper course for the judge is to pass through them undeterred" (LORD ATKIN in United Australia, Lts., v. Barclay's Bank, Ltd., [1941] A.C. 1, 29). We act in the finest common-law tradition when we adapt and alter decisional law to produce common-sense justice.

The same answer goes to the argument that the change we here propose should come from the Legislature, not the courts. Legislative action there could, of course, be, but we abdicate our own function, in a field peculiarly nonstatutory, when we refuse to reconsider an old and unsatisfactory court-made rule. Perhaps, some kinds of changes in the common law could not safely be made without the kind of factual investigation which the Legislature and not the courts, is equipped for. Other proposed changes require elaborate research and consideration of a variety of possible remedies—such questions are peculiarly appropriate for Law Revision Commission scrutiny, and in fact, the Law Revision Commission has made an elaborate examination of this very problem (1935 Report of N.Y. Law Revision Commission, pp. 449-476). That study was made at the instance of the late CHIEF JUDGE POUND of this court and was transmitted to the Legislature by the commission. Although made before the strong trend in favor of recovery had clearly manifested itself, the Law Revision Commission's comments were strongly in favor of the position taken in this opinion. The report, itself contained no recommendations for legislation on the subject but that apparently was because the commission felt that it was for the courts to deal with this common-law question. At page 465, for instance, the report said: "The common law does not go on the theory that a case of first impression presents a problem of legislative as opposed to judicial power."

Two other reasons for dismissal (besides lack of precedent) are given in Drobner v. Peters (supra). The first of those, discussed in many of the other writings on the subject herein cited, has to do with the supposed difficulty of proving or disproving that certain injuries befell the unborn child, or that they produced the defects discovered at birth, or later. Such difficulties there are, of course, and, indeed, it seems to be commonly accepted that only a blow of tremendous force will ordinarily injure a foetus, so carefully does nature insulate it. But such difficulty of proof or finding is not special to this particular kind of lawsuit (and it is beside the point anyhow, in determining sufficiency of a pleading). Every day in all our trial courts (and before administrative tribunals, particularly the Workmen's Compensation Board), such issues are disposed of, and it is an inadmissible concept that uncertainty of proof can ever destroy a legal right. The questions of causation, reasonable certainty, etc., which will arise in these cases are no different, in kind, from the ones which have arisen in thousands of other negligence cases decided in this State, in the past.

The other objection to recovery here is the purely theoretical one that a foetus *in utero* has no existence of its own separate from that of its mother, that is, that it is not "a being *in esse.*" We need not deal here with so large a subject. It is to be remembered that we are passing on the sufficiency of a complaint which alleges that this injury occurred during the ninth month of the mother's pregnancy, in other words, to a viable foetus, later born. Therefore, we confine our holding in this case to prepartum injuries to such viable children. Of course such a child, still in the womb, is, in one sense, a part of its mother, but no one seems to claim that the mother, in her own name and for herself, could get damages for the injuries to her infant. To hold, as matter of law, that no viable foetus has any separate existence which the law will recognize is for the law to deny a simple and easily demonstrable fact. This child, when injured, was in fact, alive and capable of being delivered and of remaining alive separate from its mother. We agree with the dissenting Justice below that "To deny the infant relief in this case is not only a harsh result, but its effect is to do reverence to an outmoded, timeworn fiction not founded on fact and within common knowledge untrue and unjustified." (278 App. Div. 913, 914, 105 N.Y.S.2d 417, 418.)

The judgments should be reversed, and motion denied, with costs in all courts.

[The dissenting opinion of LEWIS, J. concurred in by CONWAY, J., is omitted.]

Notes

1. Compare the decision in *Woods v. Lancet* with the decision in *Mitchell v. Rochester Ry. Co.* (Chapter 1). To what extent does the difficulty of proof in such cases pose a moral as well as a legal problem in assessing one's obligations?

   Assume that the child in the *Mitchell* case was born alive but injured as a result of the accident. Would it, or should it, have made a difference in the legal decision?

2. In *Warmke v. Commonwealth* and in *United States v. Holmes* (Chapter 3), both defendants were found guilty of manslaughter. Although malice was not an issue, motive seemed to be, despite the claim of many that the law takes little interest in motives but much in intentions. Assess this distinction in the light of these cases. Also, does circumstantial or does testimonial evidence appear to be better for determining motives?

3. There is an obvious difference between being a "citizen" and being a "loyal citizen." What different methods of investigation and reasoning are required to establish these two kinds of "facts"?

4. Name several moral presumptions. Do they operate in moral reasoning in a way analogous to the way they operate in legal reasoning? On a candid view of human nature, isn't the presumption of (moral) innocence taking very much for granted?

5. Is the rather widespread judicial distrust of the use of "general knowledge" as evidence, or as a substitute for evidence, such as was employed by Brandeis is *Muller v. Oregon,* altogether without basis, or are there good reasons which justify the distrust?

   To what extent can and should moral decisions await the pronouncements of the scientist? Are there circumstances in which that kind of fact would not be very helpful?

6. In *People v. Zackowitz,* it is said that "there must be no blurring of the issues by evidence illegally admitted and carrying with it in its admission an appeal to prejudice and passion." The primary issue at the trial was the nature of the defendant's state of mind at the time of the homicide. Did he act impulsively or with a premeditated design to kill? Why did the judge think that the admission of evidence regarding the

defendant's character and his possession of an arsenal of weapons tended "to blur the issue"? Isn't there a close relation between character and one's state of mind?

If the evidence admitted did blur the issue or make an appeal to prejudice or passion, then it clearly falls under the legal classification of "incompetent" evidence. However, "incompetent" does not mean the same as "irrelevant." Yet, the judge goes further and questions even the relevance of the statements about the defendant's ownership of weapons. Is he thereby attempting to support his judgment about the incompetence of the evidence, or is he urging an additional ground for exclusion, namely, irrelevancy. Retrace his reasoning.

Why does the judge characterize the admission of evidence for one purpose and using it for another as "illegal"? Is it any more illegal than admitting "prejudicial" evidence, or "confusing" evidence? Does he mean to make a quite different type of objection, namely, that it is "unfair" or "unjust" in a moral sense?

Glossary of Legal Terms

This list of legal expressions includes definitions which are widely accepted by lawyers and jurists. Differences, of course, exist within the legal profession regarding the proper use of many of these terms. Different legal contexts often give rise to different meanings for the same term. No attempt has been made to list all such meanings, but only those that are particularly relevant to the cases included in this volume. Also, although an attempt has been made to express these definitions in ways that are useful and understandable to the layman, the demand for technical legal accuracy has also been kept in mind. Needless to say, accomplishing this dual task has not always been easy.

ACCESSORY BEFORE THE FACT: One who, while absent at the time a crime is committed, procures, incites, or orders another to commit it. An ACCESSORY AFTER THE FACT is one who, while knowing that a crime has been committed, assists, conceals, or protects the person charged with the crime.

ACT: A voluntary bodily movement. (The most frequently cited legal definition.)

ACTION: A proceeding in a court of justice by which one party seeks to protect or enforce his rights.

ACTOR: One who does an act. (Where philosophers ordinarily use AGENT, lawyers commonly use ACTOR.)

AGENT: As contrasted with PRINCIPAL, a person who has the delegated authority of another to act for him or in his place.

APPELLANT: The party to a dispute who appeals an adverse lower court decision to a higher court.

APPELLEE: The party against whom an appeal is taken. *Cf.* RESPONDENT.

ASSAULT: An intentional and unlawful act, other than the mere speaking of words, which makes another apprehensive of immediate bodily injury or of physical contact of an offensive character. A tort as well as a crime.

ASSUMPSIT: A form of action which can be brought to recover monetary compensation for the breach of a simple contract, whether oral or written. It is distinguished from actions based on contracts under seal, such as deeds and bonds.

BATTERY: An intentional and unlawful contact upon the person of another without his consent. Neither actual harm nor apprehension of harm is essential to the action, but some bodily contact or touching is. Frequently conjoined with assault to constitute the combined tort or crime of ASSAULT AND BATTERY.

BILL OF ATTAINDER: A special act of a legislature against a particular individual pronouncing him guilty of a capital offense, and sentencing him to death, without a trial in accordance with the recognized rules of procedure. Prohibited by the U.S. Constitution, Art. I, §§ 9, 10.

CAUSE OF ACTION: (1) The grounds for holding a person legally responsible; (2) more specifically, the facts or circumstances which, if established, would justify a court in rendering a judgment on the merits of the case; (3) also sometimes used synonymously with "suit," "action," or "case."

CERTIORARI: A writ issued by an appellate court in its discretion whereby it agrees to review a decision of a lower court and calls up the record of its proceedings in the case. *Cf.* WRIT OF ERROR.

CIVIL LAW: (1) In contrast to COMMON LAW as recognized in England and the United States, it is the system of law which developed out of ROMAN LAW; (2) In contrast to CRIMINAL LAW, it is that branch of law which deals with the rights of citizens in their relations with each other rather than in relation to the state.

COMMON LAW: (1) As contrasted with the enactments of legislatures, or STATUTORY LAW, the common law is that body of principles and rules whose authority derives from the customs of the past as embodied in the judgments and decrees of the courts which recognize, affirm, and enforce such customs; (2) also and especially, the ancient unwritten law of England. *Cf.* CIVIL LAW, EQUITY.

CONDITION: (1) In the law of contracts, any event, excluding mere lapse of time, the occurrence of which creates or relieves one of a duty of performance; (2) also, a provision in a contract so providing. For a causal sense of condition, *cf.* SINE QUA NON.

CONDITION PRECEDENT: In the law of contracts, a condition which must happen or be performed before the promisor's duty to act and the question of his liability can arise.

CONDITION SUBSEQUENT: In the law of contracts, a condition the occurrence or performance of which relieves a party from a previously exsting duty of performance.

CONSIDERATION: Something of legal, but not necessarily of material or economic, value (e.g., a return promise, an act, or forbearance, as well as a price) which is offered by one party and accepted by another as an inducement to make a contract. The test or criterion of legal value or "sufficiency" in this connection is that what is bargained for and exchanged for the other's promise shall be either a benefit to the promisor or a detriment to the promisee, or, as it usually is, both. Thus, SUFFICIENT CONSIDERATION is often simply defined as a legal benefit to the promisor or a legal detriment to the promisee.

CONTRACT: An agreement, either written or oral, creating a mutual obligation between two or more competent parties, and containing an offer, an acceptance of the offer, and a legal consideration.

CORPUS DELICTI: (1) Literally, the body or object of the crime; (2) the fact that a crime has actually been committed; (3) the visible evidence of the crime, such as the body of a murdered victim, or the charred remains of a house. Proof of the corpus delicti is required for every crime. This requires evidence both that a specific injury or loss occurred and that someone's criminal act is the cause of it. It is another matter to prove that the accused was the criminal involved.

CRIME: Generally, a violation of the penal law of a state; a FELONY or MISDEMEANOR as contrasted with OFFENSES such as violations of traffic laws; as contrasted with TORT, or breaches of CONTRACT, it represents a violation of one's duty to the whole community rather than an infringement of the civil rights of individuals in their relations to one another.

DAMAGES: (1) A monetary compensation which may be awarded for loss or injury suffered; (2) also, sometimes used to refer to the loss or injury itself.

DECEDENT: A deceased person.

DEFAMATION: An injury to a person's interest in reputation resulting from a communication to others which tends to hold the plaintiff up to hatred, contempt, or ridicule, or to cause him to be shunned or avoided, or to injure him in his occupation. Cf. LIBEL, SLANDER.

DEFENDANT: The party against whom a suit or action is brought.

DEFENDANT IN ERROR: The party against whom a writ of error is issued; the appellee, who could be either the plaintiff or the defendant in the lower court action. Cf. PLAINTIFF IN ERROR.

DEMURRER: An allegation that even if the facts stated in the pleading are true, they do not constitute a cause of action or a defense, and thus do not require the demurring party, whether plaintiff or defendant, to proceed further in the case.

DEVISE: A disposition of real estate by means of a last will and testament. *Cf.* LEGACY.

DICTUM: A statement or comment made in a judicial opinion which is not necessarily involved in or essential to the determination of the issue in the case being decided. *Cf.* RATIO DECIDENDI.

DIVERSITY OF CITIZENSHIP: Grounds for jurisdiction of the federal courts under U. S. Constitution, Art. 3, Sec. 2, as to cases between citizens of different states.

DOWER: The share of a husband's real estate which his widow is entitled by law to claim at his death.

EQUITY: As contrasted with LAW generally, or more particularly with the COMMON LAW, the term denotes a distinctive system of courts, rules, principles, and procedures which historically derives from the English Court of Chancery; that branch of the law which has exclusive jurisdiction over such matters as trusts and fiduciary obligations, the rescission, reformation, and specific performance of contracts, injunctions, e.g., in labor disputes, and in general with regard to all cases in which the courts of law are unable either to provide a remedy or to provide an adequate one.

EX POST FACTO LAW: A law passed after the occurrence of an act or event which changes the legal character or consequences of the act or event. Prohibited by the U.S. Constitution, Art. I, §§ 9, 10.

FELONY: A very serious crime, such as murder, arson, or rape, which is punishable by death or imprisonment in a state or federal penitentiary. *Cf.* MISDEMEANOR.

HEIR: One whom the law designates as a successor to a deceased person's estate.

INSANITY (LEGAL): A defect of reason caused by a disease of the mind in a person such that he did not know at the time of his act that what he did was wrong, and/or did not know the nature and quality of the act.

INTESTATE: Without having made a will; also, the person who dies without having made a will.

LEGACY: A bequest or disposition of property by will. A more inclusive term than DEVISE which is restricted to the disposition of real estate only.

LEGATEE: The recipient of a legacy.

LIBEL: Defamation expressed either in print or writing, or by means of pictures, effigies, or other signs. *Cf.* DEFAMATION, SLANDER.

JUDGMENT N.O.V. (non obstante veredicto): Literally, a judgment notwithstanding the verdict. A judgment entered by the court in favor of one party, either the plaintiff or the defendant, notwithstanding a jury's finding in favor of the other party.

MALA IN SE: Acts which are wrong independently of legislation.

MALA PROHIBITA: Acts which are made offenses by legislation and prohibited as such.

MALFEASANCE: The doing of an act which a person ought not to do; often used in the sense of MISFEASANCE. *Cf. also,* NONFEASANCE.

MALICE: The intent to do harm without lawful justification or excuse; not necessarily the same as personal hate, spite, or ill will.

MALICE AFORETHOUGHT: A deliberate and premeditated intention to commit an unlawful act.

MANSLAUGHTER: (1) The unlawful killing of another without malice. It is VOLUNTARY MANSLAUGHTER if done with the intention to cause death or great bodily harm and in the sudden heat of passion caused by a provocative act; it is INVOLUNTARY MANSLAUGHTER if done without an intention to cause death or great bodily harm, and if done either in the commission of a nonfelonious illegal act (malum in se rather than malum prohibitum), or in the commission of a lawful act with reckless disregard of others. (2) The preceeding definition based on the common law has been greatly changed by statute, some statutes defining voluntary manslaughter as a lesser "degree" of murder, and involuntary manslaughter based on recklessness as "criminal negligence." (3) A useful negative definition which reveals the "catch-all" character of the term is the following: All homicides which are neither murders nor innocent homicides, meaning by the latter, homicides which are legally justifiable or excusable.

MENS REA: Literally, a guilty mind; the mental element in the crime; frequently used as synonymous with criminal intent.

MISDEMEANOR: A lesser crime than a FELONY and punishable by a fine or by imprisonment other than in a state or federal penitentiary.

MISFEASANCE: An improper doing of a lawful act. *Cf.* MALFEASANCE, NONFEASANCE.

MUNICIPAL LAW: (1) The law of a particular state or nation as distinguished from INTERNATIONAL LAW; (2) More narrowly and commonly, the law of local towns, villages, and cities.

MURDER: The unlawful killing of another with malice aforethought, either express or implied.

NEGLIGENCE: The failure to do something which a reasonable and prudent man would do, or the unintentional doing of something which such a person would not do, which constitutes the proximate cause of actual injury to another.

NONFEASANCE: The omission to do an act which a person ought to have done. *Cf.* MISFEASANCE, MALFEASANCE.

NONSUIT: An action which is terminated without an adjudication of the issues on their merits. A VOLUNTARY NONSUIT occurs when the plaintiff abandons his case and consents to a judgment against him for costs. An INVOLUNTARY NONSUIT occurs when the plaintiff fails to appear or fails to present evidence on which a jury could find a verdict.

OVERRULE: To annul an earlier decision by depriving the rule upon which it was based, as well as the case itself, of all authority as precedent. *Cf.* REVERSAL.

PLAINTIFF: The party who sues another in a civil action to obtain a relief for injuries to his rights.

PLAINTIFF IN ERROR: The party who requests the issuance of a writ of error to review the judgment or other proceeding of a lower court. He could be either the plaintiff or the defendant in the original suit. *Cf.* DEFENDANT IN ERROR.

PRECEDENT: A judicial decision which is taken as binding authority for the settlement of future similar cases arising in the same court or in other courts of lower rank within the same jurisdiction.

PROXIMATE CAUSE: An act or omission without which the injury complained of would not have occurred, and which is immediately responsible for it. Not necessarily the same as, and not to be confused with the actual cause, or "cause in fact." Better termed "legal" or "responsible" cause. *Cf.* SINE QUA NON.

QUANTUM MERUIT: Literally, as much as he deserved; a kind of damages sought in an action involving a contract for work and labor, and based on an implied promise on the part of the defendant to pay the plaintiff as much as he reasonably deserved for his labor.

RATIO DECIDENDI: The primary reason or logical basis for the decision. *Cf.* DICTUM.

RES JUDICATA: The principle that a right, question, or fact once put in issue and adjudged by a court of competent jurisdiction cannot be disputed in a subsequent suit between the same parties.

RESPONDENT: The party who answers, especially in equity and admiralty; distinguished in an appellate case from APPELLANT.

REVERSAL: The annulling or changing of an earlier decision because of some error or irregularity, without calling into question the rule of law upon which it is based. *Cf.* OVERRULE.

SINE QUA NON: Literally, without which not; the necessary condition for the occurrence of an event or infliction of an injury; commonly called the "but for" rule or test of "actual cause" as contrasted with PROXIMATE CAUSE.

SLANDER: Oral defamation. *Cf.* DEFAMATION, LIBEL.

SPECIFIC PERFORMANCE: The actual performance of the terms of a contract, as ordered by a court of equity, in cases where legal damages for a breach of contract are inadequate.

STARE DECISIS: The policy of the courts to adhere to precedent and not to disturb settled points. *Cf.* PRECEDENT.

STATUTE OF FRAUDS: A statute which has as its purpose the prevention of frauds and perjuries by requiring that certain legal transactions be in writing and signed in order to be enforceable.

STATUTE OF LIMITATIONS: A statute which assigns time limits after which certain crimes may not be prosecuted, or certain types of civil suits maintained.

STRICT LIABILITY: Liability without fault, i.e., without either wrongful intent or negligence on the part of the defendant.

TESTATOR: One who dies leaving a will or testament.

TORT: Any wrongful act, other than a breach of contract, for which a civil action can be brought.

TRESPASS: (1) A form of action at early common law which could be brought for wrongful injury to the person or property of the plaintiff produced by the application of direct force by the defendant, and for which monetary compensation was sought; (2) also, the name of a specific modern tort involving damage to property.

TRESPASS AB INITIO: A trespass "from the beginning." An act which was lawful at the time committed but which becomes wrongful and unlawful because of subsequent wrongful acts, e.g., a privileged entry upon another's land followed by a wrongful use of it or injury to it.

TRESPASS ON THE CASE: A form of action at early common law for any wrongful injury to the person or property of the plaintiff which was indirectly or secondarily caused by the defendant's act, and for which monetary compensation was sought.

VERDICT: The finding or decision of a jury regarding matters or questions submitted to them at a trial and formally reported to the court. Unanimity among the jurors is required only in criminal cases.

WRIT OF ERROR: A common law writ issued by an appellate court to review a decision of a lower court upon appellant's contention that errors were committed by the lower court. As contrasted with a writ of CERTIORARI, which depends for its issuance upon the discretion of the appellate court, this method of appeal is a "matter of right" for the appellant.

Appendix: Legal Abbreviations

The standard citation of the opinions published in the law reports gives the volume number, the name of the report, and the page number on which the opinion commences, in that order, e.g., 6 N.H. 481. N.H. stands for *New Hampshire State Reports;* N.Y. for *New York State Reports.* They are the reports of the highest appellate court of the state and are "official," i.e., published and authorized by the state. The official federal reports are cited similarly, e.g., U.S. for *United States* (Supreme Court) *Reports.*

It is customary to add a second, and sometimes a third, citation for each case, e.g., besides 6 N.H. 481, the following: 26 Am. Dec. 713. This refers to an "unofficial," i.e., private commercial, publication known as *American Decisions.* One of the largest and most inclusive sets of unofficial reports is published by the West Publishing Company, and the abbreviations for these reports include the following: Atl., N.E., S.E., Pac., So., N.W., S.W., N.Y. Supp., Fed., F. Supp., Sup. Ct.

In addition to the reports of the highest appellate courts, there are also some reports of the opinions of the intermediate appellate courts, both federal and state, e.g., Fed. for *Federal Reporter* (U.S. Court of Appeals, and other lower federal courts), and N.Y. Supp. for *New York Supplement* (certain lower appellate courts in N.Y.). With a few exceptions, these reports are unofficial.

Prior to 1790, when the U.S. Supreme Court appointed the first official reporter, all case reporting was done unofficially, and more or less unsystematically. These early reports were generally referred to by the name of the reporter, as were even the first official reporters, e.g., Dall. for Dallas, Wall. for Wallace, until about 1875 when U.S., standing for *United States Reports,* was substituted and became the standard citation of the official reports. A similar official reporting syestem was initiated in the individual states beginning in 1804. Unofficial reporters, such as those of the West Publishing Company, continue to supply lawyers with almost identically the same case reports as contained in the official reports, but usually more expeditiously and often with the added advantage of headnotes and annotations.

Nothing quite like the official reporting system as it is known in the United States exists in England. There are "authorized" reporters, but they are not official or salaried as in the United States. The earlier English reports are, like ours, referred to by the names of the reporters, but the citations now are quite impersonal, e.g., Q.B. for *Queen's Bench Reports* and A.C. for *Appeal Cases.*

I. AMERICAN FEDERAL AND STATE LAW REPORTS

A.2d	Atlantic Reporter, Second Series
Ala. App.	Alabama Appellate Court Reports
A.L.R.	American Law Reports
A.L.R. 2d	American Law Reports, Second Series
Am. Ann. Cas.	American Annotated Cases
Am. Dec.	American Decisions
Am. Rep.	American Reports
Am. St. Rep.	American State Reports
App. D.C.	Appeals Cases, District of Columbia
App. Div.	Appellate Division, N.Y. Supreme Court
Atl.	Atlantic Reporter
Brock.	Brockenbrough's Marshall's Decisions, U.S. Circuit Court
Cal. App.2d	California Appellate, Second Series
Cow.	Cowen's Reports (N.Y.)
Cush.	Cushing's Reports (Mass.)
Dall.	Dallas' United States Reports
F.2d	Federal Reporter, Second Series
Fed.	Federal Reporter
Fed. Cas.	Federal Cases
Fed. Rep.	Federal Reporter
F. Supp.	Federal Supplement
L. Ed.	Lawyers Edition, U.S. Supreme Court Reports
L.R.A.	Lawyers Reports Annotated
Misc.	Miscellaneous Reports (N.Y.; N.J.)
N.E.	North Eastern Reporter
N.W.	North Western Reporter
N.Y. Supp.	New York Supplement Reporter
N.Y.S.2d	N. Y. Supplement Reporter, Second Series
Pac.	Pacific Reporter
P.2d	Pacific Reporter, Second Series
S.E.	South Eastern Reporter
So.	Southern Reporter
Sup. Ct.	Supreme Court Reporter (U.S.)
S.W.	South Western Reporter
Tex. App.	Texas Criminal Appeals Reports

Tex. Cr. R.	Texas Criminal Reports
U.S.	United States Supreme Court Reports
Wall.	Wallace's Reports (U.S.)
Wall. Jr.	J. W. Wallace's Circuit Court Reports (U.S.)
Wend.	Wendell's Reports (N.Y.)
Whart.	Wharton's Reports (Pa.)
Wheat.	Wheaton's Reports (U.S.)

II. ENGLISH LAW REPORTS

A.C.	Law Reports, Appeal Cases
All E.R.	All England Law Reports
App. Cas.	Law Reports, Appeal Cases
B. & C.	Barnewall & Cresswell's King's Bench Reports
Black, W.	Wm. Blackstone's King's Bench Reports
Cox C.C.	Cox's Criminal Law Cases
C.P.	Common Pleas Reports
Eng. L. & Eq.	English Law & Equity Reports Reprint
Eng. Rep.	English Reports
F. & F.	Foster & Finlason's Nisi Prius Reports
Jur.	Jurist Reports
K.B.	Law Reports, King's Bench
L.J.K.B. (N.S.)	Law Journal Reports, King's Bench, New Series
L.J.Q.B.	Law Journal Reports, Queen's Bench
Q.B.	Queen's Bench Reports
Saund.	Saunder's King's Bench Reports
Taun.	Taunton's Common Pleas Reports
Term.	Term Reports

III. OTHER LEGAL PUBLICATIONS

Am. Jur.	American Jurisprudence (Encyclopedia)
Bac. Abr.	Bacon's Abridgement (English-Encyclopedia)
Bl. Comm.	Blackstone's Commentaries on the Law of England
Calif. L. Rev.	California Law Review
Cent. Dig.	Century Digest
C. J.	Corpus Juris (Encyclopedia)
C. J. S.	Corpus Juris Secundum (Encyclopedia)
Colum. L. Rev.	Columbia Law Review
Cornell L. Q.	Cornell Law Quarterly
Dec. Dig.	Decennial Digest
Harv. L. Rev.	Harvard Law Review

L. Q. Rev.	Law Quarterly Review (English)
N.Y.U.L.Q. Rev.	New York University Law Quarterly Review
R.C.L.	Ruling Case Law (Encyclopedia)
Am. Law Inst. Rest.	American Law Institute Restatement of the Law (of Torts, Contracts, etc.)
U.C.L.A.L. Rev.	U.C.L.A. Law Review
U. Chi. L. Rev.	University of Chicago Law Review
Vand. L. Rev.	Vanderbilt Law Review
Yale L. J.	Yale Law Journal

IV. COURTS

Adm.	Admiralty Court or Division
App. Div.	Appellate Division
C.A.	Court of Appeal (English)
C.C.	Circuit Court (Old Federal)
C.C. Pleas	Court of Common Pleas
Ch.	Chancery
Cir.	Court of Appeals (Federal)
Cir. Ct.	Circuit Court (State)
C.P.	Common Pleas
Crim. App.	Court of Criminal Appeals
Ct. App.	Court of Appeal(s) (State)
D.	District Court (Federal)
Dist. Ct.	District Court (State)
Eq.	Equity
Ex.	Exchequer
Ex. Ch.	Exchequer Chamber
H.L.	House of Lords
K.B.	King's Bench
N.P.	Nisi Prius
P.C.	Privy Council
Q.B.	Queen's Bench
Sup. Ct.	Supreme Court
Super. Ct.	Superior Court
Sup. Jud. Ct.	Supreme Judicial Court

V. OTHER ABBREVIATIONS

B.	Baron, a judge of the Court of Exchequer
C.	Chancellor
Cong.	Congress
Const.	Constitution

C.J.	Chief Justice; Chief Judge
J.	Judge, Justice
J.J.	Judges, Justices
L.J.	Lord Justice
M.R.	Master of Rolls
P.L.	Public Law
Stat.	Statute(s); Statutes at Large
Stat. at L.	Statutes at Large
U.S.C.	United States Code
U.S.C.A.	United States Code Annotated

INDEX

Accident, 39, 49, 97, 125, 167, 201
Act, of God, 143, 147-152, 162
  instinctive, 35
  intentional, 156-158, 165
  intervening, 54, 56, 159-163
  negligent, 16, 164-177
  overt, 153-155
  theories of, 144
  voluntary, 124
Analogy, 56, 99, 173, 180, 198
  See also Cases
Andrews, J., 78, 169
Aristotle, 7, 25
Assault and battery, 69, 79, 156
Assumpsit, 18, 191

Bacon, Francis, v, 24, 108
Belief, 60, 126, 136, 224, 258
Black, Hugo L., 217
Brandeis, Louis D., 179, 205, 226, 256
Burden of proof, 225, 236, 241
  See also Presumptions, Proof

Canons, 24, 213, 218
Cardozo, Benjamin, 34, 58, 164, 182, 194, 201, 214, 227
Cases, distinguishable, 21, 40
  exceptional, 79
  factually alike, 56, 262
Cases of first impression, 145-146, 178-184
  in particular jurisdiction, 123, 179
  as regards facts, 28, 116, 161

as regards right of action, 179
  See also Precedent
Cause, contributing, 163
  intervening, 36, 47-57, 151, 160
  proximate, 53, 55, 98, 149, 168, 172-177
Cause of action, 20, 56, 143, 165, 168, 183, 261
Chain of causes, 36, 162, 173
Civil law, 27, 29, 117
Clemency, 60
Common law, 25, 27, 100, 114, 179, 181, 207, 209, 210, 262, 263-265
Concurring opinions, 22, 217-220
Condition precedent, 11
Conduct, 143
  reasonable, 170
  wilful, wanton, and reckless, 38
  See also Act, Reasonable man
Conscience, 217
  domain of, 29
  of judges, 130, 218
  of the people, 214
Consideration, 19-22
  as material benefit to promisor, 20-21
  moral obligation as, 21
  sufficient, 20-21
Constitutionality, 209, 210, 218, 255, 258
Contract, 8-12, 20, 23, 42, 256
Contributory negligence, 15, 97, 199, 201
Crime, 27, 81, 123, 154, 168, 213, 227, 230, 231

Custom, 98

Damages, actual versus legal, 9
  as compensation, 9, 168
  as injury, 9, 16, 101, 168
  proximate, 16-17
  punitive, 170, 179, 184
Demurrer, 13, 14, 18, 20, 184
Dissenting opinions, 28-33, 78-80,
  101, 151, 152, 169-177
  See also Concurring opinions
Divine law, 26, 66
Doctrine, 16, 108, 203
  of attractive nuisance, 41
  of a case, 27, 89
  philosophical, of causation, 172-
  173
  of the state of nature, 116
  of strict liability, 83
Douglas, William O., 219
Drunkenness, 45, 73-80
  as a defense, 73
  as mitigation, 74-75
Duty, 3-40, 165, 196, 198
  to anticipate, 40, 56, 151
  to be charitable, 41
  to communicate, 130-137
  conflict of, 93-95
  of imperfect obligation, 41, 130
  to be intelligent, 36-37
  to make reparation, 4, 89, 176
  to moralize, 111
  not to harm others, vi, 93, 99,
  172
  not to sacrifice lives, 117-118
  not to slander your neighbor,
  131
  to obey the law, 67, 101
  of perfect obligation, 41
  periphery of, 152
  prima facie, vi
  to rescue, 35
  to retreat, 119-120
  to speak, 14
  to use reasonable care, 13, 38, 40,

  99, 171
  unenforceable, 21
  See also Moral duty

Equal protection of the law, 4,
  190, 208, 255
Equality, 5, 260
Equity, 207
  Aristotle's definition of, 25
  considerations of, 29
  of a statute, 24-25
Evidence, adequate, 238
  admissible, 82, 220
  as a whole, 50
  character testimony as, 154, 229-
  232
  circumstantial, 154, 250-253
  dying declaration as, 39
  inadmissible, even if true, 59,
  216, 224
  incompetent, 227-233
  law of, 224
  materiality of, 40, 79, 81, 82, 170,
  195
  obtained by force, 212
  preponderance of, 236
  real versus verbal, 216
  sufficient, 40
  uncontradicted, 39
  weight of, 241
  See also Proof
Exceptions, procedural, 40, 61, 82
  to rules, 36, 88-89, 91, 101, 197
  See also Cases
Excuses, 43-92, 110, 112, 236

Fact, 225
  disagreements over, 223
  finding of, 31, 242-249
  law versus, 266
  orders of, 246
  question of, 177
  ultimate, 246
  See also Matter of law
Fairness, 89, 176, 231

Flew, Antony, 144 n
Frankfurter, Felix, 211, 242
Fraud, 13, 32, 243, 246, 248
Freedom, of speech and press, 218,
    264
  of testamentary disposition, 30
  to contract, 258
  See also Liberty

Good faith, 9, 81, 236, 239

Hart, H. L. A., 144 n
Hobbes, Thomas, 6
Holmes, Oliver Wendell, 119, 171,
    181, 182, 199, 210, 262

Ignorance of fact, 81-82
Illegality, 111, 232, 248
Immunity, 179, 182, 198
Inadvertence, 39, 54
Injury, *see* Damages, Wrong
Injustice, 176, 209
  of rule, 9, 261
  See also Justice
Insanity, 44, 58-68, 69-72, 170
  feigned, 58
  irresistible impulse test of, 66
  test of, in M'Naghten's Case, 61-
    64
Intent, 170
  criminal, 31, 75, 76, 78, 81, 112,
    228
  of insane persons, 71
  related to legal and moral guilt,
    78-79
  specific, 77
  transferred, 167
  See also Intention
Intention, 39, 71
  to do harm, 157
  of legislators, 24-25, 98
  of testator, 23, 31
  unlawful, 157
  See also Intent
Interpretation, canons of, 24-25

  of Constitution, 214, 217
  of rule in M'Naghten's Case, 64
  of statutes, 24-25, 81, 100

Judge, fact-finding powers of, 54
  idiosyncrasies of, 220
  limits of authority of, 30-31
  question for, 135
  responsibility of, 213
Judicial legislation, 182
Judicial notice, 254-260
Jurisprudence, American, 109
  of conceptions, 197
  of country, 26
  general, 207
  mechanical, 197
  modern, 29
  of state, 27
Jury, case taken from, 48
  common sense of, 67
  findings of, 36, 39, 253
  function of, compared with
    judge's, 135
  questions for, 37, 54, 177, 200
Justice, 22, 66, 70, 114, 224, 262,
    264
  in accordance with law, 232
  considerations of, 198, 241
  ends of, 28, 219
  moral and social, 117
  notions of, 213
  principles of, 27, 30, 218
  public, 112
  sense of, 173, 217
  standards of, 264
  See also Fairness, Injustice
Justification, 43-44, 93-139, 154,
    236

Kant, Immanuel, 7, 41
Knowledge, 167
  common, 266
  general, 226, 258
  judicial notice of general, 254-
    260

legal, 54
scientific, 54, 226
See also Belief

Law of nature, *see* Natural law
Law of necessity, 113
Legality, principles of pure, 5-6
terms of pure, 63
versus morality, 4
See also Illegality
Letter of the law, 24, 99
Liability without fault, 45-46, 71,
83-90, 91
Libel, 126-137
Liberty, 214
See also Freedom
Life, dollars and cents value of, 21
reckless disregard of, 125
sacrifice of, 36, 115
See also Lives, Self-sacrifice
Lives, equal value of human, 107
greater value of others', 108
Logic, 173, 196, 230, 241

Malice, 112, 128, 136-137, 157, 170,
237
Malum prohibitum, 81
Manslaughter, 59, 105, 159, 250
Marshall, John, 22
Matter of law, 85, 98, 100, 123,
150, 176, 203, 237-238, 266
See also Fact, Judge, Jury
Maxims, 24-28, 197
Melden, A. I., 144 n
Mercy, 112
Mill, John Stuart, 41
Misrepresentation, 13, 32
See also Fraud
Mistake of fact, 81
Mitigation, 74-75, 113
Moral duty, vi, 3-7, 20-21, 25, 67,
117, 126-137
See also Duty
Moral sense, 14
Morris, Herbert, 144 n
Motive, 78, 81, 136, 252, 267
See also Intent, Intention

Municipal law, 117
Murder, 23, 58, 73, 119, 153, 230

Natural law, 6, 27, 110, 112, 113,
117, 214, 221
Negligence, 54-55, 100, 164-177
Nonsuit, 15, 17, 18, 83

Oath, 242
Obligation, *see* Duty, Moral duty
Omission, 55, 98, 143, 186
Ownership, 192, 197
See also Possession, Property

Persuasion, 224, 229, 245
See also Proof
Philosophers, v, 109, 223
Philosophy, abstract and general
character of, v
constitutional, 218, 219, 220
Pollock, Sir Frederick, 182
Possession, 191-193
Pound, Roscoe, 180, 197
Precedent, 28, 66, 202, 261-266
See also Cases of first impression
Presumptions, 22, 32, 62, 78, 124,
225, 234-241, 248-249
Principles, 30, 85, 98, 116, 124, 131,
182
Privilege, 89, 126-137, 181, 207
Promise, express, 22, 42
implied, 11, 42
subsequent, 20, 21
See also Oath
Proof, 224, 246-249
difficulty of, 183, 261-267
measure of, 245
standard of, 247
strict, 81
sufficiency of, 248, 251
See also Evidence
Property, 181, 191-193
devolution of, 24
See also Ownership, Possession
Public Policy, 16, 26, 32, 70, 71, 90,
173, 198, 241

Punishment, 33, 112, 118

Reasonable man, 25, 36-37, 99, 120, 135-136
Responsibility, 42
  for becoming intoxicated, 74
  causal sense of, 133, 160-161
  criminal, 80, 161
  degree of, 152
  to God, 112
  of insane persons, 69-72, 91
  of judges, 213
  for own death, 200
  partial, 91
  problem of how much, 45
  vicarious, 44
Right, the better, 192
  civil, 220
  claim of, 93
  constitutional, 212
  of courts to reexamine questions, 264
  human, 112, 214
  legal, 164, 192, 256, 266
  to make law, 112
  making law conform to, 262
  moral, 264
  of parents, 236
  versus harm, 93
  of way, 196
Right of action, 16, 166, 261
Right of privacy, 178-184
Risk, 35, 88, 151, 165-167
Robbery, 73, 76
Ross, Sir David, vi-vii, 43
Rules, competitive, 189, 194-198
  customary, 98
  distinguished from standards, 189
  of evidence, 224
  presumptions as, 237
  procedural (specific), 54, 73, 206-207, 245
  problem of applying, 221
  purpose of, 100
  reason for, 29-30

settled, 8, 41, 54, 183
standards reduced to, 204
statutory, 97, 123
substantive (specific), 8, 17, 31, 35, 41, 54-55, 87-89, 92, 123, 180, 193, 197
for termites, 14
for unforeseen contingencies, 114

Scrutton, L. J., 126
Self-defense, 110, 119-121, 125, 155
Self-sacrifice, 36, 105
Sense of fair-play and decency, 216
Sense of justice, 173, 216, 217
Standards, 14, 67, 166, 219, 221, 246
  of care, 99, 151-152
  of conduct, 200
  of justice, 213-214
  of proof, 246
  of reasonable man, 99
  reduced to rules, 189
  versus rules, 204
State of nature, 111, 116
Statute of frauds, 20, 22
Strict liability, see Liability without fault
Suicide, 105, 161, 186

Thayer, James Bradley, ix, 237, 241
Tort, 168, 193, 209
  of assault and battery, 69
  difference between crime and, 168
  history of law of, 168
  liability of insane persons for, 69-72
  See also Wrong
Truth
  failure to disclose, 13-14
  half-truth, 13
  misrepresentation of, 13
  sole aim of trial not, 224

See also, Belief, Evidence, Libel

Universal law, 25, 117
Utilitarianism, 45-46

Verdict, directed, 48, 69
   special, 156
Volition, 36

Wigmore, John H., 168, 230, 231

Will, 23-33
Wrong, 43, 166, 169
   legal versus moral, 61, 65
   meaning of, in definition of in-
      sanity, 60-68
   as violation of a right, 166, 168
   as violation of a statutory duty,
      101
   See also Damages, Tort